FOOTBALL'S
GREATEST
★ ★ ★ ★
STARS

FOOTBALL'S GREATEST STARS

★ ★ ★ ★ ★

ALLAN MAKI

ADDITIONAL RESEARCH AND WRITING
BY GEORGE JOHNSON

WITH A FOREWORD BY
THURMAN THOMAS

FIREFLY BOOKS

A FIREFLY BOOK

Published by Firefly Books Ltd. 2008
Copyright © 2008 Allan Maki

First printing

Publisher Cataloging-in-Publication Data (U.S.)
Maki, Allan.
Football's greatest stars / Allan Maki ; with additional research and writing by George Johnson
[ ] p. : photos. (some col.) ; cm.
Includes index.
Summary: A history of football, including the rise of the National Football League told through profiles of its key players. Also included are histories of NFL franchises.
ISBN-13: 978-1-55407-389-4   ISBN-10: 1-55407-389-8
1. National Football League -- Biography. 2. Football players --United States -- Biography. 3. National Football League – History. I. Johnson, George. II. Title.
796.332/092/2 B dc22   GV955.5.N35M355 2008

Library and Archives Canada Cataloguing in Publication
Maki, Allan
Football's greatest stars / Allan Maki ; with additional research and writing by George Johnson
Includes index.
ISBN-13: 978-1-55407-389-4   ISBN-10: 1-55407-389-8
1. National Football League--Biography. 2. National Football League--History. 3. Football players--United States--Biography.
4. Football--United States--History. I. Johnson, George, 1957- II. Title.
GV939.A1M33 2008   796.332092'2   C2008-901124-4

Published in the United States by
Firefly Books (U.S.) Inc.
P.O. Box 1338, Ellicott Station
Buffalo, New York 14205

Published in Canada by
Firefly Books Ltd.
66 Leek Crescent
Richmond Hill, Ontario L4B 1H1

Cover and interior design by Jamie Hodgson | Studio 34
Statistical and team compilations by Derek Iwanuk

Printed in China

The publisher gratefully acknowledges the financial support for our publishing program by the Government of Canada through the Book Publishing Industry Development Program.

DEDICATION

For my dad, for teaching me how to laugh,
and for my amazing wife, who keeps me laughing.

KEY TO ABBREVIATIONS

ast = assists

att = attempts

avg = average

comp = completions

FF = forced fumbles

FG = field goal/s

FGA = field goal attempts

FR = fumble recoveries

int = interceptions

KR = kick returns

pct = percent/percentage

PR = punt returns

rec = receptions

TD/TDs = touchdown/s

yd avg = average yards

yds = yards

ypc = yards per carry

XK = extra kicks made

XKA = extra kicks attempted

CAPTIONS

Pg 2–3: Under extremely wet conditions at Los Angeles Memorial Coliseum, the Minnesota Vikings and the Los Angeles Rams compete in the 1977 NFC divisional playoff, also known as the Mud Bowl. The Vikings defeated the Rams 14–7 under the guidance of quarterback Bob Lee.

Pg 5: Steve Young and Brett Favre congratulate each other after the hard fought 1997 NFC Championship game. Favre's Packers defeated Young's 49ers 23–10 to advance to the Super Bowl for the second straight year; the Packers would lose the Super Bowl to the Denver Broncos.

Pg 6: Terry Bradshaw in 1979. The Hall of Fame quarterback would lead the Steelers to their fourth Super Bowl in six seasons, and their second in a row, while also winning his second Super Bowl MVP.

CONTENTS

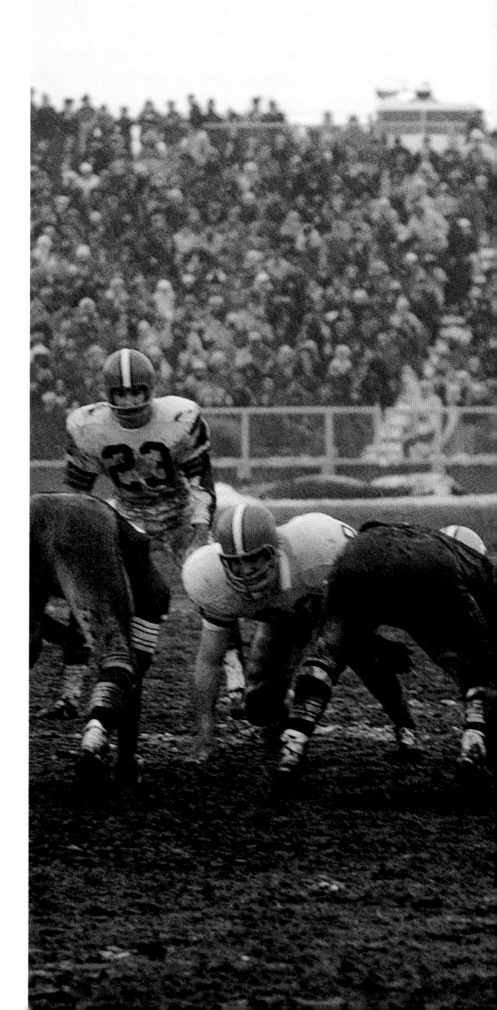

The Deacon was sipping drinks with an inquisitive sportswriter in a Toronto nightclub one evening when the question was raised: What made him one of the NFL's most dominant defensive linemen? Was it his quickness, that quarterback-crippling, inside-outside rush move?

Twenty years removed from his last game, David "Deacon" Jones shook his head and uttered a single word: "Attitude." That was the key that unlocked his greatness, Jones insisted. All those who play in the NFL boast a high degree of talent, he explained. They can run fast, hit hard, throw accurately. But what separates the prime cuts from the herd is how badly they want to succeed: their attitude.

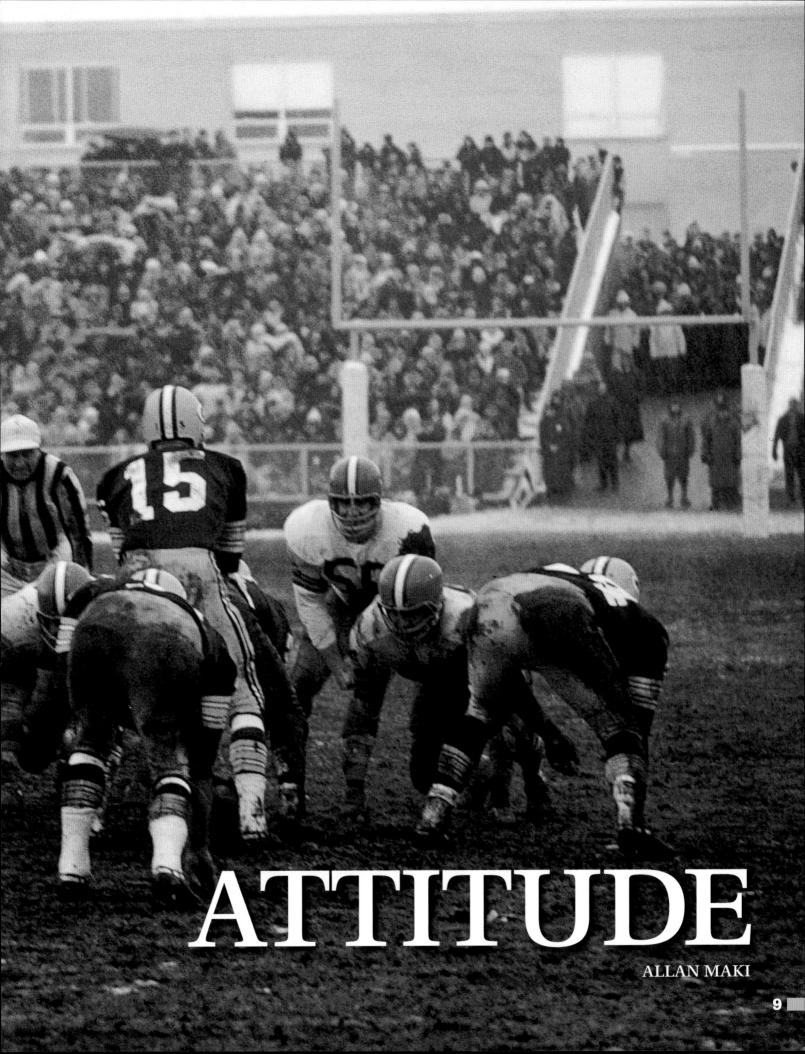

ATTITUDE

ALLAN MAKI

SIMPSON AND LEWIS ARE NOT

POPULAR PICKS, BUT AS ATHLETES,

AWAY FROM OUTSIDE TEMPTATIONS,

THEIR WORK HAD THE FOOTBALL

WORLD SHAKING ITS HEAD

IN AMAZEMENT.

That was how the Deacon saw it, and I thought of that conversation with Jones soon after I was contacted last fall by Firefly Books editor Steve Cameron. Steve had asked me to write about the NFL's 50 Greatest Players. The dilemma, aside from a tight deadline, was how to pick the foremost 50. How do you compare players from different eras? How do you value a good offensive lineman as opposed to a good inside linebacker? Do you go by durability? Versatility?

Do you pick an athlete because he took his position and played it like no one else ever had? That worked in a couple of cases (for example, New York Giants' linebacker Lawrence Taylor and Baltimore Colts' tight end John Mackey), but not for everyone. So how did we come up with our 50?

We used two criteria: only players from the late 1950s and early 1960s up to the present would be included. We wanted a contemporary collection (no offense to Otto Graham or Don Hutson). They also had to pass the Deacon's test, meaning they had to have an attitude about them. That wasn't to say every player had to preen and prance like Deion "Neon" Sanders auditioning for the Rockettes dance troupe. That was his own gimmick, his personal style.

What we wanted overall were players with an unflinching belief in themselves — men whose personal triumphs and attitudes were as impressive as the statistics and records they set.

Green Bay Packers' quarterback Bart Starr was a shining example of that. Starr was a late-round draft pick with supposedly limited skills, but his passion for the game helped him to become a master craftsman. Starr's ambition was to execute a game plan to perfection and to do it in the biggest games. In terms of his personality, he was practical and humble.

But make no mistake. Starr was a merciless competitor. He would find the weakness in an opposing defense and exploit it repeatedly. He wasn't in it for the glory. He just wanted the victory. And he collected his share.

Considering the depth of our project — and again, a pressing deadline — *Calgary Herald* sports columnist George Johnson was brought in for his able assistance. Johnson is one of Canada's premier sportswriters and when he began filing his first biographies, he,

too, was captivated by the players who had confronted adversity in their lives, if not their careers. His piece on Green Bay linebacker Ray Nitschke captures all the elements we were looking to highlight.

With Johnson aboard, we debated then settled on our 50 favorites, based on their inner traits and on-field work, and began writing. A portion of my research came from conversations over the years with some of the NFL's finest minds (coach Marv Levy, who was inducted into the Pro Football Hall of Fame in 2001, and general manager Bill Polian, who built the Indianapolis Colts into 2007 Super Bowl champions), along with some of the game's freest thinkers (NFL assistant coaches Bill Bradley and Fred Biletnikoff, and my long-time source and purveyor of all things NFL, Deep Zone. You know who you are).

Those men provided tremendous insight into the game and helped shape my thoughts as this book was assembled.

When I look back at this endeavor, I realize we excluded many remarkable athletes, for example, Dallas Cowboys' defensive lineman Bob Lilly; Oakland Raiders' cornerback Mike Haynes; Miami Dolphins' receiver Paul Warfield. But I'd argue hard and fast if any of our 50 had to be dropped to make room for someone else.

Some of you may take issue with the inclusion of Buffalo Bills' running back O.J. Simpson and Baltimore Ravens' linebacker Ray Lewis, both of whom were charged with murder in separate incidents. Simpson was found not guilty; Lewis pleaded guilty to a lesser charge. Simpson's legal battles came after his career; Lewis's came at the height of his playing days, and he has been able to restore at least part of his reputation through humanitarian efforts.

Simpson and Lewis are not popular picks, but as athletes, away from outside temptations, their work had the football world shaking its head in amazement. (Lewis's still does.) They had the gifts. And attitude!

They did a pretty good job of wanting to be the best player in football, and that's why they're included here.

So sit back, relax and marvel at the great players and moments that have shaped the NFL. Where would the game be without them?

FOREWORD
by Thurman Thomas

Reflecting on the stories in this book and the stars that I played with, against, and those who came before me, I can't help but think of my rookie season. It was 1988, and I can remember sitting in the Visitors' locker room at Chicago's Soldier Field on game day, getting ready to play. Our team, the Buffalo Bills, were 4–0 and about to take on the 4–0 Bears. It was our first big test of the season.

I was getting taped, and I heard this voice saying, "Where's that Number 34?" I had no idea whose voice it was. I thought maybe it was a coach looking for me.

But it was Walter Payton, one of my two idols when I was younger — the other was Earl Campbell. Walter had retired from the Bears but he wanted to meet me. I was this 22-year-old kid without a clue, and he was Walter Payton, the NFL's all-time leading rusher. He'd read somewhere that I wore the number 34 because of him, and Earl Campbell, too, and he wanted to talk to me.

I told Walter I had started running up hills as part of my training program because that's what he'd done during his career. He told me it was good for building endurance, and we talked some more and shook hands. After Walter left, Jim Kelly, our quarterback, came up to me and said, "Oh man, that is so cool. Give me a high five."

I said, "Are you nuts? I just shook Walter Payton's hand. I don't want to touch your hand."

My dream was to be like Walter and Earl. Being from Texas, I had followed Earl's career from his days at the University at Texas and then on to the Houston Oilers. Earl and Walter, I wanted to make my game like theirs. I knew I wasn't as physical as Earl or as experienced as Walter, but I wanted to be a great player like them. That's where it probably started for me.

Even as a kid, I used to tell my mom I was going to be a professional football player. And when I made it, I wanted Bills' fans around the world to know that when I was out on the football field, I was doing everything possible to win the game. It didn't matter if I was running the ball or I was catching the ball or I was picking up a blitz. I was a guy you literally had to peel off the football field. I gave it my all on every play.

Personally, I think that's what being a great player is about. It's not just about the winning. I look at other great athletes — Ted Williams, Barry Bonds, Charles Barkley — and they've been in the spotlight and never won a championship. Look at how great a player Barry Sanders was, or Warren Moon, and neither of them won an NFL championship.

In Buffalo, we got to the Super Bowl four years in a row from 1991 to 1994. I look back at that as a remarkable feat, and for sure I wish we could have won one, two or all four of those games. The thing is

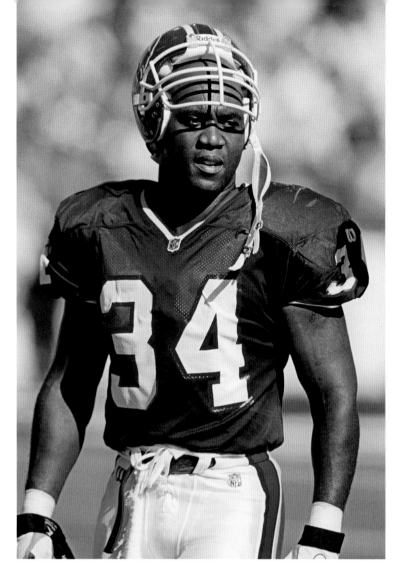

if you go to a Super Bowl and lose, it could tear your team apart. To go to four Super Bowls and lose and to keep coming back trying to win, I don't think anyone could fault us for our effort. That's what greatness is about — trying to win and competing hard.

Besides, I say we could have won a Super Bowl if we hadn't played a team from the NFC East — the Dallas Cowboys, Washington Redskins, New York Giants. If we had played the NFC North or South, then we might have won. I've always had a good sense of humor.

When I was coming out of Oklahoma State University, there were questions about me as a running back. A lot of NFL teams passed me up because of my knee, which I injured in my senior year. There were NFL scouts who figured my knee wouldn't hold up for more than three or four years.

Buffalo drafted me in the second round and I always considered myself an every-down back. I worked with Jim Kelly, Andre Reed and the other receivers staying out after practice and running routes with them, just to get some timing down and to let the coaches see I could come out of the backfield and catch the football. I understood that to catch the ball was every bit as important as running it.

Maybe I felt that way because I played in an era when it was Emmitt Smith and Barry Sanders, or Barry Sanders and Emmitt Smith. I was always third, and I understood that. People loved Em-mitt and Barry. Those two were great running backs, and are great friends of mine. I was just a guy in Buffalo trying to do what he could, although I did get my share of attention.

Kids who are about 19 years old now, they all talk to me about Tecmo Bowl. Do you know about Tecmo Bowl? It was a little computer football game. I still have kids say to me, "When I played Tecmo Bowl, I was always you. Forget Emmitt Smith or Barry Sanders; I was Thurman Thomas." It was big in 1991, the year I won the NFL's MVP. Apparently I was unstoppable.

I told you I had a sense of humor.

People have asked me what I'm most proud of in my football career. When I look back at my time in the NFL, I'm proud to say I lasted 13 years without having a serious injury. That's probably my greatest accomplishment — playing hard and staying healthy. That's also what I admired about Walter Payton, along with the type of person he was.

For Walter Payton to come into the Bills' dressing room like that before a game, just to say hi, it made a ton of difference, not just for me but for our other players, too. They were so impressed by him. We lost that game against the Bears. The score was 24–3. But meeting Walter and shaking the hand of greatness, that's one of my fondest memories. ■

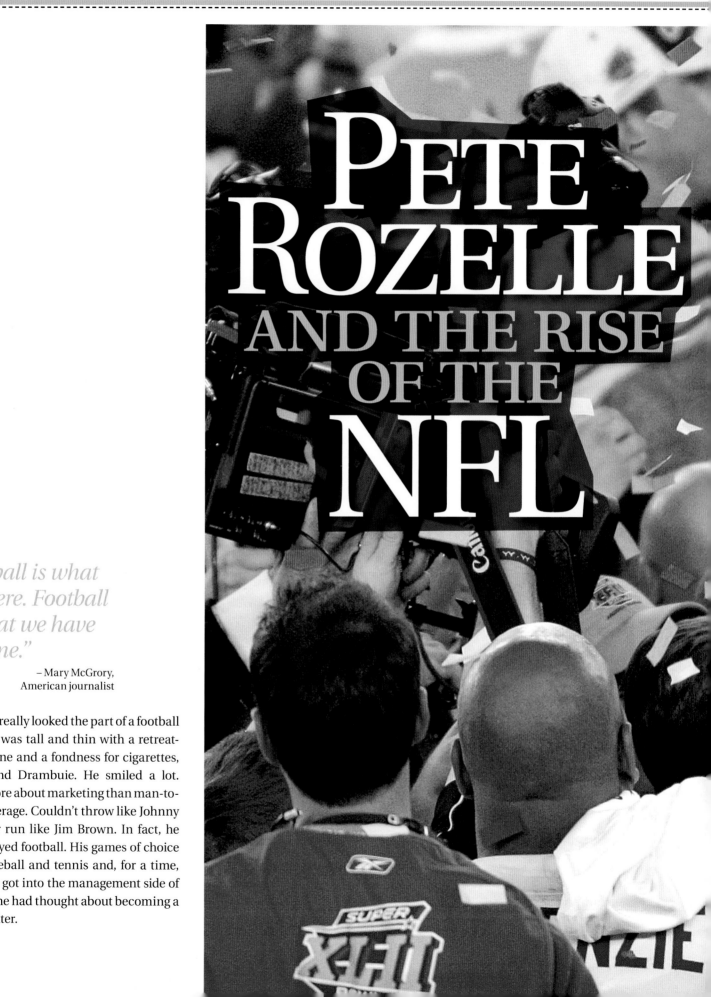

PETE ROZELLE
AND THE RISE OF THE
NFL

"Baseball is what we were. Football is what we have become."

– Mary McGrory,
American journalist

He never really looked the part of a football titan. He was tall and thin with a retreating hairline and a fondness for cigarettes, scotch and Drambuie. He smiled a lot. Spoke more about marketing than man-to-man coverage. Couldn't throw like Johnny Unitas or run like Jim Brown. In fact, he never played football. His games of choice were baseball and tennis and, for a time, before he got into the management side of football, he had thought about becoming a sportswriter.

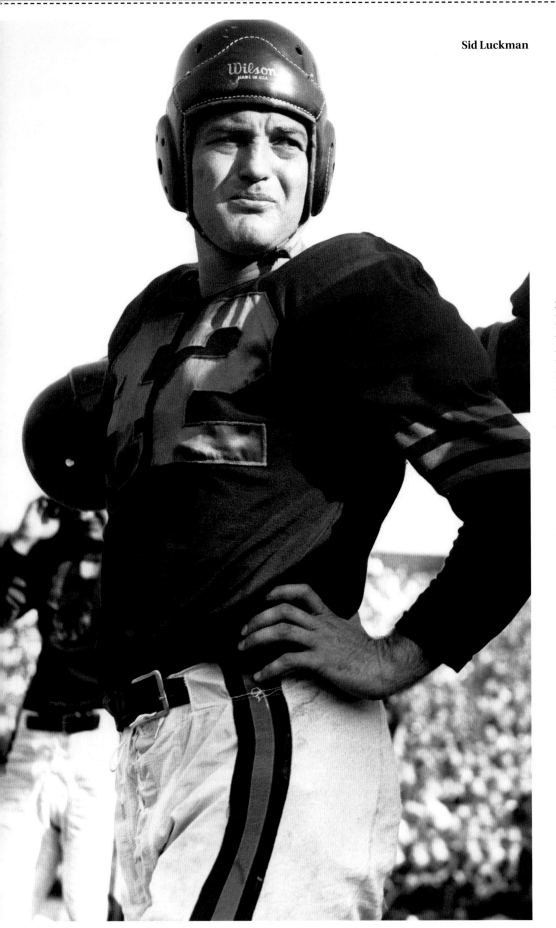

Sid Luckman

Yet Alvin Ray (Pete) Rozelle was the single most influential figure in the rise of the National Football League, and he took it to phenomenal heights: a man who used his salesman's charm and administrative moxie to transform his league into the monster that ate professional sports.

Take a look any Sunday from September to February. All across the U.S., there are 70,000-seat stadiums jammed at or near capacity, with face-painted zealots writhing on every play. Here are multi-millionaire athletes performing for the tens of millions of television viewers around the world. Great plays are highlighted over and over from a dozen different camera angles, helping to add to the anticipation and importance of the next play, the next series.

Then the Super Bowl comes along with its Janet Jackson wardrobe malfunction and its $2.6 million price tag for a 30-second TV commercial and everything goes over the moon. Its New Year's Eve at Times Square times 10.

Rozelle made all this happen. He took the NFL from its lagging position behind major league baseball and college football and maneuvered it to a place other leagues now dream of. National TV rights contracts? Rozelle negotiated those for the owners, always with staggering results. Enforced revenue sharing so the small-market teams could run with their big-market brethren? Rozelle got the New York Giants and Chicago Bears to go along with that, and hence, the birth of parity.

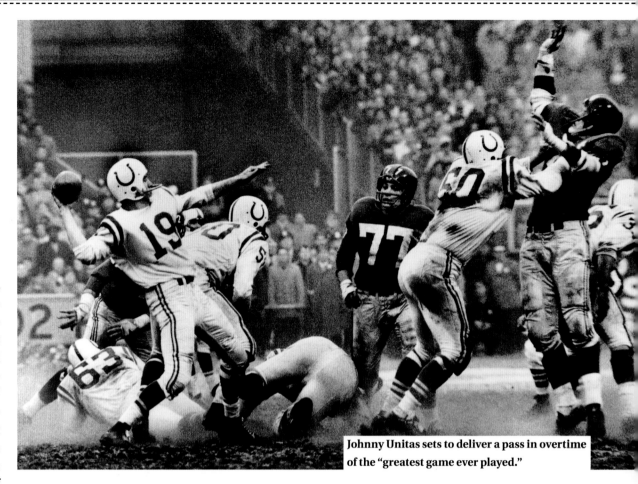

Johnny Unitas sets to deliver a pass in overtime of the "greatest game ever played."

NFL Properties. NFL Films. NFL Charities. *Monday Night Football*. In almost every way, Rozelle's long-range thinking paid off. As *Miami Herald* columnist Edwin Pope told ESPN Classic's *Sports Century* series: "I firmly believe that when the final history of the National Football League is written, the all-time hero of the NFL, the man who contributed most to changing America's Sunday afternoon watching habits, is Pete Rozelle."

Was Rozelle without his faults? Absolutely not. His decision to play games two days after U.S. president John F. Kennedy was assassinated in 1963 was considered a colossal blunder, one that Rozelle came to regret. Late in his 29-year run as commissioner, many players argued Rozelle and the NFL hadn't done enough to take care of the retired players who lacked the pension money to cover the cost of operations for football-related injuries and assisted living. The inference was telling: Rozelle could be cold-hearted and calculating if it suited his interests or the NFL's, which led to his nickname, "the arrogant czar."

But the pluses outweighed the negatives. Rozelle combined his ground-breaking accomplishments with a touch of Madison Ave. As NFL commissioner from 1960 to 1989, he was, as he stated several times, "the right man at the right time."

BEFORE ROZELLE

When Rozelle was named commissioner on Jan. 20, 1960, he replaced Bert Bell, who had suffered a heart attack and died on Oct. 11, 1959, while attending a game between the two teams he had co-founded, the Philadelphia Eagles and the Pittsburgh Steelers.

As the NFL's first commissioner, Bell used to draw up the league's schedule at his kitchen table. He bought his share of the Eagles in 1933 for $2,500. Tim Mara had paid the same amount for the New York Giants in 1925. In essence, the NFL at that time was the domain of seven men — Bell, Mara, George Halas, George Preston Marshall, Earl (Curly) Lambeau, Charlie Bidwell and Art Rooney. Their ambition was to carve out a niche among sports fans who loved college football when they weren't watching baseball playoffs and the World Series. But throughout the 1930s, the NFL did little to excite the masses.

Harold (Red) Grange, known as the Galloping Ghost, helped legitimize professional football when he signed with the Chicago Bears in 1925. But the best thing to hit the game was a change in offensive strategy known as the T-formation. With the quarterback lining up behind the center, and two running backs in the backfield, the pivot had a myriad of options from faking hand-offs to throwing deep downfield. The Bears and quarterback Sid Luckman were so efficient using the T-formation they beat the Washington Redskins in the 1940 NFL Championship game by a score of 73–0. (Yes, you read that correctly.) That was the beginning of the Bears as Monsters of the Midway, the NFL's first dynasty.

While the game was undergoing changes on the field, the NFL was a closed shop that operated solely on the wishes of its owners, particularly the southern-born George Marshall, who wanted nothing to do with black athletes. From 1934 to 1945, not one black played in the NFL. It took the 1946 Los Angeles Rams to change that when they signed former UCLA

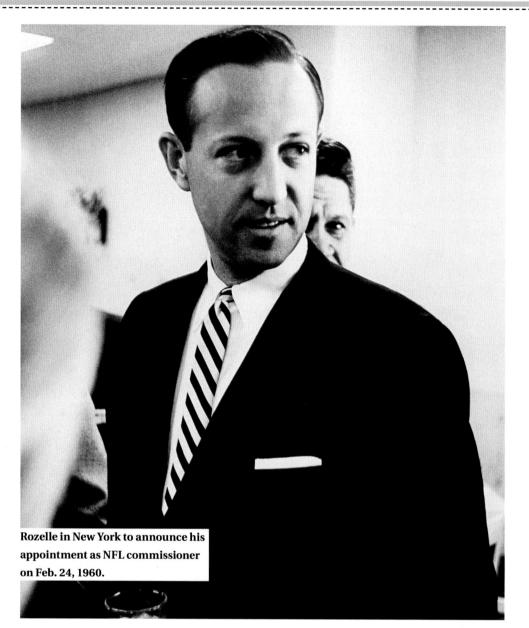

Rozelle in New York to announce his appointment as NFL commissioner on Feb. 24, 1960.

star Ken Washington. Soon after, the Cleveland Browns of the All-America Football Conference added Marion Motley and Bill Willis.

Marshall was so against the inclusion of blacks that he uttered his infamous quote, "[The Washington Redskins] will start signing Negroes when the Harlem Globetrotters start signing whites." Marshall stuck to those words until 1962 when he was told by the U.S. Interior Secretary that unless the Redskins signed a black player, the government would revoke the team's lease at D.C. Stadium (now Robert F. Kennedy Stadium). Marshall responded by drafting Syracuse running back Ernie Davis, who promptly said, "I won't play for that S.O.B." And he didn't. He was traded for another black offensive talent, Bobby Mitchell.

NFL EXPLODES INTO THE MAINSTREAM

What saved the NFL from its parochial thinking and lack of pizzazz in general was the Dec. 28, 1958, championship game. On that day, the NFL exploded into the mainstream with what is still referred to as the greatest game ever played — the Baltimore Colts against the New York Giants. The on-field theatrics were spectacular, and it was full of seminal moments, future Hall of Famers and the first overtime in NFL history. The game was also televised nationwide (watched by more than 40 million people) and it had Johnny Unitas, the first idol of the NFL's modern era.

The pressure-treated Unitas, who operated with a surgeon's precision, engineered two dramatic scoring drives, including the winning march, and thus was springboarded into the limelight. He became the focal point of an emerging game, one that was taking hold of a new generation of Americans, the post-World War II boomers whose changing lifestyle included eating TV dinners on TV trays while flipping through the *TV Guide* and watching the quintessential TV sport: football.

As the game moved toward the swinging Sixties, Rozelle began his rise to prominence. He had had a series of public relations jobs before joining the Los Angeles Rams as its PR specialist in 1952, and after a brief hiatus to help promote the 1956 Melbourne Olympics, the 33-year-old Rozelle became general manager of the Rams — a franchise that had, up till then, been losing fans almost as quickly as it was losing money.

Rozelle gave the Rams purpose and professionalism. He established a Rams store near the team's offices on Beverly Boulevard, where fans could buy all manner of merchandise, including Ram bobblehead dolls. But the California son of a depression-era store owner couldn't do enough to make the Rams a winning team and so, after three seasons as GM, as he was contemplating a change, he was asked if he'd let his name stand as a candidate for the commissioner's job.

Finding the late Bert Bell's replacement had turned into a colossal stand-off. Some of the owners wanted to stick with Austin Gunsel, the former FBI agent and NFL treasurer, who had been serving as acting commissioner. Others preferred west-coast lawyer Marshall Leahy, who wanted the league offices moved to San Francisco from Philadelphia.

After 22 ballots and seven days, on Jan. 26, 1960, Rozelle left the conference room so the owners could debate his merits. He stayed in a men's room to kill time. Whenever someone came in to use the facilities, he would straighten his tie and wash his hands. Finally notified that he'd been approved as commissioner, Rozelle displayed his gift for the appropriate quip. "At least I'm taking the job with clean hands," he said.

He had no idea how messy things were going to get.

THAT UPSTART — THE AFL

"I wonder if that S.O.B. Tex Maule is watching?"

    – NBC broadcaster Curt Gowdy commenting on-air about the *Sports Illustrated* writer who had written nary a good word about the AFL

Lamar Hunt never looked the part of a football titan, either. He, too, was tallish but with a knobby chin, a round face and horn-rimmed glasses.

Hunt was born into enormous wealth, yet wanted little to do with the family oil business. He wanted to own a football team, and after trying unsuccessfully to buy his way into the NFL fraternity, he came up with a solution: he would start his own league. And so, on Aug. 14, 1959, Hunt announced the formation of the American Football League, which was to begin play in 1960.

At first, it seemed as if Hunt and his sev-

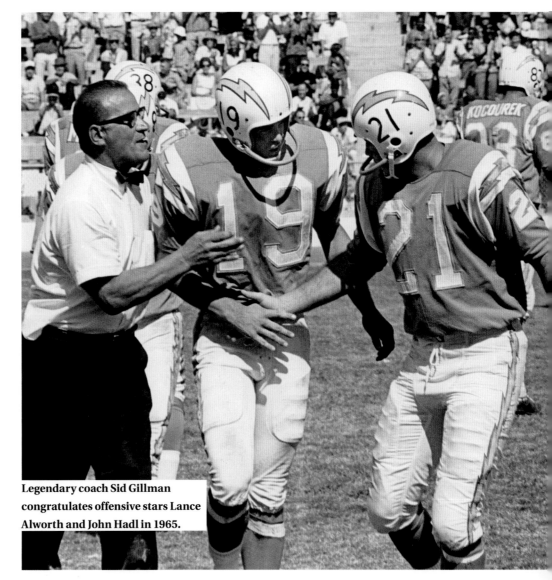

Legendary coach Sid Gillman congratulates offensive stars Lance Alworth and John Hadl in 1965.

en associates (jokingly known as the Foolish Club) had the blessings of the NFL and its commissioner, Bell. But when the NFL began granting expansion teams to the very cities the AFL had intended to cultivate, the tone was set and the battle was on. Not that the AFL was fighting from anything resembling a position of strength.

Early on, almost everything about the new league had a hand-me-down, garage-sale feel to it. The Oakland franchise fumbled its first attempt at naming the new team: a local newspaper held a name-the-team contest and for reasons never quite understood, "the Senors" won by a landslide. (Team officials later switched the name to Raiders rather than have a public address announcer say, "First and 10 for the Senors.") The New York Titans didn't even have a playbook. Head coach Sammy Baugh kept everything recorded in his head. The Denver Broncos may have been the AFL's cheapest-run organization. At the first training camp, the players slept in army-style barracks and were fed poorly. The exception was Friday when everyone was served steak. The idea was to offer meat on Friday because the Catholic players wouldn't eat it. As for the Broncos' uniforms, they were the height of ugliness, including socks with vertical stripes.

At least the Broncos had uniforms for their debut, whereas the Houston Oilers didn't. When the Oilers hit the field, most of the players wore blue and white while 14 others were outfitted in red practice jerseys. Apparently, thieves had made off with the rest of the Oilers'

Broadway Joe Namath

blue-and-white uniforms. "We looked like a bunch of rinky dinks," recalled Oilers' owner Bud Adams. True enough, they did.

History shows the AFL's first regular-season game was played on Sept. 9, 1960, with the vertically-striped-challenged Broncos taking on the Boston Patriots. The game drew 21,597 spectators, and the AFL was off and bumbling. It had few established star players and lacked the NFL's crisp professionalism. Knowing that, the AFL opted for a more wide-open brand of play. Offense was the name of the game and offense is what the AFL sold. Coach Sid Gillman saw to that.

With the Chargers, first in Los Angeles and then in San Diego, Gillman brought a meticulous, inventive mindset to a league that desperately needed both. He didn't like the short passing game that dominated the NFL. He believed in throwing the ball downfield and exciting the fans. The Chargers also had Al Davis and Don Klosterman as scouts. They would eventually bring in the likes of college stars Ron Mix, Paul Lowe, Keith Lincoln, Lance Alworth and John Hadl. The Chargers became regulars in the AFL championship games, twice losing to Houston before crushing the Boston Patriots 51–10 in 1963.

The NFL was convinced all it had to do was sneeze and the AFL would be scattered to the four corners whence it came. But the junior circuit embraced the newness of the

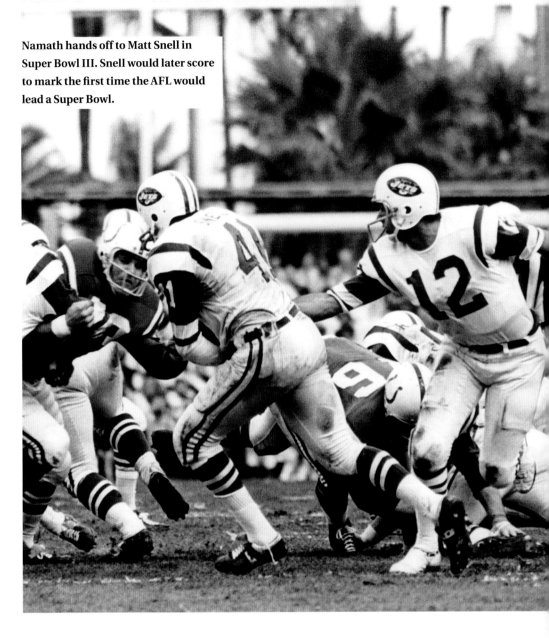

Namath hands off to Matt Snell in Super Bowl III. Snell would later score to mark the first time the AFL would lead a Super Bowl.

LIFE ON THE SUPER STAGE

QUIRKS AND QUOTES

Now entering middle-age, the Super Bowl has provided many a bad game, some good ones, some great games and a list of characters longer than Ben Davidson's handlebar mustache in the 1968 AFL–NFL championship.

One of the early stars of the Super stage was Dallas Cowboys' running back Duane Thomas, who had a Rubik's Cube personality. The more you worked with it, the more confusing it got. Thomas was equal parts strange, belligerent, brilliant and infuriating. During the week leading up to 1972's Super Bowl VI, he was required by the NFL to meet with the media. He did so by sitting in the stands with several scribes clotted around waiting for the great

man to speak. For several minutes, Thomas sat there without saying word. When he spoke, it was to ask, "What time is it?" He eventually got up and left. Apparently, it was time to go.

Thomas, however, did serve up two of the finest Super Bowl quotes ever uttered. Asked on national TV by Tom Brookeshier if he was as fast as he looked on the field, Thomas replied, decade by using two-point converts, having the players' names on the back of their jerseys and the official time on the score clock. Fans began to take to an old game made livelier. The 1962 AFL championship clash between Houston and the Dallas Texans, won by Dallas in overtime, drew 56 million television viewers.

The off-field drama was compelling, too. The AFL began to snap up collegiate stars such as Buck Buchanan, Bobby Bell, Pete Beathard and Matt Snell. The entire football community was rife with tales of intrigue about what teams were doing to ensure they got their player before the other league did. The NFL even had a clandestine procedure, dubbed Operation Handholding, to stand guard over prized recruits and ensure they signed with "the right league." NFL team officials and scouts were involved in the ploy while Rozelle,

Rozelle and Hunt

as commissioner, offered no public knowledge of its existence.

Then came the day the AFL arrived in the minds of the American sporting public: the day Joe Namath agreed to sign with the New York Jets.

Right from the snap in 1965, it was clear the Jets wanted to make a splash with Namath. They drafted him first overall compared to the NFL's St. Louis Cardinals, who took him 12th overall. The Jets offered Namath a three-year deal worth a record $427,000. The Cardinals and the NFL thought Jets' owner Sonny Werblin had flipped his lid.

> NAMATH GAVE THE JETS $427,000 WORTH OF INSTANT PUBLICITY. HE HAD THE LOOKS, THE CHARISMA AND A FOOTBALL PEDIGREE.

Werblin's background in the entertainment business had convinced him that his team, and the AFL too, needed a star and Namath, as Rozelle had said of himself, was the right man at the right time.

Namath gave the Jets $427,000 worth of instant publicity. He had the looks, the charisma and a football pedigree, having led the University of Alabama to a U.S. college championship under coach Bear Bryant in 1964. The Jets began selling out at home and on the road. Before 1965 ended, the AFL had entered into a five-year, $36 million TV agreement with NBC, with veteran announcer Curt Gowdy calling the games. That same year, the Kansas City Chiefs signed Heisman Trophy-winning running back Mike Garrett. The NFL retaliated

by signing a player (Buffalo Bills kicker Pete Gogolak) who was already under contract in the AFL.

One of the first to grasp the magnitude of the NFL/Gogolak move was Al Davis, the former Charger scout who had gone on to run the Oakland Raiders and was now AFL commissioner. "I guess [the AFL owners] thought I'd be a catalyst," Davis said of his appointment. "It was a situation that called for some constant pressure to be put on the other side."

The squeeze-happy Davis applied more pressure than a pair of vice grips. He signed eight NFL quarterbacks, including Roman Gabriel and John Brodie, to AFL contracts. Davis wasn't interested in negotiating peace. He wanted a fight to the finish.

With Davis in office for two months, a series of back-channel meetings were held between the NFL and AFL to discuss the

---

"Evidently." And when asked if winning the Super Bowl was the ultimate, Thomas responded with a question of his own. "If the Super Bowl is the ultimate game, how come they're playing it again next year?" Good point.

Dallas linebacker Thomas (Hollywood) Henderson, who said of Pittsburgh Steelers' quarterback Terry Bradshaw, "He's so dumb he couldn't spell cat if you spotted him the 'c' and 't'" After the Steelers beat Dallas, Henderson had to backpedal furiously. "I didn't say he couldn't play, just that he couldn't spell."

Russ Grimm of the Washington Redskins said he'd run over his own mother to win the Super Bowl. Oakland linebacker Matt Millen concurred: "I'd run over Russ Grimm's mother to win the Super Bowl, too."

HEROES AND ZEROES

You can't miss much at the Super Bowl. Under the media's unforgiving eye, stars become heroes and the mistake-prone become scoundrels. Joe Montana drove his San Francisco 49ers for a late, game-winning touchdown in

Super Bowl XXIII. Prior to that game, Cincinnati Bengals' running back Stanley Wilson was suspended after being caught in a bathroom using cocaine. In Super Bowl XXXIII, John Elway retired in style winning his second consecutive Lombardi Trophy. Prior to that game, Atlanta Falcons' defensive back Eugene Robinson was arrested for soliciting a female undercover police officer who was posing as a prostitute. Robinson had just received the Bart Starr Award from the Christian group Athletes in Action for his "high moral character."

possibility of a merger. The two leagues had been locked in an escalating bidding war for players. Together, they had spent $7 million on their 1966 draft picks — an unheard of amount for player salaries and bonuses. Something had to give.

At first, Rozelle wasn't interested in a merger but the NFL's owners wanted to end the spending spree. Rozelle negotiated the best deal he could. He sent Tex Schramm of the Dallas Cowboys to talk with Hunt, who seemed the most agreeable of the Foolish Club members. As part of the merger, 10 AFL teams were accepted under the NFL banner. Two (Oakland and New York) had to make indemnity payments to the NFL teams in their area. It was agreed the two leagues would officially unite in 1970, with three NFL teams: the Pittsburgh Steelers, Baltimore Colts and Cleveland Browns moving to what would be called the American Football Conference. However, an annual AFL–NFL Championship game would be played starting January 1967.

Ironically, it was Lamar Hunt, the man who wanted to own a football team so badly that he started his own league, who gave the AFL–NFL championship game its lasting moniker. After watching his daughter play with an incredible bouncy toy, the Super Ball, he thought, "the Super Bowl"? Some said it sounded too hokey. Hunt thought so, too. But the name stuck. The first thing Rozelle did was sell the broadcasting rights to the Super Bowl to both CBS and NBC. The two networks paid $1 million each for the one game. That Rozelle was able to play the two networks against each other, for the good of the NFL, was further proof of his negotiating skills.

SUPER BOWL MADNESS

"If there had been a Super Bowl back then, Nero wouldn't have burned Rome. He'd have been too busy schmoozing with corporate chieftains who arrived by sedan chair and reclined under purple robes as grapes were dropped into their mouths."

– Sports writer Dave Kindred on the Big Game

The Super Bowl is the perfect American institution, pomp and pageantry, celebrities and newsmakers and, occasionally, an entertaining football game, although that's hardly necessary. So majestic is the Super Bowl that it no longer requires breath taking action. Just start the countdown to kickoff and the show promotes itself. It is a rolling, rollicking bit of over indulgence you don't want to miss out on. The game has become so grandiose, so ingrained, that it has evolved into a world phenomenon and a parody of itself. How many media-day spoofs have you seen or read? Or Super Bowl TV commercials that never fail to amuse? It's all part of the package now.

Back in 1967, the first AFL–NFL Championship game between the Kansas City Chiefs and the Green Bay Packers was hardly the hottest ticket in Los Angeles. The Packers carried the NFL's expectations as the superior league and were aware of their responsibility. The Chiefs had some outstanding players, but were overwhelmed by the enormity of the challenge and Vince Lombardi's unstoppable Packers' power sweeps.

Ironically, Lombardi wanted no part of hyping the game and sequestered his team in Santa Barbara, 90 miles north of L.A. It was left to the likes of Kansas City defensive back Fred (The Hammer) Williamson to fire up the media with talk of how he was going to flatten Packers' receivers Carroll Dale and Boyd Dowler with his mind-numbing kung-fu karate chop "delivered perpendicularly to the earth's latitude." Late in the second quarter, Williamson was knocked cold trying to tackle Green Bay running back Donny Anderson. Asked why it took the Packers so long to get to Williamson, safety Willie Wood replied, "It took him that long to make a tackle."

Despite The Hammer's best trash-talking efforts, most everything about the first title game was pedestrian. The final crowd count of 61,946 looked small inside the mammoth

---

Then there was the case of the stolen wristwatch. When the Miami Dolphins won Super Bowl VII to go 17–0 on the year, the players hoisted head coach Don Shula on their shoulders and carried him off the field. Before he reached the dressing room, Shula noticed someone, a fan, had stolen his watch right off his wrist. Shula spotted the thief and ran after him. The coach got his watch back; the perfect ending to a flawless season.

The Super Bowl is so powerful it can even elevate the stature of a losing player and ennoble him in defeat. Don Beebee of the Buffalo Bills earned lasting notoriety in Super Bowl XXVII for chasing down Dallas Cowboys' defensive lineman Leon Lett in the fourth quarter and punching the ball out of his hands before Lett could showboat his way into the end zone. Dallas won the game anyway, 52–17. Beebee won a lot of fans.

And let's not forget Carolina Panthers' quarterback Jake Delhomme, who in Super Bowl XXXVII passed for 323 yards and three touchdowns only to be beaten by the New England Patriots on a last-minute field goal. As the Patriots celebrated, Delhomme stood on the field as long as he could to capture the disappointment. "I just wanted to watch and let it sink in and hurt a little bit," he explained afterward. "When I have a tough day, I'll just think about that feeling and it will make me dig down just a little deeper."

Delhomme won a lot of fans that day, too. Chances are he would have ditched them all for a chance to hold the trophy. ■

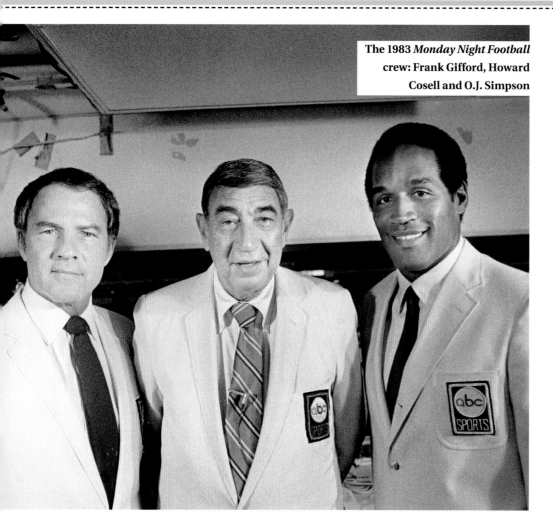

The 1983 *Monday Night Football* crew: Frank Gifford, Howard Cosell and O.J. Simpson

L.A. Coliseum. Ticket prices were $12. The game ended with the Packers winning by 25 points. The NFL's honor had been preserved and not much more happened the following year when the Packers won again, this time by 19 points over Oakland.

With the NFL's showcase event in danger of becoming a non-event, it was Namath who rode to the rescue with a pre-game boast that left The Hammer Williamson sprawled in its wake. With the Jets about to face the all-powerful Baltimore Colts in the Super Bowl, Namath predicted, "We're going to win on Sunday. I guarantee it."

This was akin to saying the Mona Lisa wasn't much of a painting. The Colts had obliterated their foes and crushed Cleveland 34–0 in the NFL championship game. Sports writers of the day, particularly Tex Maule of *Sports Illustrated*, wrote that the Jets would lose by 30 points or more. The official betting line had the Jets as 18-point underdogs.

Enter Namath, stage right. He not only backed up his prediction by leading the Jets to a 16–7 upset, he put the "super" in the Super Bowl. He made it matter and, in doing so, he became the idol of football's new era much the same way Unitas had done a decade earlier.

"Standing in the press box and watching Namath unravel the NFL myth was a thing to behold," said broadcaster Howard Cosell.

That myth was further unraveled when Kansas City whipped Minnesota in Super Bowl IV, giving both leagues a pair of championship wins before their official merger in 1970 — the same year Vince Lombardi died of cancer. Rozelle had the good gumption to name the Super Bowl trophy in honor of the venerable coach; the commissioner knew how to keep the calliope playing by cultivating captains of industry with one hand and playing to the masses with the other.

In the years following, the big game began to expand like a hot-air balloon. It took on a larger-than-life form that was part sport, part business, all entertainment. University marching bands gave way to Carol Channing, Up With People, New Kids on the Block, Michael Jackson, Janet Jackson, Paul McCartney, the Rolling Stones and Prince. Anthem singers ranged from Anita Bryant to Diana Ross, Billy Joel, Cher, the Dixie Chicks, Beyoncé and back to Billy Joel. The most unusual Super Bowl halftime theme? The XXVIII tribute to Indiana Jones and the Temple of the Forbidden Eye produced by Disney.

The Forbidden Eye? Why not?

"The Super Bowl is like the last chapter in a hair-raising mystery," Rozelle said. "No one would dare miss it."

THE MOVE TO PRIMETIME

"Everything … everything is magnified by television."

– TV sports guru Roone Arledge

Through the early 1960s, Rozelle had a vision. It was a good vision and he wanted to share it with the NFL's owners. "Let's play a regular-season game on a week night," he said. "How about Fridays?" The owners said no. That night was reserved for high school football, they argued.

So Rozelle rejigged his proposal and had a 1964 game scheduled for Monday night in Detroit between the Lions and Green Bay. It drew more than 59,000 spectators. By the time the 1969 season ended, the NFL had played six more Monday nighters and had enough faith in Rozelle's vision to allow him to sell it to a major U.S. TV network.

"There were a lot more TV sets in use on Monday night than on Sunday afternoon," reasoned the commissioner, who rightly deduced that a prime-time presence would expand the brand and attract more viewers and those all-precious advertising dollars.

CBS and NBC passed on the idea but ABC, which trailed its small-screen rivals, took the chance only after knowing Howard Hughes' sports network was ready to make a deal with the NFL. ABC producer Roone Arledge, a pretty fair visionary himself, was given the Monday Night assignment and opted for a bolder, more stimulating approach to broadcasting NFL games. His innovations came at viewers like an unblocked defensive end.

First, there was the theme music, the instrumental intro by Johnny Pearson that became a recognizable call to the couch. More TV cameras were used to give fans a vibrant look at the action with the stadium lights glimmering off the players' helmets. There was the increase of on-screen graphics, instant replays and three announcers in the booth. One of those announcers was Don Meredith, the former quarterback who had joined the expansion Cowboys in 1960 when the NFL was doing its best to thwart the AFL. He got to do the color commentary on *Monday Night Football*'s first game, featuring Joe Namath, the AFL icon who super-sized the Super Bowl.

Within a year, Meredith was joined on Monday Night by Frank Gifford, who had played for the New York Giants in the first nationally-televised championship game in 1958 that brought the NFL to the mainstream. It was a mix of personalities and possibilities; past participants forming new elements.

But the man who gave the show its tone, its swagger, its feeling of uniqueness was Howard William Cosell. No one ever loved the sound of his own voice more than Cosell. After listening to him for five minutes you either wanted your ears cut off with a rusty saw or hear another five minutes of Cosell's soap-box ramblings. Either way, he garnered reaction and that's what ABC and the NFL wanted.

Cosell's shtick was his punctuated, verbose style of announcing. He could make something as simple as a pregame coin toss sound like the lead up to the Civil War. He didn't know the x's and o's of football, but he understood story lines and he

delivered them while playing off the rigid Gifford and fun-loving Meredith, who would warble "Turn Out the Lights, The Party's Over" whenever a game got out of reach.

"We were desecrating something," ABC's Arledge told *Sports Illustrated*. "CBS had Ray Scott, and now we had this loudmouthed Cosell on TV questioning everything, yelling about what a dumb trade that was, and asking, 'Don't football players have rights?' And a lot of the owners just couldn't deal with it."

Viewers kept tuning in either to laud Cosell's clout or dismiss him as a clown. After its debut season, enough viewers had tuned in to make *Monday Night Football* the third highest-rated TV program behind *The Flip Wilson Show* and *The Mary Tyler Moore Show*. And still the innovations kept coming. At halftime, *Monday Night Football* showed the highlights from all of Sunday's games, with Cosell providing the breathless voice-over.

Then there were the guests, the visitors who dropped by the booth to share a few words, usually with a star-struck Cosell (who could curb his yapping tongue when he wanted to). Beginning in 1973, the cast of droppers-by included politicians Ronald Reagan, Henry Kissinger and Ted Kennedy, musicians John Lennon and John Denver, actor Burt Reynolds and even Kermit the Frog. Sadly, it was during a Dec. 8, 1980, Monday night game that Cosell announced to the world that Lennon had been shot and killed in New York.

"This, we have to say it, is just a football game, no matter who wins or loses," Cosell said to the nation in the wake of Lennon's death — much to everyone's agreement.

Winners and losers all had their moments on Monday night. One of the best featured a close-to-retiring Joe Montana leading Kansas City to a 31–28 win against John Elway and the Denver Broncos. Another had Green Bay quarterback Brett Favre playing the day after his father's death and throwing for 399 yards and four touchdowns. One of the worst showings? The Pittsburgh Steelers over the winless Miami Dolphins by a final score of 3–0 in 2007.

THE REST OF THE STORY

With Sundays and Mondays locked up as the sole sporting domain of the NFL, the biggest challenges for Rozelle next came from within the organization itself. Labor strife was inevitable as revenues grew and the players demanded their share. There were two player strikes in the 1980s. The first, in 1982, lasted 57 days. The 1987 strike wiped out one week of games before the NFL brought in replacement players to play the next three weeks. There were also issues over franchise relocations. Rozelle fought long and often with his former AFL peer, Al Davis, who moved the Raiders out of Oakland to L.A. when the Rams left the L.A. Coliseum to play in Anaheim.

As the 1980s wound down, so did Rozelle. He had fought off both the upstart World Football League and the U.S. Football League to maintain the NFL's dominance of the pro-football market. He had moved the game "from the back page to the front page," said New York Giants' owner Wellington Mara. "From daytime to prime time." It was time to retire, which he did in 1989.

Before he died of a brain tumor in 1996, Rozelle said he wanted to be remembered most for developing the Super Bowl into one of the biggest sporting spectacles on the planet. He'll be remembered for that and more.

"Pro football was taking off when I became commissioner," he said, "and when a sport's successful, and you're its chief executive officer, much of the credit flows to you and you develop a good track record."

You become a football titan, as much as Unitas, Brown, Lombardi and Montana. Different, for sure, but no less important. ▪

THE
TOP 20

Terry Bradshaw
Jim Brown
Dick Butkus
John Elway
Brett Favre
Forrest Gregg
Deacon Jones
Dan Marino
Joe Montana
Walter Payton
Jerry Rice
Barry Sanders
Deion Sanders
Gayle Sayers
Emmitt Smith
Roger Staubach
Fran Tarkenton
Lawrence Taylor
Johnny Unitas
Reggie White

12 TERRY BRADSHAW

QUARTERBACK

THIS GOOD OL'BOY'S NOBODY'S FOOL

Don't for an instant let that folksy charm and the good-ol'-boy demeanor con you. The Smoky and the Bandit schtick that he has transformed almost into an art form on Fox NFL Sunday broadcasts is part Terry, surely.

But the kid from Shreveport, Louisiana, was, and is, nobody's fool.

In his day, his Pittsburgh Steelers had it all. They had the rampaging Mean Joe Greene, snarling Jack Lambert and the unassailable Steel Curtain defense. They had the Mikhail Baryshnikov of wide receivers in Lynn Swann. They had a workhorse tailback in Franco Harris carrying the overland mail, and they had coach Chuck Noll pulling the strategic strings along the sidelines.

But most of all, they had a director fully equipped to draw the very best out of his ensemble cast.

"Imagine yourself sitting on top of a great thoroughbred horse," Terry Bradshaw would later say in describing the experience. "You sit up there and you feel the power. That's what it was like, playing quarterback on that team. It was a great ride."

At 6-foot-3 and 215 pounds, Bradshaw would never be confused with a jockey. But no one could argue that he wasn't the man in the saddle, driving the big, fast, unbeatable stallion relentlessly forward.

Today, he is one of the most amiable sports personalities in America. Funny. Self-deprecating. As at home in a TV booth at Lambeau Field as he is guesting with Jay Leno on *The Tonight Show*. Football fans love him for his wit, his candor and, naturally, for the four Super Bowl championships he directed in only six years.

What many conveniently forget now is that the Terry Bradshaw legend was painfully slow in developing.

In the formative years of his career (and after), Bradshaw was derided as a bumpkin, a rube. Every time he opened his mouth, it seemed, he stuck a cleat in it. His sound bites were peppered with phrases such as: "We had 10 turnovers in one game, seven fumbles and four interceptions." Or, "I may be dumb but I'm not stupid." His critics lapped it up.

Bradshaw arrived in Steeltown from Louisiana Tech as the first player select-

CAREER HIGHLIGHTS

Drafted: 1970; 1st round, 1st overall; Pittsburgh Steelers

Rookie Season: 13 games, 218 att, 83 comp, 1,410 yds, 6 TDs, 24 int, 30.4 QB rating

---

Career Year (1978): 16 games, 368 att, 207 comp, 2,915 yds, 28 TDs, 20 int, 84.7 QB rating

---

Accomplishments
NFL MVP: 1978
Pro Bowls: 3 (1975, 1978, 1979)
All-Pro: 3 (1975, 1978, 1979)
Super Bowl MVP: 2 (1979, 1980)
All-Decade Team: 1970s
Led the league in touchdown passes: 1978, 1982
Hall of Fame: 1989

Ranking on the all-time passing list in major categories
Completions: 2,025 (49th)
Attempts: 3,901 (42nd)
Yards: 27,989 (39th)
Touchdowns: 212 (22nd)
QB Rating: 70.9 (129th)

Quick Fact: In 2006, Bradshaw signed a contract with the Daytona Beach Thunder of the American Indoor Football League to be their fourth-string quarterback at the age of 57. However, the comeback was short lived as he had to have back surgery and missed the season.

Bradshaw leads the Steelers to a
35–31 victory over the Dallas Cowboys
in Super Bowl XIII.

ed in the 1970 draft. In his first five seasons, he threw 48 touchdown passes — and 81 interceptions.

In his second autobiography, *No Easy Game*, he recounted how much he had to endure to win over a city, establish a reputation, and find his feet in the pro ranks. "I always wanted everyone to like me," he wrote. "I wanted the city of Pittsburgh to be proud of me. But my first few seasons, I could count the number of people on my bandwagon on one finger.

"I had people call me a dummy and a hick. I had a lady stop me outside the stadium and tell me I stunk. I heard the people cheer when I got hurt. Rub up against enough briar patches and your hide will get pretty tough. Mine did."

Bradshaw even lost the starting quarterbacking spot to Joe Gilliam in 1974 for a short time. But by the end of that season he had regained control of the offense, and the Steelers were on their way to Super Bowl IX, a 16–6 verdict over the snake-bitten Minnesota Vikings.

It would be the first bold step in an unparalleled march to greatness.

The next year, Bradshaw and Co. were back at the big dance again, Super Bowl X. The man at the helm threw for 209 yards, including the now legendary 64-yard toss to Swann late in the fourth quarter to ice a 21–17 win over the Dallas Cowboys.

As proficient as he was in directing his offense, utilizing its assets to the fullest measure, there was a streak of the riverboat gambler about him, too. One of the characteristics that made him such a perfect fit for this nearly perfect team was his unshakable confidence.

"My nature," he explained once, "was attack. Throw it deep. Anybody can throw wide. Let's go deep." The air-out to Swann remains the most memorable example of that go-for-broke mindset.

Three seasons later in 1978, the Steelers were once again back in the title hunt. Bradshaw produced his finest regular season, and was named Associated Press NFL MVP for 2,915 passing yards and 28 touchdowns. There wasn't much more he could do professionally to convince people. Still, the snide remarks would not die.

Before Super Bowl XIII, mouthy Dallas linebacker Thomas (Hollywood) Henderson famously ratcheted up the rivalry between America's Team and the NFL's best team by saying of Terry Bradshaw, "He couldn't spell 'cat' if you spotted him the 'c' and the 't'."

Bradshaw didn't much care about spelling bees, but he certainly knew how to spell W-I-N. His 318 yards and four touchdown tosses earned him the Super Bowl MVP as Pittsburgh claimed its third championship in five years, 35–31.

Hollywood Henderson offered only a lame rebuttal.

No one knew it at the time, of course, but the 1979 season would be the swansong of that legendary Pittsburgh run. Another Super Bowl, this time a 31–19 shutdown of the Los Angeles Rams, and another MVP for the guy behind center.

Terry Bradshaw would soldier on for another four seasons, through injury and disappointment, finally retiring in 1983. He'd be a first-ballot Hall of Famer, naturally. And although the Steelers do not retire numbers, no one in his right mind would be daft enough to ask for 12. So consider it unofficially retired.

Over 14 seasons, he threw for 27,989 yards, and his touchdown-to-interception ratio is only 212-to-210, hardly impressive by conventional "great quarterback" standards. But then, Terry Bradshaw was never a conventional quarterback. Merely a great one. He just won, long before the Nike ads coined the phrase, "Just do it." ∎

	Gms	Att	Yds	Avg	TD	College
TOTAL	118	2,359	12,312	5.2	106	Syracuse

32 JIM BROWN

RUNNING BACK

IF SUPERMAN WAS A RUNNING BACK

Jim Brown and Sam Huff: the unstoppable force vs. the immovable object.

Their confrontations were the stuff of legend: Brown, the greatest running back of his age — arguably of any age — and Huff, the Hall of Fame-bound middle linebacker of the Washington Redskins. One particular duel stands out in Huff's mind. It encapsulates the rivalry and respect between the two men, as well as Jim Brown's brilliance.

On Brown's first carry of this particular game, Huff plugged the hole with his usual ferocity and stopped his adversary for no gain. As Brown picked himself up off the turf and hauled himself back into the huddle, Huff hollered, "Brown, you stink!"

The next time Brown got his hands on the ball, same result. Negligible pick-up. Again, a taunting, "Brown, you stink!"

"The third time Jimmy carried," Huff would recall years later, "he drove into the middle. But nobody stopped him. He got a couple of key blocks, exploded past me and the secondary and raced 65 yards for a touchdown. Trotting back to the Browns' bench, he turned toward me and I could see he had a big grin on his

face. Then he shouted, 'Hey, Huff, how do I smell from here?'"

Long before there was Sweetness or Barry or LaDanian or Tony D, there was Jim Brown. He was the prototype NFL running back: strong, powerful, fast. Gone from the game for over three decades now, his name still resonates whenever people speak of the top players of all time. Huff once said that the only way to handle Jim Brown was "to grab, hold, hang on and wait for help."

The image of him hitting the line and powering past is what lingers — the pure, raw brute force of it all. Brown left such a legacy that he was voted the best football player ever by *Sporting News* in 2002. A quote attributed to an unnamed defender, perhaps merely fanciful, but nonetheless dead accurate, gives a fair impression of the man's impact: "That Jim Brown. He says he isn't Superman. What he really means is that Superman isn't Jimmy Brown!"

This was a pile driver of a back, legendary for brushing off tacklers and taunts alike. He was one of the few in his sport who wasn't tied to numbers, as unparalleled as they were. He played only nine seasons

CAREER HIGHLIGHTS

Drafted: 1957; 1st round, 6th overall; Cleveland Browns

Rookie Season (1957): 12 games, 202 att, 942 yds, 4.7 yd avg, 9 TDs

----

Career Year (1963): 14 games, 291 att, 1,863 yds, 6.4 yd avg, 12 TDs; 24 rec, 268 yds, 11.2 yd avg, 3 TDs.

Accomplishments
Rookie of the Year: 1957
Pro Bowls: 9 consecutive (1957–1965)
NFL MVP: 4 (1957, 1958, 1963, 1965)
Hall of Fame: 1971

Ranking on the all-time list in major rushing categories
Attempts: 2,359 (20th)
Yards: 12,312 (8th)
Touchdowns: 106 (5th)
Yards from scrimmage: 14,811 (15th)
Rushing/receiving TDs: 126 (7th)

Quick Fact: Jim Brown was an All-American in both football and lacrosse at the University of Syracuse (1956).

Brown runs against the Giants in 1963 on his way to the NFL MVP.

before retiring in the summer of 1966 to pursue his ambitions an actor and devote more time to the racial struggles of African Americans, but he led the league in rushing in eight of those seasons. Naturally, he was a Pro Bowl selection every year.

"You gang-tackled him, did whatever you could, give him extracurriculars. He'd get up slow, look at you, and walk back to the huddle and wouldn't say a word, just come at you again, and again," said Chuck Bednarik of the Philadelphia Eagles. "You'd just say 'What the hell? What's wrong with this guy for heaven sake? When is he gonna stop carrying the ball? How much more can he take?'"

The answer: Anything any defender had to give.

Brown gave this bit of advice to Baltimore Colts' tight end John Mackey: "Make sure when anyone tackles you, he remembers how much it hurts."

"He lived by that philosophy," said Mackey, "and I always followed that advice."

Brown hit. People hurt. And they remembered. At 6-foot-2 and 228 pounds, he could run around you, past you or through you.

"I always made it a practice to use my head before my body," Brown once said in an interview. "I looked upon playing football like a businessman might. The game was my business, my body and my mind were my assets, and injuries were my liabilities."

Brown spent his youth on St. Simons Island, off the Georgia coast, being raised by his great-grandmother. His father, a gambler called "Sweet Sue," had run off. His mother had gone north to look for work. When the young Jim Brown rejoined his mother, who was doing housework for a family in Manhasset, Long Island, he got involved with a gang called the Gaylords.

Football pulled him out of trouble. "It changed my life," he said. "Otherwise, I could have been some kind of gangster."

Brown could certainly dish it out on the football field, but off the field he has spent a lifetime giving back to the community. These days, he works with Cleveland and L.A. kids caught up in a gang lifestyle through the Amer-I-Can program, which he founded in 1988.

His almost superhuman exploits on the field as well as his social conscience made him an idol to millions.

"I had two heroes growing up, John Wayne and Roy Rogers," former heavyweight champ George Foreman admitted. "Then one day I saw Jim Brown."

Anyone who saw him play could never forget him. In 1965, his last season, Brown piled up 1,544 yards, and the Browns reached the championship game against Green Bay. At that time, he held NFL records for most seasons leading the league in rushing (8), most lifetime carries (2,359), most yards (12,312), highest average gain (5.2 yards per carry) and most TDs rushing (126). And he had propelled Cleveland to the 1964 title.

No one had, or has, done more in less time. Jim Brown walked away leaving fans begging for more.

During a lifetime spent in the public eye, he made the cover of *Time* magazine in 1964 and posed nude for Playgirl a decade later. He's been enshrined in the Pro Football Hall of Fame, the College Football Hall of Fame and the Lacrosse Hall of Fame. Director Spike Lee made a documentary on his career and life called *Jim Brown: All American*.

As an actor, Brown was certainly never All-Pro. No Laurence Olivier or Spencer Tracy. There were relatively small but memorable turns in such films as *The Dirty Dozen, Rio Conchos, Any Given Sunday, tick, tick, tick ...*, and others. Undoubtedly his greatest role was as Jim Brown, pile driver without peer. That part was worthy of an Oscar. That part, he was born to play. ▪

51 DICK BUTKUS

MIDDLE LINEBACKER

BORN TO BE A BEAR

"I wouldn't ever set out to hurt anybody. Unless it was, you know, important — like a league game or something."

– Dick Butkus

The ferocity, the anger, that unparalleled rage to be the best and to get it done at any cost, long ago passed into the realm of sporting legend. The story of Dick Butkus apparently trying to bite Miami guard Larry Little in a pileup and then take a nip at an official, whether true or not (Butkus denies it, Little affirms it and the official never gave his view of the situation), has taken on almost mythic proportions. In another game, against Detroit, he was accused of provoking three on-field fights and poking a finger through the facemask and into an eye of Lions' tight end Charlie Saunders.

If the name Johnny Unitas embodies cool efficiency, Lynn Swann balletic grace and Brett Favre inspirational toughness, only one word comes to mind when you mention Dick Butkus: Pain.

"It makes me mad sometimes," Butkus once complained. "Some people think I have to get down on all fours to eat my couple pounds of raw meat every day. Nobody thinks I can talk, much less write my name."

Oh, but he left his signature on the NFL in the 1960s. He could hit like an ornery mule, fill a gap in the defensive line and strike fear in the heart of anybody daft enough to hold onto the football for any significant length of time. His image, that of the wild man with a moustache in the dead-of-night Chicago Bears' No. 51 black jersey, defined an era.

Some memorable quotes have been uttered about Butkus's play over the years: Detroit Lions' GM Russ Thomas called him "an annihilating SOB," while Green Bay running back MacArthur Lane once said, "If given a choice I'd rather go one-on-one with a grizzly bear. I pray that I can get up every time Butkus hits me."

Pittsburgh quarterback Terry Hanratty summed up his play when saying, "If he doesn't tackle you, you can still hear him coming. You know he's going to be there eventually. It's savage." While teammate Ron Smith said of Butkus, "He'll be all right as soon as he has his couple cups of blood."

Put simply, Dick Butkus made brutality attractive. He is the gold standard: every linebacker who has come after him is subject to comparison, and every linebacker has ultimately been found wanting.

Born and raised in the Roseland section of the south side of Chicago, from Lithuanian stock, one of nine kids, Dick Butkus was seemingly born to be a Bear. Butkus has always credited his hunger to succeed on being a poor kid who wanted more.

Eventually, he and his city would become synonymous. Inseparable in the public consciousness.

At 6-foot-4 and 245 pounds, Butkus could not only roam from sideline to sideline, but also possessed superb instincts for reading a play, skills he was never given full credit for. Drafted in the first round by his hometown team, handed a reported $235,000 contract to keep him away from the rival AFL, he led the Bears in tackles, interceptions, forced fumbles and fumble recoveries during his rookie season. Not only did he inspire the Bears' defense, he *was* the Bears' defense.

Baltimore Colts' veteran offensive lineman Jim Parker called Butkus "the best rookie I've ever seen in my time in the league." Countless others agreed.

During his career, the big Bear would make 22 interceptions from the position and recover 27 fumbles. What set him apart from virtually every other linebacker (with the exception of Green Bay icon Ray Nitschke) was a voracious appetite for physical contact — for confrontation. He absolutely loved to be challenged to one-on-one battles.

"Some people," admitted Butkus, "think I'm kept in a cage and let out on Sundays."

To stoke the inner fire, he would use an old, but effective, parlor trick.

"When I went on the field to warm up," he recalled, "I would manufacture things to make me mad. If someone on the other team was laughing, I'd pretend he was laughing at me or

the Bears. It always worked for me."

And worked against whatever team Chicago was supposed to play that afternoon.

Alex Karras, one of the meanest hombres of the Butkus era, paid homage to the king of linebackers when he said, "He's one of those rare superstars, like Wilt Chamberlain or Lew Alcindor [Kareem Abdul-Jabbar] in basketball or Gordie Howe in hockey in his great years, where just by being on the field, the game changes. If you had 11 like him going against you, you wouldn't get any points on the scoreboard. Ever." Unfortunately, the Bear teams that Butkus led too often weren't up to his extraordinary level. So he had to make do with individual accolades.

A series of knee injuries forced him to retire in 1973, after only nine seasons. But he'd packed more into those years than lesser-motivated men had in 15. He's been inducted into the College Football Hall of Fame and joins the legendary Red Grange as one of only two players whose jersey numbers have been retired at the University of Illinois.

The Pro Football Hall of Fame was, of course, a lock, in 1979, in his first year of eligibility. And in 1985, the Downtown Athletic Club of Orlando, Florida, created an award in his name for the country's top collegiate linebacker.

More than the accolades and the honors, though, we are left with the visceral memory of No. 51, eyes ablaze, arms flying, looking like a madman escaped from the asylum, putting his body on the line to lay another thunderous smack on a ball carrier. That image is the essence, the spirit of the indomitability of pro football.

"With the highest respect," said teammate Mike Ditka on one occasion, "I've got to say that Dick is an animal."

The quintessential Monster of the Midway. ▪

	Gms	Att	Comp	Yds	TD	Int	College
TOTAL	234	7,250	4,123	51,475	300	226	Stanford

7

JOHN ELWAY

QUARTERBACK

THE SENTIMENTAL FAVORITE

"You learn a lot more from the lows because it makes you pay attention to what you're doing."

– John Elway

If ever there was a sentimental favorite, someone for the fence-sitters to root for, it had to be John Elway on the afternoon of Jan. 25, 1998, at Qualcomm Stadium in San Diego. The toothy, bashful, matinee-idol Bronco quarterback who, in 15 seasons, had accumulated everything a man could want in his chosen profession — wealth, fame, the devotion of a city and the respect of his peers … everything, that is, but one thing. That day, Elway shed the title of lovable loser forever. That day, he took the Mile High City higher than it had ever been before. That day, the demons were exorcised and the growing whispers of all heart and no head were forever banished.

The Denver Broncos, after all, had a history of spectacularly melting in the Big One — three Super Bowl appearances for Elway, four for the Broncos: three losses for Elway, four for the Broncos.

Quarterback Brett Favre and the defending champions, the Green Bay Packers,

were favored in that afternoon in January at Super Bowl XXXII. True to form, Favre marched the Pack for a touchdown on the game's opening drive. It seemed that fate would spit derisively in the face of John Elway and his compatriots yet again. But this time, the script turned out differently. This time, Elway simply refused to roll over and play dead. In a back-and-forth contest, the old pro directed two fourth-quarter TD drives, and the Broncos held on to win 31–24.

Running back Terrell Davis may have scooted for three touchdowns and gone home toting the MVP honors, but there was no doubt who had been the inspiration behind the renaissance. The fans in San Diego chanted him into the dressing room in tribute. The sound of "El-way! El-way!" reverberated around the stadium. "John left it out on the field tonight," praised Broncos' linebacker Bill Romanowski. "He played his heart out. He left his soul on that field."

"This guy is almost 40 years old," echoed linebacker John Mobley, "and he is laying his life and body on the line." For John Elway, a quest that for so long seemed

CAREER HIGHLIGHTS

Drafted: 1983; 1st round, 1st overall; Baltimore Colts

Rookie Season (1983): 11 games, 259 att, 123 comp, 1,663 yds, 7 TDs, 14 int, 54.9 QB rating

----

Career Year (1993): 16 games, 551 att, 348 comp, 4,030 yds, 25 TDs, 10 int, 90.2 QB rating

----

Accomplishments
Pro Bowls: 9 (1987, 1988, 1990, 1992, 1994, 1995, 1997–1999)
All-Pro: 5 (1986, 1987, 1993, 1996, 1997)
NFL MVP: 1987
Super Bowl MVP: 1999
All-Decade Team: 1990s
Hall of Fame: 2004

Ranking on the all-time passing list in major categories
Completions: 4,123 (3rd)
Attempts: 7,250 (3rd)
Yards: 51,475 (3rd)
Touchdowns: 300 (5th)
QB rating: 79.9 (47th)

Quick Fact: John Elway holds the record of most times being sacked (516).

Elway celebrates after his last NFL game, a 34–19 victory in Super Bowl XXXIII.

tantalizingly out of reach had finally come to an end.

"I've experienced the highest of highs and lowest of lows," he said. "I think to really appreciate anything, you have to be at both ends of the spectrum. I've always joked about Joe Montana not appreciating his Super Bowls nearly as much as I do because he never lost one. We lost three before we won one."

And it felt so damn good, the Broncos went out and did it again the next season. In what was to be Elway's swansong in professional football, he steered the only team he'd ever played for to another title, throwing the ball for 336 yards and touchdown while scoring one himself along the ground, as Denver blew away the overmatched Atlanta Falcons 34–19 at Pro Player Stadium in Miami. Elway was named MVP of Super Bowl XXXIII. It would be his last game.

One of the most highly-publicized players ever to enter the NFL, following a stellar collegiate career at Stanford (as well as two summers of minor-league baseball for the New York Yankees' organization), Elway was chosen first overall by the Baltimore Colts in 1983. He balked, convinced that the Colts offered him no chance to compete on a successful team, and used his baseball option as leverage. If Baltimore wouldn't trade him, he'd take his chances on the diamond. He held firm.

In this game of blink, the Colts eventually relented, dealing Elway's rights to Denver in exchange for quarterback Mark Hermann, offensive lineman Chris Hint and a first-round draft choice in 1985.

The Broncos were, naturally, ecstatic. In sports parlance, this big, rawboned kid had everything you could want from a competitive and a marketing standpoint. A gun for an arm. Size. Toughness. And that Ultra Brite smile aligned with a boyish charm. In fact, Elway had everything an organization dreams for when looking to anchor a franchise. It would turn out to be one of the most lopsided trades in memory.

Almost immediately, Elway began to pay dividends. He became not only one of the great quarterbacks of an era, but he also morphed into the face of his franchise. For a decade and a half, he was Denver's favorite adopted son. Professionally, he had grown up in front of their eyes. They considered him one of their own.

When John Elway retired, on top — a place many doubted he'd ever reach — he ranked second all-time in passing yards (51,475), attempts (7,250) and completions (4,123). He had engineered 47 come-from-behind victories for the Broncos and had won five of the six AFC championship games he took part in. His record of 148–82–1 is one of the finest ever by a quarterback. He finished tied (at nine) for the second most Pro Bowl selections at the position, and no one man has played in more Super Bowls than John Elway's five. He'd done it all.

History would, doubtlessly, have looked slightly more ambiguously on the Elway legacy had he not corralled those two late Super Bowl titles. Regardless, the statistics and the impact he made on the Broncos, and the league as a whole, stand on their own. With his induction to the Hall of Fame, Elway joined the likes of Johnny Unitas and Bart Starr, Roger Staubach and Terry Bradshaw, Joe Montana and Dan Marino, as a quarterback for the ages.

"I don't know if I like being the sentimental favorite," the man who had almost everything protested uneasily, on the eve of what would turn out to be his first taste, Super Bowl XXXIII in San Diego.

By that time, John Elway had little choice. ▪

4 BRETT FAVRE

QUARTERBACK

FOOTBALL'S ANSWER TO THE PONY EXPRESS

In an age of transience, of quick fixes and fleeting fads, he remained a welcome constant. Game in and game out, season in and season out — he was football's answer to the Pony Express. "Through wind and sleet and hail and dead of night …" (Not to mention those sno-cone Sunday afternoons at Lambeau Field come December). Always delivering the mail.

"You're never guaranteed about next year," Brett Favre is noted for saying. "People ask you what you think of next season … you have to seize the opportunities when they're in front of you."

There will be no next season, no more opportunities for Brett Favre.

Mar. 4, 2008, marked the end of an era, not only in Green Bay, but across the National Football League.

After years of hinting and debating and weighing options, Brett Favre decided to move on in his life, and did so on his own terms — something not many players are able to do.

As the heart and soul of the Packers, Favre was one of the game's most fearless competitors. He didn't just seize opportu-

nities; he leapt at them, lunged like a lion in the zoo at feeding time. It's impossible to think of a quarterback with a greater zeal than the No. 4 in Packer green and gold.

It was no coincidence the cover of *Sports Illustrated*'s Dec. 4, 2007, Football in America issue featured a close-up of Favre under the headline "For the Love of the Game." He embraced it like few others.

Cheer for the Green Bay Packers or loathe them, everyone with a passing interest in the game respected Brett Lorenzo Favre, the most famous son ever to come out of Gulfport, Mississippi. He played too tough, cared too much, stood too tall for anyone to quibble with much conviction.

Favre had been described as a gunslinger, a riverboat gambler, a throwback to the days of Slingin' Sammy Baugh — an old-time hero for a modern world. A less craggy John Wayne, the quiet, heroic man of action.

He maybe hasn't the Super Bowl ring collection of, say, Joe Montana or Terry Bradshaw or Tom Brady, but no one in the history of the game has done more at the position. Look it up.

CAREER HIGHLIGHTS

Drafted: 1991; 2nd round, 33rd overall; Atlanta Falcons

Rookie Season (1991): 2 games, 5 att, 0 comp, 0 yds, 0 TDs, 2 int, 0.0 QB rating

Career Year (1995): 16 games, 359 comp, 570 att, 4,413 yds, 38 TDs, 13 int, 99.5 QB rating

Accomplishments
NFL MVP: 3 (1995–1997)
Pro Bowls: 9 (1992, 1993, 1995–1997, 2001–2003, 2007)
All-Pro: 6 (1995, 1996, 1997, 2001–2003)
All-Decade Team: 1990s
Career Starts: 273 (ranked first all-time for QBs; includes playoffs)

Ranking on the all-time passing list in major categories
Completions: 5,377 (1st)
Attempts: 8,758 (1st)
Yards: 61,655 (1st)
Touchdowns: 442 (1st)
QB rating: 85.7 (19th)

Quick Fact: Leads the NFL with the most seasons with over 3,000 yards passing (15).

Favre celebrates a touchdown pass on Jan. 20, 2008; his last NFL game.

The man has played in 275 consecutive games, including playoffs, over 17 seasons. His 442 touchdown passes, 61,655 yards, 5,377 completions, 8,758 attempts and 160 wins are all career records.

So are those 288 interceptions, a number that often infuriated Green Bay fans. And yet that statistic only serves to underline Favre's bravado, his willingness to take chances and accept responsibility for their consequences. There was never any phoniness, any pretense, about Favre.

"I mean, we don't see him in a thousand commercials," said Terry Bradshaw, another good ol' boy star quarterback, "so when we see [him in] one like Wrangler, I say, 'He really must like those jeans! He really must wear them!' It's refreshing."

Over the years, Brett Favre became more than an athlete; he was an icon. Football fans have lived through much with him, and not just the joys and sorrows on the field. His addiction to painkillers. The death of his father. The death of his brother-in-law, in an all-terrain vehicle accident on Favre's property. The news that his wife, Deanna, had been diagnosed with breast cancer. The destruction of the Favre family home when Hurricane Katrina stormed through Mississippi.

For 17 years we followed his story. He was on the air longer than Bonanza. Adored by millions, fawned on by former players and coaches turned TV announcers. And now, finally, Brett Favre gets a little time to himself.

It's worth remembering that Favre was initially drafted by the Atlanta Falcons in the second round of the 1991 draft, and after one season with four pass attempts and zero completions as a backup, the Falcons dealt him to Green Bay for a first-round pick in 1992. His legendary run of 275 began that same year on Sept. 27. The week before, he'd come on the field in relief of Green Bay starter Don Majkowski, who'd been injured. Since then, across the league 212 different quarterbacks have suited up to start a game, and 17 different men have served as Favre's backup: the loneliest job since the Maytag repairman or being Cal Ripkin's insurance at the hot corner in Baltimore.

The peak of Favre's career came in 1996, the year he led the Packers to a 13–3 record, plus playoff wins against San Francisco and Carolina. In Super Bowl XXXI, at the Louisiana Superdome, close to home, Brett Favre threw for 246 yards and two touchdowns as Green Bay blitzed New England 35–21.

There would be another trip to the Big Dance and a slew of individual honors, but in the wake of the Packers heart-wrenching NFC championship overtime loss to the New York Giants in 2008, the invariable rumors of Favre's retirement began to circulate, again.

This time, however, they weren't merely rumors.

When Green Bay head coach Mike McCarthy answered his cell phone one evening while attending his daughter's basketball team banquet, he was stunned to hear Favre on the other end saying he was leaving the game, for good.

"I had to remove myself from where I was standing because I was taken aback," said McCarthy. "In my opinion, I think he would have played again at the level that he just played [in 2007]. The film reflects that. The statistics reflect that. I thought he played at a very high level and definitely had a lot left in his tank."

"I know I can still play," Favre said the day he called it a career, struggling to explain his decision, "but it's like I told my wife, I'm just tired mentally.

Then again, anything is possible. If Favre made it back onto the field in 2008, no one would be surprised. Not in the slightest. ■

75

FORREST GREGG

TACKLE/GUARD

THE QUINTESSENTIAL FOOTBALL PLAYER

It's a photograph that says a thousand words, all of them about the man in it. Standing there, his football helmet and face mask caked with mud, his face bathed in dirt, his football uniform soaked to the point where you can barely see his jersey number 75, is the 27-year-old offensive tackle Vince Lombardi would eventually call "the finest football player I've ever coached."

In that photo, taken in 1960 during a Green Bay Packers–San Francisco 49ers game, Forrest Gregg is on the sidelines, shouting something (to teammates, the referee, who knows?) and looking every bit what a football player is supposed to look like. Tough. Gritty. A guy wanting to get back into the action so he could dirty himself up some more.

Of all the star players Lombardi coached in tiny Green Bay, Wisconsin — Paul Hornung, Willie Davies, Bart Starr, Ray Nitschke, Herb Adderly, Willie Wood — Gregg earned the highest praise, despite playing one of the more anonymous positions: right offensive tackle. Left tackles garner their share of notoriety because most

quarterbacks are right-handed throwers, which means they need someone sizeable and skilled to protect their blind side. And in Green Bay, all the offensive line publicity went to Jerry Kramer, Fuzzy Thurston and later Gale Gillingham, the pulling guards who cleared the way for the Packers' fabled power sweep.

But Gregg was so good at what he did that he neutralized defensive ends all by himself without much help, if any, from additional blockers. That's saying plenty, since the defensive ends of Gregg's day included Gino Marchetti of the Baltimore Colts, Carl Eller of the Minnesota Vikings and Deacon Jones of the Los Angeles Rams, three of the best to ever crunch a quarterback.

"Forrest, at right tackle, and I played next to each other for most of my 11 seasons," recalled Kramer in his book *Distant Replay*. "He was a master of technique, of position. He would shield, slide, maneuver, and almost always get the job done … When we lined up for a play, and the defense suddenly shifted, we would never have to adjust. I'd say, 'Forrest,' and he would say, 'Yeah,' and I'd know exactly what he was going to

CAREER HIGHLIGHTS

Drafted: 1956; 2nd round, 20th overall; Green Bay Packers

Accomplishments
Pro Bowls: 9 (1959–1964, 1966–1968)
All-Pro: 9 (1959–1967)
All-Decade Team: 1960s
NFL 75th Anniversary
All-Time Team: 1994
Played on seven NFL championship teams, three Super Bowl winners
Hall of Fame: 1977

Quick Fact: Forrest Gregg coached the 1979 Toronto Argonauts of the Canadian Football League.

Gregg, muddy as usual after a gritty sequence with the legendary Packer defense.

do and he'd know what I was going to do."

Gregg came out of Southern Methodist University in 1956 as a second-round draft pick by the Packers. (In that same draft, the Packers selected Starr in the 17th round.) He cracked the starting lineup as a rookie and set what was the iron-man record of his era, playing in 188 consecutive games all the way to 1971. In Green Bay, Gregg was one of the leaders on a football team that won five NFL championships, including the first two Super Bowls. While the Packers were never the most imaginative team offensively, they were nearly flawless in their execution, all of it beginning up front along the line, a position Lombardi had once played himself. In their 1966 NFL championship win over the Dallas Cowboys, the Packers game plan consisted of just 14 plays, eight running, six passing. Gregg and his blocking partners did their job to perfection.

In fact, Gregg was so good, so light on his feet at 249 pounds, he became known as "the best dancer since Fred Astaire," and the accolades followed. He played in nine Pro Bowls and was voted to both the 1960s All-Decade Team and the NFL's 75th anniversary team. He finished his career with the Dallas Cowboys and earned a third Super Bowl with the team's victory over the Miami Dolphins. He retired soon after, at age 38, having won six NFL championships. And then he went to work as a coach. He began as an assistant with the San Diego Chargers and Cleveland Browns before taking over as Cleveland's head man in 1974. Gregg coached the 1979 season with the Toronto Argonauts of the Canadian Football League, who won only five of 16 games, and was succeeded by Willie Wood, a former Green Bay teammate. He

returned to the NFL and guided the Cincinnati Bengals to Super Bowl XVI where they lost, 26–21, to the San Francisco 49ers.

After Cincinnati, Gregg agreed to coach the Packers, where he replaced former teammate, Bart Starr, who had held the position for nine years. The Green Bay media wanted to know if Gregg, who had greatly admired Lombardi, would be as tough as his former coach. "That's impossible," Gregg answered. "I can be demanding, but not that demanding."

In his four seasons with the Packers as coach, the best Gregg could produce was a pair of 8–8 seasons. He returned to his alma mater, Southern Methodist, to revive a football program that had been suspended for two years due to NCAA violations. He later returned to the sidelines in the CFL with the short-lived Shreveport Pirates and was the vice-president of football operations for the Ottawa Renegades before they folded in 2006.

"I think it's tougher to retire from playing," Gregg said in an interview with profootball-hof.com. "There's a time for everything and things must come to an end. You have to accept that both as a player and a coach. In coaching, you're not limited in age — although people think you go brain dead after 60."

Asked if he thought the 1960s Packers are the greatest football team of all time, Gregg replied, "Absolutely and without a doubt. You know how that old saying goes, 'Look at the scoreboard.'" Gregg embodied the Packers of the 1960s. He was an efficient player who was as smart as he was talented. He practiced hard and studied harder and was driven by a sense of fair play. Once, someone told Gregg that if he went low on Carl Eller, his Minnesota nemesis, he could "tear him up" since Eller had bad knees. Gregg wouldn't go for it. "[Eller] is a helluva guy. He's such a good clean competitor, I wouldn't do anything like that."

Ah, but battle him one-on-one for two-and-a-half hours in the cold and the mud, Gregg loved that. He loved it like few others and did it better than most. ▪

75

DEACON
JONES

DEFENSIVE END

THE MAN WHO NEVER SACKED

According to the NFL, David (Deacon) Jones spent 14 years in the trenches, appeared in eight Pro Bowls, was named to the league's 75th-anniversary team and was inducted into the Pro Football Hall of Fame in 1980 — and not once did he sack a quarterback.

Oh, he did a few things — scored two safeties, made two interceptions, recovered 15 fumbles, ran back two kickoffs and kicked an extra point. But tackle a quarterback?

Nope. Never happened. Not even for the man who invented the term sack and a nasty helmet-rattling technique known as the head slap, which begs the question: If Deacon Jones is considered one of the most dangerous pass rushers the NFL has ever seen, just how revered would he have been had the league recorded quarterback sacks as an official statistic back when he played in the 1960s and 1970s?

It wasn't until 1982 that the NFL began keeping tabs on sacks. Anyone who played prior to that time was left with a collective zero next to his name, even if his name was synonymous with terrorizing offensive lines from New York to Los Angeles.

"Since when does 'all-time' begin in 1982?" Jones has asked repeatedly, claiming his sack count was over 200, the all-time career count set by Bruce Smith.

Unofficially, NFL fans and researchers have pegged Jones's total at 173.5. The Los Angeles Rams' organization is believed to have kept at least a partial log stating that in 1964 Jones broke the 20-sack barrier (with 22 in 14 games), and then upped the count to 26 sacks, along with 100 tackles, in 1967.

"Deacon Jones is one of my really good friends, and like my mentor," said New York Giants' defensive end Michael Strahan, who holds the acknowledged record of 22.5 sacks in a 16-game season. "According to Deacon, he has like 3,000 sacks. And it grows each year. Those guys who played before they had all the stats, they do have some kind of legitimate gripe."

Anyone who played against Jones would agree that he was a man ahead of his time. He stood 6-foot-5, weighed 272 pounds and had the quickness of a leopard. He could make tackles from sideline to sideline, all

over the field. On top of that, he was part of what was the first dominant defensive line in NFL history, the Fearsome Foursome, which included Lamar Lundy, Rosey Grier and Merlin Olsen in its heyday.

"We started the trend. We proved that defensive lines can control the game," Jones said in an interview with ESPN.com. "I don't think you'll find, even now, four men who had as much talent and doled out as much damage and devastation as our group. After our group came the Purple People Eaters, the Steel Curtain, Dallas's Doomsday team and that Baltimore [Ravens] team. The dominant teams all had great defensive lines, and we had something to do with that trend. That's why they've changed so many rules. They don't want games controlled by defensive lines."

Jones, who was hailed as the Secretary of Defense, was never shy about expressing his abilities. What was far more remarkable was everything he endured to make it as a pro football player. Growing up in Florida in a family of 10, Jones picked watermelons and pitched them into trucks to earn money. In town, he couldn't drink from the same water fountains as whites. He couldn't use the same restrooms as whites. He had to sit in a blacks-only section in restaurants. He had to stay in the black wing of the local hospital when he needed an operation. When Jones enrolled at South Carolina State, he took part in a march protesting the treatment of black youths who had been arrested for eating at a lunch counter. Jones said the police and fire department dispersed the marchers with hoses and dogs, and that he was pinned against a wall by a blast of water. For taking part in the march, Jones lost his football scholarship and enrolled at Mississippi Vocational, where he and others were later rounded up by the police and told to leave the state and never come back. The players' participation in the protest march at South Carolina State was the reason for their expulsion.

The Rams were only so-so on Jones and drafted him in the 14th round. When he got to

training camp, he knew he had to make an impression. Fueled by an overwhelming desire to prove himself in the mostly white world of professional football, Jones pillaged blockers and plundered quarterbacks and became a Pro Bowl regular for seven consecutive seasons, from 1964 to 1970. (He earned an eighth Pro Bowl invitation in 1972 as a member of the San Diego Chargers.) He finished his career with the 1974 Washington Redskins, where he partook in two indulgences: before every game at RFK Stadium, Jones would spit on the statue of George Preston Marshall, the former team owner who refused to sign black players for as long as he could; and, he got to kick an extra point. It was the Redskins' George Allen, who had coached Jones with the Rams, who let the veteran attempt a convert, and it was good.

These days, Jones is using all his life experiences to help those who need it most — young students from inner-city neighborhoods. The Deacon Jones Foundation offers a seven-year program for under-privileged teenagers to help them get to university and become leaders and volunteers in their community. It's a project he has tackled as hard as any quarterback. "I'm probably the toughest [expletive] here," he said. "Ain't no question about that with me. I'm the toughest guy here ... I'm clean. I mean, I ain't got no marks on me. I don't know nobody else who can say that who came out of any sport. I ain't got no marks on me, so I've got to be the baddest dude I know of."

Officially or unofficially. ■

	Gms	Att	Comp	Yds	TD	Int	College
TOTAL	242	8,358	4,967	61,361	429	252	Pittsburgh

13

DAN MARINO

QUARTERBACK

THE PURITY OF THE PASS

There are, in sport, a rare few blessed with gifts so sublime that they captivate us by their sheer maddening effortlessness, their purity of line. For close to two decades of unrivalled passing opulence in Miami, there was Dan Marino's release: quick and accurate. He delivered the ball crisply — like the snap of a wet towel being cracked in the wind — with the precision of a watchmaker's hand: quite simply, a thing of beauty.

"I know I've got to just keep throwing the ball," Marino said. "That's what I do best."

Better, arguably, than anyone ever has.

Nurtured by the ideal coach in Don Shula, and blessed with an array of game breakers at receiver that included Mark Duper and Mark Clayton, Marino didn't merely play quarterback, he redefined the position, taking what quarterback Dan Fouts and Air Coryell had in San Diego and expanding on the premise that the best, quickest way to move the football was by throwing it.

"Sure, luck means a lot in football," Shula acknowledged. "Not having a good quarterback is bad luck." If so, Don Shula was the luckiest man in the NFL.

Other quarterbacks have left their legacies: Brett Favre is legendary for his toughness, Joe Montana for dramatics, Johnny Unitas for his reading of a game. But throwing the ball? That was Marino's domain. Only Joe Namath could rival him for purity in that department. Interceptions didn't faze him. He never shied away from a mistake. Caution was for losers. Marino kept throwing the ball, undeterred, until he finally rammed it down your throat.

Remember the movie, *The Matrix*? Keanu Reeves' character Neo studies and studies until he is mentally able to slow everything around him down to a standstill — until he can catch the bullets. Dan Marino could catch the bullets. And — this is the most amazing part of it — he could catch them right away. He would become the first rookie ever to start in a Pro Bowl.

"You were basically at Dan's mercy," said defensive back Ronnie Lott of the 49ers. "All the great ones see the game so quickly that when everybody else is running around like a chicken with his head cut off, they know exactly where they want to go

CAREER HIGHLIGHTS

Drafted: 1983; 1st round, 27th overall; Miami Dolphins

Rookie Season (1983): 11 games, 296 att, 173 comp, 2,210 yds, 20 TDs, 6 int, 96.0 QB rating

----

Career Year (1984): 16 games, 564 attempts, 362 comp, 5,084 yds, 48 TDs, 17 int, 108.9 QB rating

----

Accomplishments
Rookie of the Year: 1983
Pro Bowls: 9 (1984–1988, 1992, 1993, 1995, 1996)
All-Pro: 1984–1986
NFL MVP: 1984
Comeback Player of the Year: 1994
AFC Offensive Player of the Year: 1994
NFL passing title: 1984
NFL passing touchdowns: 1984–1986
Hall of Fame: 2005

Ranking on the all-time passing list in major categories
Completions: 4,967 (2nd)
Attempts: 8,358 (2nd)
Yards: 61,361 (2nd)
Touchdowns: 420 (2nd)
QB rating: 86.4 (15th)

Quick Fact: Dan Marino was drafted by the Kansas City Royals to play baseball in 1979, the same year future Hall of Famer John Elway was drafted by the Royals.

Marino, at Rich Stadium in 1989, throws one of his 4,967 career completions.

with the ball. It's like they see everything in slow motion."

Precisely.

Marino adjusted his game over 17 seasons, alternating between long-ball thrower, precision mid-range passer and proven leader, all with the same franchise. When talk surfaced near the end of the road that he might consider joining another organization to prolong his playing career, the possibility was met with disbelief. The Pope is Catholic, Dan Marino was a Dolphin. End of story.

The one sticking point in the vast Marino legacy is that he never piloted a Super Bowl winner. He didn't need to, at least not to validate his brilliance as a quarterback. He made the cover of *Sports Illustrated*, the front of a Wheaties box and kept the deep blue south-Florida sky filled with tight spirals.

"There are times on the field," he once wrote, "when I feel like I can't miss, when I'm in complete control and everything just clicks. The ball is always on time, it's always catchable, and I'm making the right decisions on who to throw to. Those are the times when I want to pass on every play because I feel like we're unstoppable."

Growing up in a working-class neighborhood in Pittsburgh, where his father, Dan, would get up at 3 a.m. to deliver bulk copies of the *Pittsburgh Post-Gazette* newspaper, Marino learned the value of hard work. Like Wayne Gretzky, Marino let his skills do the talking. In an age of non-conformity where others would generate headlines with their mouths and their antics, Marino took the high road, working hard for everything he earned.

In 1984, the hard work continued to pay off. In his second year after replacing David Woodley as Miami's starter, Marino was close to unstoppable, as he put together one of the greatest individual seasons in history, on the way to being named the NFL MVP. He broke no fewer than six passing records that year, including touchdown tosses (48) and yards (5,084). The Dolphins finished the regular season 14–2 and reached Super Bowl XIX against Joe Montana and the San Francisco 49ers.

Marino would finish that game 29 out of 50 for 318 yards, one touchdown and two interceptions. The Dolphins lost 38–16. It would, sadly, be Dan Marino's only Super Bowl appearance.

"I am extremely proud of the fact that I was able to play 17 years for the Miami Dolphins," he said in announcing his retirement before the 2000 season began, the dream of that elusive title worn away by the onslaught of time. "And I'm going to miss it. I'm going to miss everything about it. I'm going to miss the relationships with the players, I'm going to miss the fans, I'm going to miss the great friends that I have made over this time. I am going to miss all the good times that we've had together. But most of all, I'm going to miss Sunday afternoons."

Sunday afternoons miss Marino, too.

Five of his career-passing marks have since been broken by Brett Favre and one other by Peyton Manning (who was surpassed by Tom Brady in 2007), but Marino's 61,361 career yards still stands.

On Sunday, Sept. 17, 2000, at halftime of a home game against the Baltimore Ravens, Marino's signature No. 13 was the second jersey number ever retired by the Dolphins. The other? Bob Griese's No.12. A life-sized bronze statue of him was erected at Pro Player Stadium, and Stadium Street was rechristened Dan Marino Boulevard.

He is irreplaceable. Since Marino retired, the Dolphins have auditioned more starting quarterbacks than any Dolphin fan would care to remember. All have been found wanting.

Many copies. One original. ■

16 JOE MONTANA

QUARTERBACK

THE COMEBACK KID

Most of all, he had cool. Steve McQueen in a battered bomber jacket astride a '37 Crocker motorcycle sort of cool. Naturally cool, without trying. He was that guy in school everyone gravitated to because it didn't matter how hard the test or how pretty the girl — you just knew. And you just knew he knew, too.

He was Joe. The Comeback Kid. Believer in lost causes.

"He's like Lazarus," San Franciso 49ers' teammate Tim McKyer said one time. "You roll back the stone, Joe limps out — and throws for 300 yards."

What sets Joe Montana apart from virtually every other quarterback before or since was his flair for the dramatic, the theatrical. His face should've been plastered on the cover of *Playbill* as often as *Sports Illustrated*.

There isn't an illusionist alive who wouldn't kill to know Joe Montana's secret. He convinced his audience that he could, in fact, manipulate time. Take it in his hands, turn it over, bend it, shape it, and make it do his bidding — quite a trick.

In Joe's mind, nothing was out of reach.

No deficit too great. No mountain too daunting. He gave the impression that he could climb Everest in trainers and a windbreaker.

His amazing 31 fourth-quarter comebacks are why *Sports Illustrated* voted him its all-time clutch quarterback in 2006. Attempting to find consensus on the best Montana comeback is like trying to find common ground on the best Beatles tune, or the best actor to portray Bond; everyone has an opinion, and seldom is it the same.

In four Super Bowl appearances — all victories, by the way — Montana completed nearly 70 percent of his passes and didn't throw a single interception in 122 attempts. In three of those games he was named MVP, stepping back only once to allow his favorite receiver, Jerry Rice, to command the spotlight.

Beyond the cool and the list of accomplishments, early on there was something of the underdog in the cowboy who would go on to conquer the City by the Bay, and that was appealing, too.

He began his collegiate career at Notre Dame, listed seventh on the quarterback

CAREER HIGHLIGHTS

Drafted: 1979; 3rd round, 82nd overall; San Francisco 49ers

- -

Rookie Season: 16 games, 23 att, 13 comp, 96 yds, 1 TD, 0 int, 81.1 QB rating

- -

Career Year (1989): 13 games, 386 att, 271 comp, 3,521 yds, 26 TDs, 8 int, 112.0 QB rating

- -

Accomplishments
Pro Bowls: 8 (1982, 1984, 1985, 1986, 1988, 1990, 1991, 1994)
Super Bowl MVP: 3 (1981, 1984, 1989)
NFL MVP (AP): 2 (1989, 1990)
All-Decade Team: 1980s
Comeback Player of the Year: 1986
Passing titles: 1987, 1989
Passing touchdown leader: 1982, 1987
Hall of Fame: 2000

- -

Ranking on the all-time passing list in major categories
Completions: 3,409 (9th)
Attempts: 5,391 (9th)
Yards: 40,551 (9th)
Touchdowns: 273 (9th)
QB rating: 92.3 (5th)

- -

Quick Fact: Holds the career Super Bowl record for most touchdown passes (11).

Joe Cool passes against the Atlanta Falcons in 1990 on his way to his second MVP honor.

The next year, Montana followed that up in Super Bowl XXIV with an even more dominating performance, shredding the Denver Broncos for five touchdown passes in a 55–10 rout.

He just kept topping himself.

When he finally retired in 1995, Joe Montana held NFL playoff records for completions, yards and touchdowns, as well as for a single-season (1989), and owned the second highest-rated passing efficiency in league history. He had been lavished with a slew of individual awards and had four Super Bowl rings.

Typically, he spread the praise around as easily as the football. "The beauty of Bill's system was that there was always a place to go with the ball," Montana said, with typical humility. "I was just the mailman, just delivering people's mail. And there were all kinds of houses to go to."

When he walked away from the game he had come to embody, after a swansong two seasons in Kansas City, Joe Montana cited his young family as a major reason. These days, he owns horses and produces wine under the label Montagia.

"When I was playing, I missed my two girls' [activities]," he explained at the time. "They look up, and myself and my wife are not there. To me, it's more important to be home with my boys. The Super Bowl is a great event, but I've moved on with my life. I want to be there for the boys."

He'd spent enough years being there for his other boys; for coach Bill, for Jerry, Roger, John, Dwight and the rest. Fifteen years was enough. In the end, you could say, Joe Cool just ran short of urgency. He never ran out of time. ▪

depth chart. In 1977, only three years later, he led the school to a national championship.

It seems ludicrous now, but Montana was considered too slight and his arm strength rated only "average" by NFL scouts, who'd charted his days with the Fighting Irish. Even a wild comeback win in the '79 Cotton Bowl, Montana completing the winning TD pass with two seconds to play — a foreshadow of things to come — wasn't enough to completely convince the skeptics.

He lasted until the third round in his draft year, chosen 82nd overall by the 49ers. The rest, as they say, is history.

With Bill Walsh's legendary West Coast Offense, the kid from New Eagle, Pennsylvania, took over control of the team in 1981 and efficiently went about setting a new standard for the position. Ironically, the play that began the Montana legend, the six-yard pass to Dwight Clark in the Dallas Cowboys' end zone with less than a minute to play that thrust the 49ers into Super Bowl XVI, wasn't planned. The moment remains an image frozen in time: Clark leaping high in the air to snare the ball, forever to be remembered by NFL fans as simply The Catch. Montana later admitted he'd been trying to heave the ball out of the end zone so he could regroup on the next snap. If that isn't being touched by the heavens, nothing is.

Exactly how anointed Joe Montana was would be all too apparent in 1989. In the closing moments of Super Bowl XXIII, Montana drove the 49ers an improbable 92 yards, threw a 10-yard touchdown pass to John Taylor with 34 ticks left on the clock, to give the 49ers a 20–16 win over the Cincinnati Bengals. The man himself endeavored to explain his knack in the clutch:

"It's a blur," he admitted. "I hyperventilated to the point of almost blacking out. I was yelling so loudly in the huddle that I couldn't breathe. Things got blurrier and blurrier."

34 WALTER PAYTON

RUNNING BACK

SWEETNESS AND THEN SOME

An infectious joy of being, the possibilities of life itself, combined with a relentless pursuit of excellence. They are only part of why so many were so moved, so stricken, took the loss so personally, when Walter Payton died of a rare liver disease, primary sclerosing cholangitis, at age 45. It was as if we'd lost a member of our own family.

As quarterback Jim Harbaugh, a rookie with the Bears in 1987, said upon Payton's passing, "Sweetness … there may not have been a better nickname for a player."

The sight of him near the end, a man once so in command of his physical prowess, now so gaunt and frail, at an overwhelmingly emotional press conference to discuss his illness, shocked many.

But it gave strength to just as many more.

Out of the skeletal frame, an immense bravery shone brightly. A bravery beyond running between the tackles on fourth down and a yard when everyone in the stadium knows the quarterback is handing you the ball.

"Am I scared?" Walter Payton said that day early in 1999. "Hell, yeah, I'm scared. Wouldn't you be scared? But it's not in my hands anymore. It's in God's hands."

Nine months later, he was in God's hands.

At his memorial service held at Soldier Field, his family and hundreds of friends turned out to say goodbye to a legend.

"Many of you knew my father as a football player and as a business man," said his son Jarrett, then 18, and now a running back for the CFL's Montreal Alouettes. "I knew him as my dad, and he was my hero.

"My mother, my sister and I will miss him, but we know he's in a place where there's no sickness, no pain."

The emotional service lasted for more than two hours.

"I've got a little girl, she's four years old," defensive tackle Dan Hampton, a teammate of Payton's for nine years, said then. "Ten years from now, when she asks me about the Chicago Bears, I'll tell her about a championship.

"And I'll tell her about great teams and great teammates and great coaches and how great it was to be a part of." Hampton's voice began to quaver. "But the first thing I'll tell her about is Walter Payton."

Drafted: 1985; 1st round, 4th overall; Chicago Bears

Rookie Season (1985): 13 games, 7 TDs, 196 att, 679 yds, 3.5 yd avg

----

Career Year (1984): 16 games, 381 att, 1,684 yds, 4.4 yd avg, 11 TDs

----

Accomplishments
Pro Bowls: 9 (1976, 1978–1981, 1984–1987)
NFL Player of the Year: 2 (1977, 1985)
NFL Offensive Player of the Year: 1977
Hall of Fame: 1993

Rank on the all-time list of major rushing categories
Attempts: 3,838 (2nd)
Yards: 16,726 (2nd)
Touchdowns: 110 TDs (3rd)
Yards from scrimmage: 21,264 (3rd)
Rushing/receiving TDs: 125 (8th)

Quick Fact: In his first NFL game, Walter Payton carried the ball eight times for zero yards.

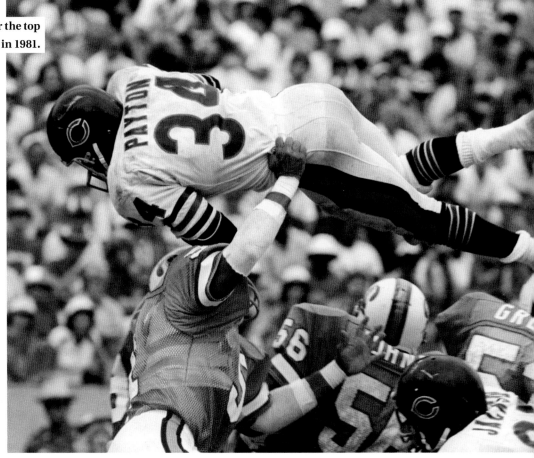

Not big, at 5-foot-10 and 200 pounds, he was blessed with tree trunks for legs, soft hands, a hide as tough as old shoe leather (he missed only two games in 13 seasons) and an indomitable will. The sight of his patented high kick as he ripped opposing defenses apart remains one of the iconic images of the game.

Amazingly, Payton was as good a blocker as he was a runner, and as good a receiver as he was a blocker. He could throw the ball as a change of pace and, in a pinch, punt. He could, to use a well-worn phrase, do it all.

Payton was tagged with the nickname Sweetness in college while playing at Jackson State and finishing fourth in Heisman Trophy balloting in his senior year. Jim Harbaugh was right — it simply could not have been more appropriate.

A sweetness of style, a sweetness of spirit, a sweetness of philosophy — that's what set Walter Payton apart.

In *The Football Book*, Paul Zimmerman of *Sports Illustrated* recalled an astonishing feeling he had while interviewing Payton one unforgettable night. "His eyes sparkled in that half light," Zimmerman wrote, "and I got this weird feeling there was a glow around him, that he was giving off sparks, that there was some kind of fire burning inside, lighting him up. It was the fire of pure energy."

On the field, Payton towered above the pack: he was a two-time league MVP, a nine-time Pro Bowler, the 1977 Pro Bowl MVP and a 1985 Super Bowl champion with the Bears. He ran for 16,726 yards during his career, a record at the time. Ten times he lugged the ball for 1,000 yards or more in a season. Caught 492 passes, too. One amazing afternoon against the Minnesota Vikings, Payton ran riot, for 275 yards, a record that lasted until Viking rookie Adrian Peterson broke the pinball machine with 296 in 2007.

Typical of Payton's insatiable drive to achieve professionally, when he eclipsed Jim Brown's career rushing mark, he sent up a flare for all those who would follow.

"I want to set the record so high that the next person who tries for it," he said, "it's going to bust his heart."

Nothing could bust Walter Payton's heart. Everything else might wear out, eaten insidiously away by the ravages of disease. But not the heart. That stayed strong until the last.

Off the field is where Payton carved his most extraordinary niche. A quiet, gentle man, unshakeable in his faith and unlimited in his caring for his community, everyone was drawn to Sweetness. It sounds trite in these jaded times, a cliché almost, but he knew the secret of life.

Which is why almost a decade after his death, the Payton legend only grows stronger. His popularity in Chicago and fame nationwide are undiminished. In the pantheon of immortal Chicago athletes, Sweetness ranks with the deities, up there on a par with Bobby Hull, the Golden Jet; Ernie Banks, Mr. Cub; and His Airness, Michael Jordan. That glow, those sparks, the energy Paul Zimmerman wrote of, can never be extinguished.

Sweetness, and then some.

"He was the best football player I've ever seen," said his longtime coach, Mike Ditka, in summation. "And probably one of the best people I've ever met."

As an epitaph, a man could do worse. ▪

80

JERRY
RICE

WIDE RECEIVER

THE BEST THERE EVER WAS

Joe Rice didn't stand for excuses or even a few minutes of sleeping in. Every summer morning come 5 a.m., he'd be up and hauling his boys out of bed so they could go to work with him.

Joe was a mason and young Jerry's job was to catch the bricks his brothers tossed at him so he could hand them to his dad for placing. Sometimes Jerry stood on a wooden scaffold two stories high and caught bricks until his hands were calloused but sure. A typical day went to sundown in the unforgiving heat of a Mississippi July and August.

That was how it began for Jerry Rice, the greatest football player of our time. Without knowing it, everything he learned and did as a child, everything he yearned to perfect as a teenager was the foundation for what he would accomplish in the NFL. It was all laid out in Crawford, Mississippi, just like the bricks his father used to set row by row, one on top of another.

There have been hundreds of great football players over the decades, men who aspired and inspired with equal fervor. Rice was one of those who kept doing his best game after game, season after season, until he retired and the numbers showed that he had accomplished what no other receiver or football player had ever done.

The sixth son of Joe and Eddie B., Rice didn't just set records; he etched them in granite. He didn't just outdistance his closest challengers, he humbled them. In every offensive category, he sits at the top, hopelessly out of reach for the next-best player, as good as that player is. From his 208 career touchdowns (Emmitt Smith is second with 175), to his 274 consecutive games of catching at least one pass (Andre Reed is second at 183), Rice defied his defenders with seldom seen splendor and style.

For his efforts, he won every award that mattered — NFL MVP, Super Bowl champion and Super Bowl MVP. Once, when asked to comment on his many achievements and accolades, Rice insisted they were only part of the narrative.

"To me it was never about what I accomplished on the football field," he explained, "it was about the way I played the game. I played the game with a lot of determination, a lot of poise, a lot of pride and I think

CAREER HIGHLIGHTS

Drafted: 1985; 1st round, 16th overall; San Francisco 49ers

Rookie Season (1985): 16 games, 49 rec, 927 yds, 18.9 ypc, 3 TDs

----

Career Year (1995): 16 games, 122 rec, 1,848 yds, 15.1 ypc, 15 TDs, 104 total points, one 41-yard TD pass

----

Accomplishments
Pro Bowls: 13
Pro Bowl MVP: 1995
Super Bowl MVP: 1988
Player of the Year: 1987, 1993 (AP)

Current Regular Season NFL Records
Receptions: 1,549
Receiving yards: 22,895
All-purpose yards: 23,540
Touchdown receptions: 197
Total Touchdowns: 208
Receiving yards gained in a single season: 1,848
Seasons with at least 50 receptions: 17
Seasons with at least 1,000 receiving yards: 14
Games with at least 100 receiving yards: 76
Consecutive games with at least one reception: 274
Consecutive games with at least one TD reception: 13

Quick Fact: Became the first non-kicker to score 1,000 points in his career.

23 touchdowns for the season.

The next season, in Super Bowl XXIII, he caught 11 passes for 215 yards and a touchdown and was named MVP. In Super Bowl XXIV, he caught seven passes for 148 yards and scored three touchdowns. In Super Bowl XXIX, he caught 10 passes for 149 yards and scored three touchdowns again, this time with a shoulder he had separated earlier in the game.

Rice never stopped working on his game with more practices, more time studying game film, more drills aimed at exploiting the weaknesses in the defensive backs assigned to cover him. When Montana moved on, Rice and quarterback Steve Young kept the show rolling. When Rice left for the Oakland Raiders, he maintained his expectations with a high level of consistency. In his three seasons with the Raiders (2001–2004), Rice averaged 79 catches for 1,078 yards and six touchdowns. As sure as the sun sets in the west, Jerry Rice can catch a football.

He joined the Seattle Seahawks four games into the 2004 season, and attended the Denver Broncos' training camp in 2005 before choosing to retire. By then, the name Jerry Rice stood for unbridled excellence. He set the bar so high it may never be cleared.

From making the hardest catches look easy, to forcing himself to run more sprints because he had to be better than everyone else, Rice proved to be a hard-working stickler. He had no choice, he insisted. That was the way it had to be for him, the way he was raised as the country kid who caught bricks before galloping after his ambitions with a football tucked under an arm.

In Jerry Rice, what we saw was an individual who really just loved the game, and played it like no other. ▪

what you saw there … was an individual who really just loved the game."

The love of football came to Rice early in his childhood. He and his brothers played sandlot games the way they chased the horses that ran wild in the countryside — for fun, with reckless abandon. His first taste of organized football came in Grade 10 after he was caught skipping school. The story goes that Rice played hooky one day, only to be caught by his high school principal, Ezell Wickes. When Rice saw the principal, he took off like a frightened colt.

The next day, Rice was called into Mr. Wickes' office and strapped for his transgression. Still, the principal was so impressed with Rice's running ability that he talked to the school's football coach, who convinced Rice to play.

Rice relied on his natural gifts and capacity for work to become an all-state receiver, but attracted no interest from the major universities. Only one school offered him a scholarship, so he went to Mississippi Valley State, a Division 1-AA school. There, he became one of the most prolific players in the U.S. by starring in coach Archie Cooley's run-and-shoot offense that averaged more than 55 points per game in one season. It was Cooley who said of Rice, "He can catch a BB on a dead run at night."

The San Francisco 49ers were so taken by Rice's catching ability that they traded up in the 1985 draft so they could select him as a target for quarterback Joe Montana. It was a decision that paid off many times over, especially in the critical games where Rice rose to new heights and so did his numbers.

In 1987, Rice caught 22 touchdown passes, a record that was broken in 2007 by Randy Moss of the New England Patriots. But here's the catch: Moss scored his 23 touchdowns in 16 games. Rice did his 22 in just 12 games (the 1987 season was shortened by a players' strike). Not only that, Rice's 22 touchdowns came off 65 catches, which meant one of every three receptions went for a major. For good measure, he scored on a short run, giving him

20 Barry SANDERS

RUNNING BACK

THE BEST TEN YEARS OF FOOTBALL

It was never enough to know what made Barry Sanders run. What people wanted to grasp was what made him quit? How could he walk away from the game at age 30? What about the records, the fortune and adulation?

He wasn't hurting physically. Certainly, he wasn't hurting for money, not with $20.9 million left on a four-year deal with the Detroit Lions. How could he retire without really explaining why? Where was his loyalty, his sense of responsibility?

"I tell you what I heard from 'Ol Blue Eyes one time — Frank Sinatra," Sanders said, five years after his retirement shocked the football universe. "He said the same question was put to him, 'What do you owe the fans?' And he said, 'First of all, I owe them a good performance.' I really listened to that and really took a hold of that.

"First and foremost, I owe people everything that I was as a football player when I stepped onto the field … and I think I did that. Once I left the field, I've never been good or comfortable with all the other stuff, of what you owe everyone else as far as the media and fans and people like that, and

I may have been clumsy with those things at times. But none of my actions have been intentionally directed towards the fans or the city of Detroit."

No NFL running back has been more exciting to watch and less understood than Sanders. He didn't just perform in shoulder pads, he conducted recitals. He didn't run, he accelerated and exhilarated; a master showman who made opponents wish they had taken up another occupation — anything besides playing defense.

Sanders was a uniquely built, stunningly gifted athlete. He stood 5-foot-8, weighed 203 pounds. As fast as he was running a straight line, it was his ability to maneuver without losing top speed that allowed him to out-distance his adversaries. And strength? Even as a pick-up basketball player, Sanders could dunk the ball from a standing position. He had it all.

He set all kinds of records in college, where he produced five consecutive 200-yard games and scored at least two touchdowns in 11 consecutive games; and the NFL, where he rushed for more than 1,500 yards five times in his career and scored 15

CAREER HIGHLIGHTS

Drafted: 1989; 1st Round, 3rd overall; Detroit Lions

Rookie Season (1989): 15 games, 280 att, 1,470 yds, 5.3 yd avg, 14 TDs

----

Career year (1997): 16 games, 335 att, 2,053 yds, 6.1 yd avg, 11 TDs

----

Accomplishments
Rookie of the Year: 1989
Pro Bowls: 10 (1990–1999)
All-Pro: 8 (1989–1991), (1993–1997)
NFL MVP: 2 (1991, 1997)
NFL Offensive MVP: 3 (1991, 1994, 1997)
Leading rusher: 4 (1990, 1994, 1996, 1997)
Touchdown leader: 2 (1990, 1991)
Hall of Fame: 2004

Ranking on the all-time list in major rushing categories
Attempts: 3,062 (5th)
Yards: 15,269 (3rd)
Touchdowns: 99 (8th)
Yards from scrimmage: 18,190 (5th)
Rushing/receiving TDs: 109 (T-14th)

Quick Fact: Sanders holds the NFL record for the most carries for negative yardage (336 carries for −952 yds).

Dec. 21, 1997, Sanders is the third player ever to rush for more than 2,000 yards in a season.

touchdowns on runs of 50 yards or more.

"If there was ever an artist, he was a Picasso," Hall of Fame running back Marcus Allen said of Sanders. "He was one of the few that would make other athletes' jaws drop. You'd go, 'Oh man, did you see that?' You'd call up another top running back and go, 'Yo, [Eric] Dickerson, did you check that out?'"

It was impossible to keep tabs on Sanders' highlights. Picking out his best run was like trying to name your favorite Beatles' song. There was that amazing recovery against the Buffalo Bills, the one where he was in the clutches of a tackler and falling when all of a sudden he stuck out his left arm, pushed himself off the turf, regained his balance, cut back and raced away in the opposite direction.

Or the one where he froze that Minnesota Vikings' defensive back with an outside-inside juke en route to a long gain. Or the one where he had the New England Patriots' defender turning in circles trying to locate his man, let alone tackle him. Or the one where he exploded through the right side of the Indianapolis Colts' defense as if it were nothing but party streamers. Or the one …

There were so many "ones."

But while Sanders reveled in personal triumphs, his Detroit Lions' team was hardpressed to be average. The Lions during Sanders' years (from '89–'98) were 78–82, and made the postseason five times. Only once did they win a playoff game. In that 1991 contest, a 31–6 trouncing of the Dallas Cowboys, Sanders scored on a 47-yard run in the final minutes. The following week, Detroit was crushed 41–10 by the Washington Redskins with Sanders kept to 44 yards on 11 carries.

The Lions' shoddy postseason record, combined with Sanders' drop in yardage, opened the doors for critics to claim the Hall of Fame running back was largely overrated. Their argument was based on Sanders playing the bulk of his career inside a domed stadium and that once outdoors, in the playoffs, he was far less effective. (Statistical note: Sanders scored a touchdown for every 35 touches in his 153 career regular-season games while averaging a touchdown for every 112 touches in his six career playoff games.)

Sanders left himself wide open to detractors when he retired late in July 1999. It happened in the most unanticipated fashion with Sanders faxing a letter to his hometown newspaper, the *Wichita Eagle*. In his statement, Sanders said, "The reason I am retiring is very simple. My desire to exit the game is greater than my desire to remain in it."

Sanders declined to elaborate, which prompted a run of conspiracy theories. Sanders wanted more money, wanted to be traded, hated his coach Bobby Ross, hated the Lions for releasing his friend Kevin Glover two years earlier and not doing enough to field a winning team.

Sanders said little even when the media argued he owed his teammates a definitive explanation, especially with him only 1,457 yards shy of breaking Walter Payton's then record for most career rushing yards.

It took Sanders time to articulate his reasons for quitting: "I'm very competitive when it comes to winning and losing and playing well," he said. "And I did put up big numbers. There were some times in 1997 when I could have gone back in to pad my numbers, but I wasn't as competitive with the numbers as I was about winning and losing."

There was always talk Sanders would return to the NFL, but he never did. Like Jim Brown, Sanders stepped away from the field ensuring a life-long debate that he could have played longer and done more amazing things had he chosen to stick around.

"Ten years is a lot of football," he said. It was enough for him and much too little for his fans. ■

21 DEION SANDERS

DEFENSIVE BACK

COUNTDOWN TO PRIME TIME

He was a left-handed, spray-hitting, base-stealing Mr. Virtuoso, who played in a World Series, a Super Bowl, and could cover 40 yards in 4.57 seconds running backwards.

He was Neon Deion, Prime Time. A two-sport attraction who hit a home run with the New York Yankees the same week he scored his first NFL touchdown as a member of the Atlanta Falcons.

Some loved him, others hated him, but there was no denying Deion Sanders was a monstrous talent who could do it all, make any play, steal any thunder. But in 1997, Sanders tried to end it all by driving his black Mercedes over a 30-foot cliff. Why? Because nothing mattered to the game's biggest showman, not the fame, not the money. Sanders' life was a bottomless pit he couldn't fill with the richest contract or the hottest car.

"When I hit bottom," Sanders wrote in his autobiography, *Power, Money & Sex: How Success Almost Ruined My Life*, "the car started sliding awkwardly, rocking back and forth, until I came down hard and slid to the bottom of the hill. Miraculously, I walked away without a scratch."

He was not, however, unchanged.

Sanders considers himself a happy man these days, more relaxed and fulfilled. His faith has given him the depth of character to match the many feats he accomplished as his era's greatest two-sport athlete.

As the trash-talking, bandana-wearing, brash and bejeweled Prime Time, Sanders was larger than life. In his major-league baseball career, he played for four teams, including the 1992 Atlanta Braves, who made it to the World Series. In the Fall Classic, against the Toronto Blue Jays, Sanders batted .533 with eight hits, two doubles, four runs and an RBI, all while playing with a broken bone in his foot.

In football, he was vastly, outrageously superior. He ran back kicks and punts, intercepted passes and was as dangerous a scoring weapon as any of the Falcons' receivers. In fact, Sanders would occasionally line up at wide receiver and race downfield to catch passes. In his five years in Atlanta, Prime Time scored 10 touchdowns — three on defensive plays, three on kick-off returns, two on punt returns and two on pass receptions.

CAREER HIGHLIGHTS

Drafted: 1989; 1st round, 5th overall; Atlanta Falcons

Rookie Season: 15 games, 39 tackles (28 solo, 11 ast), 2 forced fumbles, 5 int; Special teams: 15 games, 28 PR, 307 yds, 1 TD, 35 KR, 725 yds

---

Career Year (1994): 14 games, 36 tackles (36 solo), 14 pass deflections, 6 int, 303 yds, 3 TDs

---

Accomplishments

Pro Bowls: 8 (1991–1994; 1996–1999)

All-Pro: 9 (1991–1999)

Led the league in non-offensive touchdowns: 3 (1990, 1991, 1998)

Holds the record for non-offensive touchdowns: 19

Led the league in punt returns for TDs: 3 (1989, 1990, 1998)

Led the league in kickoff re-turns for TDs: 2 (1990, 1991)

NFL Defensive Player of the Year: 1994

NFL All-Decade Team: 1990s

Quick Fact: Deion Sanders is the only player to play in the World Series (1992 Atlanta Braves) and the Super Bowl (San Francisco 49ers, Dallas Cowboys).

He over-celebrated every one of them.

"How do you think defensive backs get attention?" asked Sanders, who had drawn plenty of attention in his days as a baseball-football-track star at Florida State University. "They don't pay nobody to be humble."

Sanders was equally a braggadocio when he high-stepped his stuff for the San Francisco 49ers and Dallas Cowboys. He won Super Bowl XXIX with the 49ers and Super Bowl XXX with the Cowboys, and all along the way he was to rival receivers what a detour sign is to frustrated motorists.

"When we played against him last year, we talked about not even bothering to throw his way," New Orleans Saints' receiver Michael Haynes said at the time. "It was part of our game plan to keep the ball away from him. There were routes we wouldn't run toward Deion. He can take away that much."

With the Cowboys, Sanders continued to strut and be well-paid for his bravado. He could shut down entire offenses, intercept passes, then taunt his former teammates as he ran down the sidelines en route to an easy touchdown, as he did against Atlanta. He was living the dream life, even performing rap songs entitled, "Must be the Money." Everywhere you looked in 1997, there was Neon Deion, smiling, shilling, primping, playmaking. He was a one-man corporation. Who could have asked for more?

Then came the fall. His wife sued him for divorce and refused to bring their children to Cincinnati, where he was playing baseball for the Reds. Suddenly, the money no longer mattered. Not even an outstanding year — one that saw him on the field for 50 percent of the Cowboys' offensive plays and 80 percent on defense — could fill the void within him.

"I had just had the best season of my career. Everything I touched turned to gold," he wrote in his autobiography. "But inside, I was broken and totally defeated … I remember sitting at the back of the practice field one afternoon, away from everybody, and tears were running down my face. I was saying to myself, 'This is so meaningless. I'm so unhappy. We're winning every week and I'm playing great, but I'm not happy.'"

After driving his car over a cliff and surviving, Sanders began to reshape his life through religion. He learned to separate Prime Time from real time. He left Dallas and signed with the Washington Redskins. A year later he retired, then un-retired to join the Baltimore Ravens for the 2004 season. That year he intercepted a pass and returned it for a touchdown, the 12th of his career, tying a league record.

After re-retiring, this time for good, Sanders worked as a football commentator before finding some solace in charitable deeds. He mentored two young football players: Devin Hester, the Chicago Bears' high-speed kick returner, and U.S. college running back Noel Devine. He raised money for victims of Hurricane Katrina by challenging professional athletes in football, baseball, basketball and hockey to donate to relief efforts.

He also stuck his foot in it by supporting former Atlanta quarterback Michael Vick, who pleaded guilty to funding an illegal dog-fighting operation in 2007 and was sentenced to 23 months in jail. Sanders wondered, "Are we using him to bring an end to dog fighting in the United States? The only thing I can gather from this situation is that we're using Vick."

Still, the new Deion Sanders is happier than he's been in more than a decade. His life isn't a mix of conflicting sports, juggled schedules and empty desperation. It's calmer.

And Sanders can handle that. ∎

40

GALE SAYERS

RUNNING BACK

THERE'S MAGIC IN THE AIR

Gale Sayers didn't merely run with a football, he slalomed. He was a restless wave of a running back, shifting to and fro, weaving in and out, until he at last found an open portal in the defensive line, and then he was gone.

"He's the only guy I think could be running, stop on a dime, tell you whether it was heads or tails and not even break stride," marveled Green Bay Packers' defensive back Herb Adderley.

Apparently hemmed in, changing direction, slithering out of the desperate grasp of tacklers, making his cut at precisely the right instant, Sayers left bamboozled defenders clawing at air. Pro football had not seen his like before. Watching old film of Gale Sayers today, he gives you, more than anything, this exhilarating sense of … freedom.

To defenders, he must have seemed an almost ghostly presence: an apparition clad in white or black, wearing No. 40. As difficult to contain as a drop of mercury. Sayers could run with power and purpose, certainly, but what we remember most is his speed and elusiveness. It sounds ab-

surdly simple and clichéd, but it was nonetheless true: he just made people miss. Sayers once said he could instinctively "feel" defenders getting close to him. Certainly, there seemed to be some form of special intuitive power at work. Magic, they came to call him in Chicago. The legendary Papa Bear, coach George Halas, dubbed him the greatest back since Red Grange. Although their styles were different, Sayers in a heartbeat became heir apparent to the great Jim Brown.

He had come out of the University of Kansas, nicknamed the Kansas Comet, a fourth pick in the 1965 NFL draft, snubbing a more lucrative offer from the Kansas City Chiefs of the upstart AFL, to join the Chicago Bears.

In his second regular-season game, Gale Sayers touched the ball once. And scored a touchdown. By game five, he couldn't be kept out of the starting lineup. That day, one screen pass, in particular, trumpeted the arrival of a new star in the pro football firmament: An 80-yard touchdown ramble after latching onto the ball, shedding Los Angeles Rams along the way. "I hit him so

Drafted: 1965; 1st round, 4th overall; Chicago Bears

- -

Rookie Season: 14 games; Rushing: 166 att, 867 yds, 5.2 yd avg, 14 TDs; Receiving: 29 rec, 507 yds, 17.5 yd avg, 6 TDs; 16 PR, 238 yds, 14.9 yd avg, 1TD; 21 KR, 660 yds, 31.4 yd avg, 1 TD

- -

Career Year (1967): 14 games; Rushing: 229 att, 1,231 yds, 5.4 yd avg, 8 TDs; Receiving: 34 rec, 447 yds, 13.1 yd avg, 2 TDs; 23 KR, 718 yds, 31.2 yd avg, 2 TDs

- -

Accomplishments

Pro Bowls: 4 (1965–1967, 1969)

All-Pro: 5 (1965–1969)

NFL Comeback Player of the Year: 1969

Led NFL in rushing attempts: 236 (1969)

Led NFL in rushing yards: 1,231 (1966); 1,032 (1969)

Led NFL in rushing yards/ game: 87.9 (1966); 95.1 (1968); 73.7 (1969)

Led NFL in points scored: 132 (1965)

Led NFL in touchdowns: 22 (1965)

Led NFL in all-purpose yards: 2,272 (1965); 2,440 (1966); 1,689 (1967)

- -

Quick Fact: Gale Sayers became the youngest person ever inducted into the Pro Football Hall of Fame in 1977 at the age of 34.

Sayers runs in his rookie season, 1965, against the Giants with a block from James Cadile.

hard," said the Rams' All Pro defensive tackle Rosey Grier of that play, "that I thought my shoulder must have busted him in two. I heard a roar from the crowd and figured he'd fumbled, so I started scrambling around looking for the loose ball. But there was no ball and Sayers was gone."

The rookie also threw a touchdown pass that day from an option play. The Bears won, 31–6. Gale Sayers had arrived. But there was more to come. The afternoon of Dec. 12, 1965, was a cold, wet day at Wrigley Field. Some people have labeled the game that day as "the greatest individual game ever played." In the bog of Wrigley, Gayle Sayers piled up 336 all-purpose yards and scored a phenomenal, record-tying six touchdowns, despite being pulled by Halas for most of the fourth quarter with the Bears comfortably in front.

"I think in the mud I ran more flat-footed, made my cuts not on my toes but on the balls of my feet and my heels," he recalled. "That kept me on balance."

Sayers captured Rookie of the Year honors in 1965 for his 867 yards rushing, 507 yards receiving and 22 touchdowns, a league record. His second season was no less spectacular. Sayers rushed for 1,231 yards, caught passes for 447 more and scored 12 touchdowns — eight via the run, two through the air and two more on kickoff returns. His stats dipped in 1967, mostly because the Bears were a team in decline. Then, the next season, the unthinkable happened. After nine games, Sayers had amassed 1,463 yards rushing, and was averaging 6.2 yards a carry. But on Nov. 10, 1967, in mid-cut, he was tackled by the 49ers' Kermit Alexander. Sayers crumpled to the field in pain. He'd torn multiple ligaments in his right knee.

Surgery ended Sayers' season, and at that time, cast doubt on his career. But if he was a man of few words, he was also nothing if not incredibly courageous and single-minded. A punishing rehabilitation followed. Looking back on that time, he said, "I learned if you want to make it bad enough, no matter how bad it is, you can make it." When Gale Sayers returned to the Bears the next season, he wasn't the same player. Oh, he could still "feel" the defenders, yes. Avoiding them proved a far greater challenge, though. That electric speed, the impossible-to-explain elusiveness, had been compromised. More and more yards had to be won down in the trenches, between the tackles, in the tough areas.

Sayers still led the league in rushing. It was arguably his greatest accomplishment in the game. A second knee operation, in 1970, did what few defenders had been able to in four and a half unforgettable seasons: cut down Gale Sayers in his tracks.

In 1970, he published his autobiography, *I Am Third*, in part detailing his friendship with teammate Brian Piccolo, who had lost a courageous battle against cancer. The book inspired a made-for-TV movie, *Brian's Song*, starring Billy Dee Williams as Sayers and James Caan as Piccolo. When Sayers accepted the NFL's Most Courageous Player Award that year, he dedicated the tribute to his friend. His words of that night, repeated by an actor after Piccolo had passed away, touched an immediate, emotional chord in a nation: "I love Brian Piccolo, and I'd like all of you to love him. When you hit your knees to pray tonight, please ask God to love him, too."

The Comet, they had christened him in his prime. And a Comet he proved to be, flashing across the sky, burning oh-so brightly, taking our breath away, only to fade from view too soon, leaving us awed and unfulfilled at the same time.

Only 34 when enshrined, Gale Sayers remains the youngest man ever voted into the Pro Football Hall of Fame. ▪

	Gms	Att	Yds	Avg	TD	College
TOTAL	226	4,409	18,355	4.2	164	Florida

22 E<small>MMITT</small> S<small>MITH</small>

RUNNING BACK

EVERYTHING THAT'S GOOD ABOUT FOOTBALL

Play-by-play man Brad Scham's call of the moment, Oct. 22, 2002, is as instantly familiar to Texans as Al Michaels's call of the Feb. 22, 1980, "Miracle on Ice" is to the nation.

"I-formation, two receivers right. Second and seven from the Dallas 30. [Chad] Hutchinson hand-off Smith — 35, 40-yard-line! Right on the mark! That should do it! Move over, Sweetness! Make a place for Emmitt!"

Nobody had to make a place for Emmitt Smith. He made his own.

"Thirteen years ago," recalled wideout Michael Irvin during an emotional post-game celebration, marking running back Smith's passing of Walter Payton atop the NFL's all-time rushing list. "A rookie walked into my room. He was my roommate. We talked about the things we wanted to accomplish on the field.

"The first thing he said to me — and we were not a good team at the time — was that he wanted to win Super Bowls for you guys. And he did that. He said he wanted to win rushing titles, and he did that. He said he wanted to win MVPs, and he did that. His last goal, which I thought was fantasy,

was to become the all-time leading rusher in the NFL.

"And today he did that."

On that afternoon, in front of the home fans at Texas Stadium, Emmitt Smith ran into the record books.

What people conveniently forget now, in the soft glow of hindsight, is that he was, by that point in his career, generally thought to be a spent force. Observers had begun wondering aloud if Emmitt Smith hadn't stayed too long at the fair. As he reached out to history that Oct. 22, he was en route to the lowest rushing total in his career, a count below the Herculean standards he'd set with 11 consecutive years of 1,000 yards or better. There were opinions voiced that maybe he should've had the good sense to retire. Lucky thing Emmitt Smith hadn't the sense to listen to others.

If he had, he might've also believed the scouts who had written him off as too small and too slow when he came out of the University of Florida. He could've subconsciously agreed with all those teams that so cavalierly bypassed him in the 1990 draft. If he had had that kind of sense, Smith

CAREER HIGHLIGHTS

Drafted: 1990; 1st round, 17th overall; Dallas Cowboys

Rookie Season (1990): 16 games, 241 attempts, 937 yds, 3.9 yd avg, 11 TDs

----

Career Year (1995): 16 games, 377 att, 1,773 yds, 4.7 yd avg, 25 TDs

----

Accomplishments
NFL Rookie of the Year: 1990
Pro Bowls: 8 (1990–1995), (1998, 1999)
NFL MVP: 1993 Bert Bell Trophy
NFL MVP: 1993 AP and Football Writers Association
Super Bowl MVP: 1995

Ranking on the all-time list major rushing categories
Attempts: 4,409 (1st)
Yards: 18,355 (1st)
Touchdowns: 164 (1st)
Yards from scrimmage: 21,579 (2nd)
Rushing/receiving TDs: 175 (2nd)

Quick Fact: The only NFL Player to be named the NFL's MVP and win ABC's Dancing with the Stars Championship (2006).

Smith gains yards against the Cardinals in 1999; his last Pro Bowl season.

could never have passed Payton, would never have left an indelible mark on pro football.

What Emmitt Smith had, in abundance, was more powerful than sense. It was self-belief, an inner faith that if a person wanted something badly enough, he could get it.

"For me," Smith once said, "winning isn't something that happens suddenly on the field when the whistle blows and the crowds roar. Winning is something that builds physically and mentally every day that you train and every night that you dream."

As philosophies go, that carries a powerful motivational punch.

Smith thrived in a decade that also included the phenomenal Barry Sanders. Just as Ali had Frazier, Wilt had Russell and Nicklaus had Watson, Emmitt had Barry. The two men differed stylistically, and arguments raged through the '90s about who was the better back. But there's little doubt that the greatness of one drove the greatness of the other.

In the final analysis, though, Emmitt Smith was the one to persevere. The one to pass Payton.

"You can just look at my age and say, 'Yeah, he's 33, he should go,'" he told S.L. Price of *Sports Illustrated* as he approached the iconic figure of 16,726 yards accrued in a career. "Yeah, I'm 33. But have I lost my step? Have I lost my vision? Have I lost my power? Have I lost my ability to make a person miss? If I answer yes to all those questions you might be right. But don't tell me I should quit just because of my age. That's what makes this frustrating. You have to know who you are. I know who I am."

When Smith arrived in Big D, the Cowboys were hardly America's Team. They weren't, in fact, much of a team at all. Coach Jimmy Johnson had the gargantuan task of trying to rebuild a 1–15 loser.

With Smith running and Troy Aikman playing catch with Irvin, the Cowboys would go on to glory. In his career, Emmitt Smith would win three Super Bowls, play in eight Pro Bowls and win the 1993 NFL MVP Award. Like his hero, the man he supplanted at the summit of football's Olympus, Walter Payton, Smith did it all with class and distinction. Here was someone who had his head screwed on right.

For instance, he came out of Florida early for the NFL draft, but having promised his mother he'd get an education, returned to school during the offseasons, earning his Bachelor's degree in Public Recreation in 1996.

"He personifies everything that's good about football," said Seattle Seahawks' coach Mike Holmgren.

Appropriately, after spending 2003 and 2004 with Arizona to close out his career, the Cardinals released Smith and he signed a one-day, no-pay contract to retire as a Dallas Cowboy.

Deep inside, Emmitt Smith, the guy many believed was too slow and too small, never wavered in his conviction that he had a date with destiny.

"I think about it all the time," Smith once told *Sports Illustrated* as he closed in on the man they called Sweetness. "I'm chasing after legends, after Walter Payton and Tony Dorsett and Jim Brown and Eric Dickerson. After guys who made history. When my career's over, I want to have the new kids, the new backs, say, 'Boy, we have to chase a legend to be the best.' And they'll mean Emmitt Smith."

The 18,355 yards he amassed in 15 seasons remains the touchstone figure they're all still trying to catch. ∎

	Gms	Att	Comp	Yds	TD	Int	College
TOTAL	131	2,958	1,685	22,700	153	109	New Mexico Military Institute, Navy

12 Roger STAUBACH

QUARTERBACK

CAPTAIN COMEBACK WAS A COWBOY

In an era of change and rebellion, Staubach was a welcome, old-fashioned super hero, representing less turbulent times. Genial. Straitlaced. Rigidly conservative. Devoutly Catholic. To push the theme you might almost say "prim." He came to symbolize those great Cowboy teams that went to four Super Bowls in an eight-year span.

Somehow, Roger Staubach seemed above it all.

In an interview aired on CBS in 1975, though, he showed he wouldn't let the image compromise his sense of humor.

"Everyone in the world compares me to Joe Namath, you know." he told interviewer Phyllis George, "As far as off the field, he's single, a bachelor, a swinger; I'm married with a family and he's having all the fun. I enjoy sex as much as Joe Namath, you know, only with one girl. It's still fun."

The remark, coming from Staubach the Square, had all of America talking. Just as the man's quarterbacking had all of the NFL talking through 11 seasons of excellence.

As conventional as he was outside the white lines in his personal life, Roger Staubach could be considered a bit of a hell-raiser on the football field. He wasn't christened "Roger the Dodger" for nothing. His ability to avoid trouble netted him 2,264 rushing yards and 20 touchdowns during his seasons in Texas.

Armed with a dizzying array of offensive weapons — former Olympic gold medal sprinter Bob Hayes, Drew Pearson on the outside; pocket-sized dynamo Robert Newhouse, Calvin Hill and the sublime Tony Dorsett charging out of the backfield — Staubach was the choreographer of a brilliant ensemble.

His uncanny knack for bringing the Cowboys back from the abyss transformed the son of a Cincinnati salesman into NFL royalty. He directed 23 come-from-behind victories in the fourth quarter during his career, 14 of those in the final two minutes or overtime.

"Roger," said Dallas tight end Billy Jo Dupree, "never knew when the game was over."

Staubach's Hail Mary pass to Drew Pearson with the Cowboys trailing the favored Minnesota Vikings in the 1975 NFC Divisional tilt with virtually no time left on the score clock has gone into the realm of legend.

CAREER HIGHLIGHTS

Drafted: 1964; 10th round, 129th overall; Dallas Cowboys

- -

Rookie Season (1969): 6 games, 47 att, 23 comp, 421 yds, 1 TD, 2 int, 69.5 QB rating

- -

Career Year (1979): 16 games, 461 att, 267 comp, 3,586 yds, 27 TDs, 11 int, 92.3 QB rating

- -

Accomplishments
Pro Bowls: 6 (1971, 1975–1979)
All-Pro: 5 (1971, 1976–1979)
NFL All-Decade Team: 1970s
Super Bowl MVP: 1972
Led the league in QB Rating: 4 (1971, 1973, 1978, 1979)
Hall of Fame: 1985

- -

Ranking on the all-time passing list in major categories
Completions: 1,685 (77th)
Attempts: 2,958 (82nd)
Yards: 22,700 (70th)
Touchdowns: 153 (65th)
QB Rating: 83.4 (25th)

- -

Quick Fact: Roger Staubach served four years of military service before he could pursue his professional football career.

But as Staubach knew, the last-minute theatrics were born not so much out of inexplicable inspiration as through preparation, repetition and the readiness to hold his nerve in any situation. As a field general, he was tough, single-minded, commanding and innovative. Tom Landry, the taciturn coach of the Cowboys, called Staubach the greatest leader he had ever had the good fortune to come across.

"Confidence," Staubach once said, "doesn't come out of nowhere. It's a result of something … hours and days and weeks and years of constant work and dedication. Spectacular results come from unspectacular preparation."

Roger Staubach certainly arrived in the NFL prepared. His path to football immortality was hardly a conventional one, but that makes the story all the more compelling. Originally selected by the 'Boys in the 10th round of the 1964 draft as the reigning Heisman Trophy recipient, he was unable to play pro football until his Naval commitment, including a voluntary one-year tour of duty in Vietnam, had ended.

In his junior year, he had led the Naval Academy's Midshipmen to a 9–1 record and the No. 2 ranking in the nation. Coach Wayne Hardin called him the finest quarterback the Navy had ever seen.

So the talent was obvious. The timing was troublesome. Undoubtedly, that's why he went so late in the draft. The wait was ultimately worth it for the Cowboys.

When Staubach left the Navy in 1969, he was a 27-year-old rookie. By 1971, he was the starter in Big D, taking control from incumbent Craig Morton after Dallas sputtered out of the gate 4–3.

Staubach guided the Cowboys to 10 consecutive regular-season victories, and culminated an astounding NFL debut as a starter by beating the Miami Dolphins 24–3 in Super Bowl VI. His 119 yards passing and two TDs at the New Orleans Superdome that afternoon earned Roger Staubach MVP laurels. He'd taken his sweet time getting there, but he'd arrived in style.

The next decade would see Staubach and the Cowboys set standards for other quarterbacks, other franchises, to emulate.

Staubach would engineer Dallas's marches to three more Super Bowl appearances, beating Denver 27–10 in 1978, back in New Orleans, while losing a pair of title clashes to the Terry Bradshaw-led Pittsburgh Steelers, both times at Miami's Orange Bowl, in 1976 and 1979.

Upon retiring at the close of the 1979 season, in part over concerns of possible lingering aftereffects from a series of concussions, Staubach became more engrossed in a business he'd begun while still playing: real estate. In that, like anything else he has ever thrown his energies into, Staubach made a rousing success.

During his years at the helm of "America's Team," Captain America had thrown for 22,700 yards and 153 touchdowns. His career passer rating of 83.4 was, at the time, the highest career mark ever. He had played in six Pro Bowls (although, ironically, was never chosen All Pro), led the league in passing four times and took home the NFL Players Association MVP Award in 1971.

He'd proven his versatility a hundred times over, winning games and championships with his arm and his feet and his head. In his first year of eligibility, 1985, to no one's surprise, Roger the Dodger took his place in Canton, Ohio, alongside the greatest in the game.

Roger Staubach may have gotten a late start, but it'd be difficult to argue that he hadn't made up for lost time. ▪

10 Fran TARKENTON

QUARTERBACK

BLOOD, SWEAT AND RECORD BOOKS

It'd be too convenient, too clichéd, to make the claim that Fran Tarkenton reinvented the quarterbacking position. However, it would by no means be out of line to say he stretched its limits, in much the same way he stretched the defenses of his day.

Before him, the overwhelming majority of quarterbacks dropped back in the pocket to throw the football. And stayed there, come hell or high water. That was the accepted way to play. The pocket was their womb, their cocoon. Inside it, they felt safe and protected. Tarkenton changed all that. He broke containment. He created chaos. He gave defensive coaches new, multiple dangers to consider.

"People looked down on scrambling quarterbacks when I broke in," Tarkenton noted ruefully, later in his career. "Now those who can't scramble are at a disadvantage."

The son of a preacher, born in Richmond, Virginia, Fran Tarkenton was drafted in the third round of the 1961 draft by the Minnesota Vikings, coming off a fine college career at Georgia, where he was mentored by the legendary coach Wally Butts.

Right from the get-go, he showed vast potential. His first pro start resulted in a 250-yard passing day and a 35–13 upset of the Chicago Bears.

He'd spend six seasons with the Vikings at old Metropolitan Stadium in Bloomington, bickering with head coach Norm Van Brocklin about the effectiveness of his scrambling style before requesting — and receiving — a trade to the New York Giants in time for the 1967 campaign. In the Big Apple, he provided an interesting contrast to the brash, outspoken quarterback of the other team in town, Joe Willie Namath.

The Giants, though, were no powerhouse. Still, in 1970, Tarkenton had them fighting, unsuccessfully, for a playoff spot. They wound up 9–5. It would be his high-water mark in New York.

By 1972, Tarkenton was back in the Twin Cities. But these weren't the same sad-sack Vikings he'd left in '67. A steely-eyed coaching recruit from the Winnipeg Blue Bombers, Bud Grant, had been installed on the sidelines and Minnesota was putting the pieces in place for a concerted championship push.

CAREER HIGHLIGHTS

Drafted: 1961; 3rd round, 29th overall; Minnesota Vikings

Rookie Season: 14 games, 280 att, 157 comp, 1,997 yds, 18 TDs, 17 int, 74.7 QB rating

----

Career Year (1969): 14 games, 409 att, 220 comp, 2,918 yds, 23 TDs, 8 int, 87.2 QB rating

----

Accomplishments
Pro Bowls: 9 (1964, 1965, 1967–1970, 1974–1976)
All-Pro: 6 (1970, 1972–1976)
NFL MVP (AP): 1975
Led the league in pass attempts: 2 (1975, 1978)
Led the league in pass completions: 3 (1975, 1976, 1978)
Led the league in pass attempts per game: 3 (1975, 1976, 1978)
Led the league in TD passing: 1975
Led the league in passing yards: 1978
Led the league in QB rating: 1969
Hall of Fame: 1986

Ranking on the all-time passing list in major categories
Completions: 3,686 (7th)
Attempts: 6,467 (7th)
Yards: 47,003 (5th)
Touchdowns: 342 (3rd)
QB rating: 80.4 (42nd)

Quick Fact: During the infamous "Hail Mary" divisional playoff game in 1975, in which the Minnesota Vikings lost to the Dallas Cowboys, Tarkenton's father, Dallas Tarkenton, had a heart attack and died during the third quarter while watching the game on TV with his other two sons.

Tarkenton's Vikings fail to rally against Oakland in Super Bowl XI, losing 32–14.

These were to be Tarkenton's years of greatest glory, and most profound disappointment. Always a bridesmaid, never a bride, the Vikings were among the regular-season elite over the next few seasons. But they could somehow never hit pay dirt come Super Bowl time. In one stretch of inexplicable agony, Minnesota lost three Super Bowls in a four-year span: In January of 1974, the Vikes were paddled 24–7 by the Miami Dolphins in Houston. The next year, in Super Bowl XI, 16–6 by the Pittsburgh Steelers at New Orleans and two years later 32–14 by Oakland, in Pasadena, California.

In three trips to the Big Dance, Tarkenton's offenses had delivered a paltry 27 points. Not good enough.

The most punishing, non-Super Bowl disappointment of Tarkenton's career came squished in between all those title challenges, in the 1975 season. The Vikings finished with a chart-topping 12–2 record that year. The Purple People Eater defense, headed by Carl Eller, Allan Page and Jim Marshall, was at its ravenous best. And the elusive Fran Tarkenton had never been more effective, winning the MVP award for his brilliance during the year.

But the Minnesota dream, riding hot on the heels of their stellar regular season, came cruelly undone during the NFC Divisional Playoff, when a controversial Roger Staubach-to-Drew Pearson touchdown pass — controversial because to this day Vikings' partisans claim Pearson interfered with defensive back Nate Wright while running his pattern — helped Dallas slip past the Purple Gang 17–14.

The play would only add to the image of Tarkenton as quarterback of the damned and the unluckiest man in pro football.

Tarkenton would play two more seasons following his final Super Bowl shot, walking away from the game at the close of the 1978 campaign after prepping his successor, Tommy Kramer.

"If it's not fun," he said, "you are not doing it right."

And football was simply not as much fun anymore. At 39, he knew instinctively that the time had finally arrived.

Even outside the game, Tarkenton continued to keep his feet moving. In retirement, Scramblin' Fran did a stint on ABC's *Monday Night Football*, hosting the cultish *That's Incredible!* TV show alongside John Davidson and Cathy Lee Crosby, and was shrewd enough to get into the computer software business on the ground floor.

In the opinion of some analysts, Fran Tarkenton's three Super Bowl defeats in four years — the perceived inability to win that magical "big one" — automatically prevents his joining the ranks of the elite all-time NFL quarterbacks. But at the time of his retirement, Tarkenton owned every major passing record of worth, with 47,003 yards passing, 3,686 completions and 342 touchdowns. Add to that his 3,674 yards rushing, 125 regular-season victories, six All-Pro selections and nine Pro Bowl appearances—and the stats make a mighty persuasive counter-argument in his favor.

This is a Hall of Famer, never forget, someone whose jersey, that famous No. 10, has been retired by the Vikings.

"Success, in my view," Tarkenton once said, obviously alluding to the one blemish on his résumé, "is the willingness to strive for something you really want. The person not reaching the top is no less a success than the one who achieved it, if they both sweated blood, sweat and tears and overcame obstacles and fears. The failure to be perfect does not mean you're not a success."

Fran Tarkenton may have never won a Super Bowl. But, hey, neither did Dan Marino. If success were to be solely measured in blood, sweat and tears, Fran Tarkenton would be as successful as they come. ▦

56 LAWRENCE TAYLOR

LINEBACKER

SEX, DRUGS AND FOOTBALL

Say L.T., and everyone, particularly those poor souls in the quarterbacking fraternity, knows exactly who you are talking about.

The No. 56 in New York Giants' blue, shedding his block from the outside linebacker position the way a snake sheds its skin, exploding into the backfield, drawing a bead on some poor unsuspecting guy with a Sack Me! sign taped to the back of his jersey. Then … impact! Followed by the aftermath.

The Lawrence Taylor saga, so familiar to football followers, is symbolic of our age: full of controversy, suspensions, sex and self-destructive drug use. It's also overflowing with exponential impact and achievement. Not that L.T. ever did things the easy way.

During a 1993 interview on TV newsmagazine *60 Minutes*, Taylor admitted to sending prostitutes to opponents' hotel rooms the night before games in order to tire them out. He confessed that he had used samples of teammates' urine to beat league drug tests, and to being hooked on cocaine.

But if L.T. couldn't seem to get out of his own way beyond the white lines, no one seemed able to get in his way when he was on patrol between them. He was arguably the most dominant single defensive player the league has ever known.

Double-teaming Lawrence Taylor seldom, if ever, worked. More than dominating his side of the ball, he actually dictated the way offenses lined up. He was a force of nature more than anything. He never felt beaten on a play. Teams were forced to make special provisions for him. Bill Parcells called Taylor the greatest player he ever coached.

"You try to stay within the rules for the sake of the game," said Taylor one time, "but you can always turn up the intensity."

Intensity was never an issue for Lawrence Taylor. He always seemed stuck on maximum overdrive. The title of his autobiography — *LT: Over the Edge* — pretty much summed it all up. His life. His game. His persona.

Taylor and New York took a shine to each other the moment the raw but gifted linebacker was drafted out of North Carolina, second overall in 1981 (the New Orleans Saints, unfortunately, had opted

CAREER HIGHLIGHTS

Drafted: 1981; 1st round, 2nd overall; New York Giants

Rookie Season: 16 games, 1 int, sacks: N/A, 1 fr

Career Year (1986): 16 games, 20.5 sacks, 105 tackles, 2 forced fumbles, 5 pass deflections

----

Accomplishments
Pro Bowls: 10 (1981–1990)
All-Pro: 10 (1981–1990)
Led the NFL in sacks: 20.5 (1986)
NFL Defensive MVP: 3 (1981, 1982, 1986)
NFL MVP: 1986
NFL Defensive Rookie of the Year: 1981
Hall of Fame: 1999

Quick Fact: When Lawrence Taylor won the NFL's MVP award in 1986, he was the first defensive player to do so since 1971.

for University of South Carolina Heisman Trophy-winning running back George Rogers with the top pick).

Giants' general manager George Young was so taken by Taylor's abilities that even before the draft he predicted Taylor would be better than NFL legend Dick Butkus.

"Sure, I saw Dick Butkus play," Young said. "There's no doubt in my mind about Taylor. He's bigger and stronger than Butkus was. On the blitz, he's devastating." L.T. and his new city had much in common: Both were bigger-than-life, badder-than-bad, exhilarating, intoxicating, and infested with a wild, self-destructive streak. It was love at first sight.

Not one to ease into anything, the new kid in town proved to be an immediate sensation, being named the league's 1981 Defensive Player of the Year in his rookie season — his first of three nominations. In 1986, he upped the ante by being named NFL MVP. Only three other defensive players have been so honored. The NFL didn't start recording sacks until Taylor's second season, in 1982. So if you factor in the 9½ sacks he was unofficially credited with in his rookie year, he amassed 142 in 184 games, an incredible ratio.

That he lasted 13 years and was so productive, given his drug and alcohol problems, is nothing short of astounding. In a perverse way, it served to underscore what a giant talent fans in New York had been privileged to watch.

A 1988 game against the New Orleans Saints is widely remembered for personifying Taylor's almost fanatical competitive attitude. Suffering from a torn pectoral muscle, the single-minded linebacker, putting aside the pain, wore a sling/harness to keep his shoulder in place.

He only recorded seven QB sacks that day.

The year Taylor became eligible for Hall of Fame induction (1999), debate sprang up that perhaps his bad-boy image, and all those indiscretions he so readily admitted to, should keep him out of Canton. The shrine of the game, they argued, was reserved for immortals, not immorals.

"If they don't vote me in the Hall of Fame," Taylor countered defiantly, "then they need to close that place down."

They did. They don't.

They might have argued all day long and into the night about Lawrence Taylor's off-the-field misdeeds, but there was simply no way around all those sacks, the 10 Pro Bowls, the individual awards and two Super Bowl rings. His career, however compromised by his off-field actions, screamed out for such recognition.

No one could dispute that he had established a new standard for the linebacker position.

Ever the rebel, L.T., now drug-free and living clean, arrived for induction in Canton decked out unconventionally in a black T-shirt under his yellow Hall of Fame sports jacket, instead of the customary shirt and tie. Oh, and he was wearing sandals — with no socks. But when the time came to speak, the longtime annihilator spoke eloquently, and from the heart.

"It's a great honor to be here," said the man who was so good at his job that he was known far and wide simply by his initials. "I think what I want to leave the people is that life, like anything else, can knock you down.

"You know, anybody can quit. Anybody can do that. A Hall of Famer never quits. A Hall of Famer realizes that the crime is not being knocked down. The crime is not getting up again." ▪

19 JOHNNY UNITAS

QUARTERBACK

THE GOLDEN ARM

Perhaps tight end John Mackey summed up the man and his aura best: "It's like being in the huddle with God." Johnny Unitas, the kid from the tough streets of Pittsburgh, made something of an unlikely deity.

Those sloped shoulders. Crooked legs. Shy grin. Bowed right arm from throwing so many passes. The high-topped black football boots and that trademark crew-cut. So iconic was Johnny U that in one episode of *The Simpsons*, more than two decades after he had retired, grandpa Abe Simpson exclaims, "Now, Johnny Unitas … there's a haircut you could set your watch to!"

Unitas arrived in Baltimore in 1956 after playing for the semi-pro Bloomington Rams. He had been earning six dollars a game, on a field strewn with rocks and shattered glass that had to be sprinkled with oil before every game to keep the dust down. He was also working as a pile driver at a construction company at the time to make ends meet.

The Golden Arm was no stranger to hard work. He grew up in a single-parent home after his father died when he was only five years old. His mother worked two jobs to support four children. Unitas later said he learned more from her than any coach.

After a standout collegiate career at Louisville, he was famously drafted in the ninth round, but then released by the hometown Pittsburgh Steelers in 1955. Apparently, the Steelers had too many quarterbacks to offer him a decent look. After being cut, a downcast Unitas hitchhiked home. "Unfortunately," recalled Steelers' owner Dan Rooney, in one of the great understatements in all of sport, "we did not give him a chance." It was an oversight a city and its franchise would long lament. Not that the Baltimore Colts were falling all over themselves to sign some kid named Johnny Unitas. The Colt's coach at the time, Weeb Ewbank, recalled that an anonymous fan sent a letter to the team extolling the virtues of this lanky, rawboned quarterback. Ewbank figured "What the hell!" and offered the guy $7,000 if he stuck around. "I always accused Johnny of writing [the letter]," Ewbank would later joke.

On Oct. 21, 1956, Johnny U tossed his first-ever NFL pass, which was picked off and run back for a touchdown. In the same

Drafted: 1955; 9th round, 102nd overall; Pittsburgh Steelers

Rookie Season (1956): 12 games, 198 att, 110 comp, 1,498 yds, 9 TDs, 10 int

----

Career Year (1959): 12 games, 378 att, 190 comp, 2,899 yds, 32 TDs, 14 int, 92.0 QB rating

----

Accomplishments

Pro Bowls: 10 (1957–1964, 1966, 1967)

NFL Championships: 2 (1958, 1959)

NFL MVP: 3 (1964, 1967, 1959)

Led the NFL in passing yards: 4 (1957, 1959, 1960, 1963)

Led the NFL in passing TDs: 4 (1957–1960)

Led the NFL in pass completions: 3 (1959, 1960, 1963)

Led the NFL in pass attempts: 4 (1957, 1959–1961)

Led the NFL in passer rating: 3 (1957, 1958, 1965)

Hall of Fame: 1979

Ranking on the all-time passing list in major categories

Completions: 2,830 (18th)

Attempts: 5,186 (14th)

Yards: 40,239 (11th)

Touchdowns: 290 (7th)

QB rating: 78.2 (56th)

Quick Fact: Holds NFL record for most consecutive games with a TD pass: 47 (1956–1960).

Johnny U orchestrates the winning drive of the 1958 NFL Championship game.

game, he then ran into teammate Alan Ameche on the next possession. Chicago recovered the fumble and scored. Another botched hand off later would set up yet another Bears' major. Baltimore lost that day 58–27 — hardly an auspicious debut.

Undeterred, Unitas would go on to lead the Colts to three NFL championships, win three MVP awards, a record 10 Pro Bowl appearances and four All-Pro citations, becoming the quarterback standard for decades. He would be the first man to throw for 40,000 yards in a career. His 47 consecutive games with at least one touchdown toss remains one of the iconic records in sport, up there on Olympus beside DiMaggio's 56-game hitting streak and Glenn Hall's 502 consecutive games tending goal for the Chicago Blackhawks.

Johnny U helped usher in the modern, TV-dominated NFL in the so-called "greatest game ever played," the Dec. 28, 1958, championship clash against the New York Giants at Yankee Stadium. With only 90 seconds to work, Unitas completed four passes to set up a game-tying field goal. "We've got 80 yards to go and two minutes to do it in," a teammate remembers him saying on the field to start the march. "We're going to find out what stuff we're made of." Unitas later engineered an 80-yard drive in sudden-death overtime, capped by Ameche's one-yard touchdown plunge. Telecast live and coast-to-coast on NBC, the drama of that game ushered in a new era of mushrooming popularity for the NFL. It also made Johnny Unitas a star from coast-to-coast. "I don't know what he uses for blood," marveled former quarterback Sid Gillman, "but I guarantee you it isn't warm. It's ice-cold."

To today's football fanatic, the No. 19 in blue might seem something of a relic: the short, slipped steps of a pure old-time pocket passer. Don't be fooled, though. No one tougher, no one smarter, no one more courageous has ever played the position. Johnny Unitas defied eras.

He also defied medical logic. There's something heroic, even romantic, about those who suffer for their art. And Unitas suffered. This was a man as tough as tungsten, just like his hometown. Broken ribs. Punctured lung. Shoulder contusions. Knee surgeries. He ripped a tendon in his right arm almost off the bone and missed most of the 1968 season. He ruptured the Achilles in his right foot playing paddleball with teammate Tom Matte at a YMCA in April 1971 and was supposed to be sidelined for six months. He made it back in half the time. "What made him the greatest quarterback of all time wasn't his arm or his size, it was what was inside his stomach," said former Giants' general manager Ernie Accorsi, who worked with Unitas during his final years in Baltimore.

Johnny Unitas retired in 1973, holding 22 records at the time. He'd completed 2,830 passes for 40,239 yards and 290 touchdowns. He was voted into the Pro Football Hall of Fame six years later. In 1999, *Sports Illustrated* voted him the fifth best player of all time, second among quarterbacks only to Joe Montana. But the old-timers, those who'd been there, seen it all unfold and remembered, knew better. On Sept. 11, 2002, while working out, Johnny Unitas died of a heart attack in Baltimore at the age of 69. Baltimore mourned. A nation that had become obsessed with the game, a game he helped reinvent and popularize, stopped to pay tribute. God had left the huddle and gone up to heaven.

"There is a difference between conceit and confidence," Unitas once said. "Conceit is bragging about yourself. Confidence means you believe you can get the job done."

No one did it better — before or since. ■

	Gms	Int/Yds	TD	Sks	Fr	College
TOTAL	232	3/79	0	198	20	Tennessee

92 REGGIE WHITE

DEFENSIVE END/DEFENSIVE TACKLE

SUNDAYS, SACKS AND SERVICE

When the news that Reggie White, Green Bay's marauding Minister of Defense, had been found dead of cardiac arrhythmia at his home in Cornelius, North Carolina, on Boxing Day, 2004, it was the world of pro football that was thrown for a substantial loss. He was only 43.

Reggie was the guy who usually did the sacking.

It seemed impossible, though, that arguably the most influential defensive lineman ever was gone long before his time.

Nothing, no one, people thought, could as much as slow Reggie White down, much less stop him from reaching the quarterback; from strapping on the pads, no matter how banged up his body might be; or from voicing his opinion on a wide range of subjects, however controversial.

"He may have been the best player I've ever seen," said Packers' quarterback Brett Favre in tribute. "Certainly he was the best I've ever played with or against."

Those sentiments were echoed around the NFL.

Another former quarterbacking teammate (and later opponent), Rick Mirer, remembered his dealings with Reggie. "I had the pleasure of getting hit by him several times. The way he just threw around 300-pound guys, I've never seen anyone do that. He was just head and shoulders above anybody else I saw. He just ... dominated."

For further verification, consult Phil Simms. The one-time New York Giants' star was the victim of 15 of the 198 quarterback sacks White administered over 15 glorious seasons. Why, if Simms had been found in bed late at night, perspiring heavily, after experiencing visceral nightmares about Reggie White, he could have been forgiven.

The list of the Minister's quarterbacking victims is extensive. Seventy-five different men in all felt his wrath: the aforementioned Simms, sacked 15 times and Neil Lomax, 13 times, led the way. Over the years, White hunted down great ones, such as Troy Aikman (7 times), John Elway (5.5) and Dan Marino (2), along with the likes of Danny Kanells and Blair Kiels and Anthony Dilwegs, whose main claim to NFL fame is that they made it onto Reggie's list.

The big man from Tennessee, all 6-foot-5

CAREER HIGHLIGHTS

Drafted: 1984; 1st round, 4th overall; Philadelphia Eagles

NFL Rookie Season (1985): 13 games, 13 sacks, 2 fr

Career Year (1987): 16 games, 21 sacks, 1 fr, 1 TD

Accomplishments
Pro Bowls: 13 (1987–1999)
All-Pro: 13 (1986–1998)
Defensive MVP: 3 (1987, 1991, 1998)
Defensive Rookie of the Year: 1985
All-Decade Team: 1980s
All-Decade Team: 1990s
NFL 75th Anniversary
All-Time Team: 1994
Hall of Fame: 2006

NFL records held at retirement in 2000
Most sacks in career: 198
Most consecutive seasons with 10 or more sacks: 9 (1985–1993)
Most seasons leading the league in sacks: 2 (1987, 1988)
Most sacks in a Super Bowl: 3 (1997)

Quick Fact: Reggie White, from 1985 to 1992, recorded more sacks (124) than games played (121).

and 300 pounds of him, really was a Chattanooga Choo-Choo. When his train pulled out of the shed and built up a head of steam, nothing could stand in his way. At least, nothing human.

No one who ever played the position instilled quite the same degree of fearful respect. Oh, Bruce Smith of the Bills, unquestionably a wonderful defensive lineman, may have eclipsed White's all-time sack mark, by two. But Smith rang up that total in 19 seasons, four more than the Minister.

Reggie White was such an overwhelming force exploding into the backfield that he could dictate offensive strategy. He collected 23.5 sacks in 34 games for the Memphis Showboats of the United States Football League in 1984 and 1985, and joined the Philadelphia Eagles for the 1985 NFL season when the USFL went belly up, and he quickly became an NFL superstar. During eight seasons in Philly, White piled up 124 sacks. Amazingly, during his time in Eagle green, his sack total eclipsed the number of games he played.

In 1993, White used free agency to move to the Green Bay Packers. In six seasons there, he registered 68.5 sacks and helped the Pack to two Super Bowls, earning a ring in XXXI.

He didn't miss a beat, hadn't lost a step.

In 1998, White played what would be his last season in Green Bay, choosing to retire after being named the NFL's Defensive Player of the Year, and getting selected to his 12th consecutive Pro Bowl. Retirement, which wasn't an easy decision for White (there was much flip-flopping on White's part), didn't last long. He was convinced by the Carolina Panthers to come back and play, but his one season there in 2000 proved to be his last. He then retired from the game with nothing left to prove.

Ordained an Evangelical minister, Reggie White was, to many, a personal and professional contradiction. The relentless Sack Master between the lines, a gentle, peaceful man off the field. Never afraid to voice an opinion, to underline his conviction, White angered and upset many with his outspoken, fundamentalist views on homosexuality. He was accused of being archaic and hate-mongering.

"God," he said once, "places the heaviest burden on those who can carry its weight."

The Minister of Defense could carry plenty, which is what made his death, at the age of 43, so hard to believe. He had, in life, seemed something close to invincible.

In his chosen profession, he remains, quite simply, unmatched. In 1999, *Sporting News* ranked him 22nd on its list of the 100 Greatest Football Players. In 2005, three teams — the University of Tennessee, the Eagles and the Packers — all retired White's famous No. 92.

His nine consecutive seasons with at least 10 sacks remains an NFL record.

At his Hall of Fame induction ceremony at Canton in 2006, White's wife Sara and son Jeremy delivered the acceptance speech for a husband, a father and a football player. Jeremy, echoing the feelings of so many there that day, said in part:

"Reggie will be remembered by some as the man who sacked quarterbacks on Sundays … But to others, he will be remembered for his faith in God. And yet to others he will be remembered, yet again, as a father, a friend and a husband. Even though Reggie is not here to receive this great honor the NFL has allowed him to receive, I know he is with us. He is with us in spirit, but most of all he is with us in our memories. As long as we continue to remember anyone we have lost, they are never completely gone. They are with us."

Amen. ▮

OF MEN AND MOMENTS

"Most football players are temperamental. That's 90 percent temper and 10 percent mental."

– Doug Plank,
Defensive Back, Chicago Bears

Doug Plank didn't say every football player was that way, but he could have. Plank himself was as rough as knotty pine and could hit like a two-by-four. He understood the essence of pro football. He understood just what it took to play a violent game in rain or snow with the clock ticking down and tens of thousands of people cheering against you, and that those people wanted you to be trampled underfoot or, at the very least, humbled and scarred for life.

89

Jim Marshall sacks Chiefs' quarterback and game MVP, Len Dawson, in Super Bowl IV.

It's no wonder it takes all kinds to play in the NFL; as such the league has been a clearinghouse for the athletically blessed, the quiet and withdrawn, the loud and petulant, as well as the certifiably loony. Over the years the game has treated fans to a mixed-nut assortment of characters and character games.

To be clear, the word character is used here in its fullest form. We're not just talking about the swift and the strong who can split a pair of tacklers the way scientist Ernest Rutherford dissected the atom. We're including malcontents and foul-ups, scoundrels and flakes — off-tackle, off-the-wall eccentrics who broke the rules because they insisted there weren't any. They may have given their coaches nuclear ulcers, but those same players produced memorable moments of another kind.

THE MEN

Wrong-Way Marshall

Take Jim Marshall of the Minnesota Vikings for example. Marshall was a member of the team's fabled defensive front, the Purple People Eaters, who were named after Sheb Wooley's 1958 song, "The Purple People Eater."

Defensive end Marshall was a remarkable talent. Weighing just 235 pounds, he played 21 years in the NFL and started 302 consecutive games. To keep his streak alive, Marshall often played through injuries, aches and strains. Twice he checked himself out of a hospital to suit up on game day. The first time, he was recovering from pneumonia. The second time, he had accidentally shot himself in the side while cleaning a shotgun.

When Marshall retired at age 41, he had recorded 127 sacks, recovered an NFL record 29 fumbles, played in two Pro Bowls and a Super Bowl, and yet, all of that paled in comparison to one moment, one play.

It happened in a 1964 game between the Vikings and the San Francisco 49ers, who were playing at home in Kezar Stadium, nestled in the green confines of Golden Gate Park. The 49ers were on the move offensively, when one of their receivers was hit and fumbled the ball. An alert Marshall scooped it up and ran untouched 66 yards for what he thought was a Minnesota touchdown. But Marshall ran the wrong way and crossed the goal line into his own end zone, where he scored a safety for the 49ers.

Weren't his teammates yelling at him to turn around? (Marshall thought they were simply shouting the encouragement, "Go, Jim, Go.") Did he know something was askew when San Francisco lineman Bruce Bosley walked up to him and said, "Thanks, Jim"? (Oh yeah. That's when it hit home.)

Marshall's gaffe became not just a running gag, pardon the pun, but the defining moment of his career. Never mind that in the same game, he recorded a sack and recovered a second fumble to help the Vikings to a 27–22 win. Forevermore, he was wrong-way Marshall, the guy who thought all end zones looked alike.

"The No. 1 question is, 'I've always wondered what you thought at that moment?'" said Marshall. "And I say, 'Think of the worst thing you've ever done — the thing you're most ashamed of — and it was seen by 80 million people. Then think of people coming up to you and reminding you of it for the rest of your life. That gives you a sense of what I've gone through."

Despite the embarrassment, Marshall bore his infamy with grace. He later learned to laugh at its irrelevance after surviving a near-death experience in the mountains of Wyoming.

In January 1971, Marshall encountered a hellacious blizzard while traveling through Beartooth Pass. He was with a party of 16 and was almost killed when he drove his snowmobile over a cliff. The machine came close to rolling over Marshall, who fell 30 feet before climbing back to the top of the cliff with the help of a friend.

That was the start of a 36-hour ordeal that saw Marshall and Vikings' teammate Paul Dickson fight to stay awake so they wouldn't freeze to death. At one point, Marshall burned $1 bills then his cheque book to start a fire to stay warm.

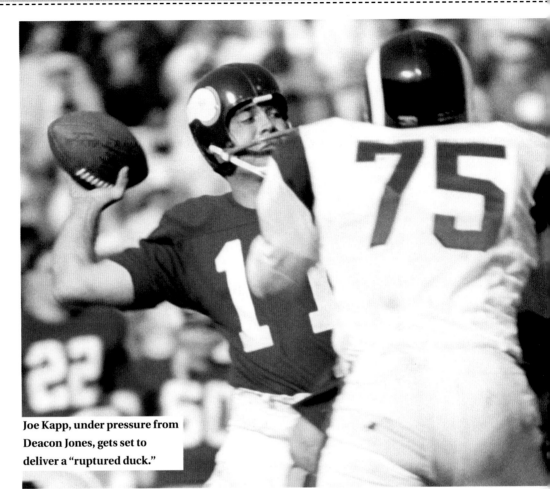

Joe Kapp, under pressure from Deacon Jones, gets set to deliver a "ruptured duck."

They eventually saw a rescue party and were told one of the group's members had frozen to death. Marshall never again complained about playing in the cold and snow of Minnesota — or running the wrong way in San Francisco.

Joe Kapp and the Magnificent Seven

One of the NFL's true characters had a day for the ages when he tied a league record by throwing seven touchdowns in a single game. Sid Luckman was the first to do it in 1943. Three others had duplicated the feat since then, but in 1969, Minnesota Viking's Joe Kapp stepped forward and joined the Magnificent Seven club with a showing that defied all logic.

Kapp, you have to understand, was not a great passer. He never threw the ball with his fingers on the laces, a tactic all the winged-arm wonders have used over the decades. His excuse was, "All the laces are different." Sometimes, when the ball was tough to grip, Kapp would wash his hands in mud puddles along the sideline. Even with a good grip and no laces, Kapp's throws fluttered through the air like broken badminton birdies or, as Detroit Lions' defensive lineman Alex Karras called them, "ruptured ducks."

And still, Kapp threw for seven touchdown passes in a single game against the Baltimore Colts, who had one of the better defensive units of the time. Did it make sense? Not at all. But Kapp was about winning, about doing whatever it took to get the job done. When told his passing style lacked the classic look of Bart Starr or Johnny Unitas, Kapp snapped, and replied, "Classics are for Greeks."

Kapp had won a Rose Bowl and a Grey Cup in the CFL before joining the Vikings. In one of his early NFL games, he lined up under center against the Los Angeles Rams' fearsome foursome defensive front of Deacon Jones, Merlin Olsen, Lamar Lundy and Roger

Brown and shouted at them, "All right, let's see how tough you sons of bitches are."

Once, after a heartfelt loss, Kapp later got into a fight with one of his own teammates, linebacker Lonnie Warwick.

"Most quarterbacks like to run out of bounds," said Minnesota coach Bud Grant, who watched Kapp charge into some of the game's toughest tacklers, just to prove a point. "Mine likes to run over people."

The Man Who Hated Rules

For sheer lunacy, no one caused more head scratching than the aptly-named Joe Don Looney. Considered "the greatest player who never was," Looney squandered his size, speed and abilities on acts of defiance and strangeness.

Dozens of players and coaches insisted Looney had it all — power, slashing speed, good hands, everything from the neck down. But he could never conform to conformity. He hated rules and being told what to do. He refused to do anything if it didn't feel right.

At the University of Oklahoma, he told coach Bud Wilkinson, "Take me out. My biorhythms are out of sync." Looney sat on the bench, didn't move for several minutes; then jumped up and proclaimed, "Coach, my biorhythms are fine. Put me in." Wilkinson did and Looney scored on a long touchdown romp.

Drafted by the New York Giants, Looney didn't believe in curfews and being told when to go to bed. With the Baltimore Colts, he used to sneak out of training camp and sleep in graveyards and was once fined $100 for being 15 minutes late to a meeting. He asked coach Don Shula, "Why wasn't I paid $100 for being 15 minutes early [the day before]?" With the Detroit Lions, Looney uttered his most memorable quote. Told to run in a play from the sidelines, Looney said to coach Harry Gilmer, "If you want a messenger, call Western Union."

Looney also refused to tape his ankles. When ordered to, he taped over his socks instead.

John Matuszak in 1976, his first season with the Raiders and his first Super Bowl victory.

"If the end zone is where happiness is, I'd be living there," Looney once said. "It's not, so I'm living here."

He didn't stay long in the NFL, just eight seasons, and he didn't accomplish much while he was there. He eventually did a tour of duty during the Vietnam War, converted to Hinduism, and died in a motorcycle crash at the age of 45. His legacy is one of unfulfilled promise and a lot of laughable tales.

Ol' Tooz

John Matuszak was another raging individualist. He stood 6-foot-8, weighed close to 300 pounds, and played for an Oakland Raiders team that got its colors and tackling style from the Hell's Angels. Nicknamed Tooz, he was a natural-born partier. Animal House on two legs.

As the Raiders prepared to boot-stomp the Philadelphia Eagles in Super Bowl XV, Matuszak vowed he was going to make sure none of his teammates broke curfew, especially with the game being held in New Orleans, where the temptations were as thick as gumbo.

"I'll keep our young fellows out of trouble," he said. "If any players want to stray, they gotta go through the Ol' Tooz." The very next night Matuszak was seen partying into the early-morning hours and fined $1,000 for his troubles.

Matuszak won a pair of Super Bowls but he is also remembered as an actor. Arguably his finest performance came in *North Dallas 40* where he played — wait for it — a football player confused by his place within the cosmos. "Every time I call it a game, you call it a business," Matuszak roared at his coaches. "Every time I call it a business, you call it a game."

Matuszak almost died once when he was playing for the Kansas City Chiefs. Having mixed beer with sleeping pills, the Tooz collapsed at a bar. Chiefs' coach Paul Wiggin was called to the scene and accompanied Matuszak in an ambulance ride to the closest hospital. Along the way, Matuszak's heart stopped and Wiggin revived it by thumping on the big man's chest. That was in 1974. Fifteen years later, at the age of 38, Matuszak died from heart complications.

Burning to Be a Success

Tom Rossovich lived his football life to the fullest. He was the Philadelphia Eagles' first-round pick in the 1968 draft, after a stellar career at Southern Cal, where his roommate was actor-to-be Tom Selleck. Rosso, as he was known, had that 1960s style about him. He had a puffy Afro hair style, and wore tie-dyed shirts and bell-bottom jeans. He was equal parts free-spirited and nonsensical. Once, he drove a motorcycle off a pier and into the ocean. He used to open beer bottles with his teeth and, when that got a little too tame, he'd grab a glass and start eating it. He'd also munch on cigarettes, paper, insects — whatever suited his fancy, if not his palate.

Rossovich's flair for the unusual is best remembered for a 1971 *Sports Illustrated* cover story. On the front of the issue, with the headline "He's Burning to be a Success," was a photograph of Rosso with his Afro on fire.

Rossovich once opened his mouth to say something and a bird flew out. True story.

"You know how I learned to play middle linebacker? From [Chicago's] Dick Butkus," Rossovich said. "Not from him personally, but at the time I was living with Steve Sabol of NFL Films and [Eagles' defensive tackle] Gary Pettigrew, and I said, 'They moved me to middle linebacker. I need to know how Butkus plays middle linebacker.' So Steve would bring all the highlights and I would study Dick Butkus for hours and hours and hours and hours."

Rossovich spent four seasons in Philadelphia and was voted to the Pro Bowl in 1969. He was traded to the San Diego Chargers, where he suffered a knee injury and watched his career fizzle out. He turned to acting where he reunited with Selleck and even appeared in several episodes of *Magnum P.I.* Not once, though, did Rosso upstage his former roomie by lighting his hair on fire.

Owens the Terrible

The most publicized character in today's NFL goes by the moniker "Terrible," as in Terrible Terrell Owens. So far — and with

Owens things are always open to change — the mercurial receiver has insinuated that one of his quarterbacks was gay while another wasn't in shape. He fired his agent, demanded his multi-million dollar contract with Philadelphia be renegotiated, and made enough negative comments about the Eagles to finally be suspended.

After being released, he signed with the Dallas Cowboys and the theatrics continued. In one episode, in 2006, he was found "unresponsive" in his home. The Dallas Police alleged it was the result of an accidental overdose of pain medication. Owens' publicist said it was an allergic reaction to the medication combined with the dietary supplement Owens was taking. Owens eventually fired his publicist for bringing about so much adverse publicity.

His many on-field high jinks have also kept Owens in the headlines. His touchdown celebrations have included pulling a Sharpie marker out of his sock and autographing the football before handing it to someone in the crowd; running to mid-field in Dallas, as a member of the opposition, and celebrating on the team's giant-sized star; lying down in the end zone and using the football as a pillow; and finally, running to the front-row seats where he grabbed a fan's bag of popcorn and poured it through the facemask of his helmet.

"A lot of people think I'm stuck up. Pretty much that I'm arrogant," Owens said of his persona. "I only do that when I'm on the field."

He does it well.

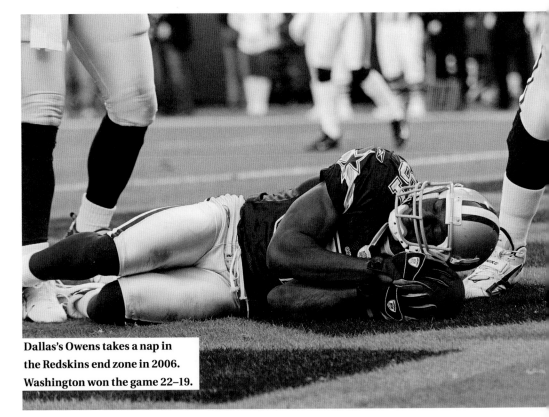

Dallas's Owens takes a nap in the Redskins end zone in 2006. Washington won the game 22–19.

Just Having a Bit of Fun

Chicago quarterback Jim McMahon had a penchant for fun. In 1985, when the Bears dominated the league with a 15–1 record, McMahon got himself into a pair of controversies. First, he mooned a helicopter hovering over the team's practice session. "I was just showing them where it hurt," said McMahon. He then defied the orders of commissioner Pete Rozelle by wearing headbands adorned with handwritten messages such as POW–MIA (Prisoners of War–Missing in Action) and Pluto (the name of a friend who was suffering from cancer). "Outrageous is nothing more than a way to wake people up," said McMahon.

Jim McMahon defies commissioner
Rozelle's headband orders.

THE MOMENTS

The commonest way to wake up NFL fans is to give them a performance they can't possibly forget, and the last 35 years or so have been crammed with remarkable efforts and character games. Some have been so staggering that they evoke instant recall with the mention of only a few words, such as The Drive, The Catch, The Comeback or Hail Mary. Today, you would be hard-pressed to find a football fan who hasn't heard all of these phrases. For example, every football fan knows what a Hail Mary is: the quarterback throws the ball up for grabs, says a prayer, and hopes one of his receivers can make the catch. It's a desperation move. Then again, desperation has been the mother of many a fine invention . . .

The Hail Mary

The year was 1975 and the Cowboys had to play the Vikings on their frozen tundra in an NFC playoff game. (Jim Marshall played in that game for Minnesota and always knew which end zone was his.) The Cowboys were trailing 14–10, starting at their 15-yard line with less than two minutes remaining in the fourth quarter. Roger Staubach, the Cowboys'

artful quarterback, got his offensive unit to the 50-yard line with only 24 seconds showing on the clock.

From a shotgun formation, Staubach took the snap, stepped up into the pocket and flung the ball downfield in the direction of receiver Drew Pearson. What happened in the next few seconds was a convergence of fate. Minnesota defensive back Nate Wright tripped over Pearson's leg and fell to the turf. Safety Paul Krause couldn't get over in time to tackle Pearson, who caught the ball on his hip and slipped, untouched, into the end zone for the touchdown.

The Vikings were mortified, then angry. They wanted a pass interference call against Pearson but didn't get it. Spectators littered the field with garbage. One fan flung a bottle that hit field judge Armen Terzian in the head, bonking him for 11 stitches. (The Vikings' faithful would later joke that the clink off Terzian's noggin was the real Hail Mary of the day.)

Staubach never saw the touchdown since he had been tackled soon after he released the ball. In the winners' dressing room, he told reporters, "I closed my eyes and said a Hail Mary." A catch-phrase was born.

To this day, Staubach and Pearson are approached by football fans who want to talk about their dramatic completion.

"It's amazing that you find so many Viking fans around the country," Pearson told *The Dallas Morning News.* "Some people bring their ticket stubs from the game for me to autograph. Others tell me, 'I remember exactly where I was when I saw that catch. You ripped my heart out.'"

The Drive

In the 1986 AFC championship game, John Elway's Broncos trailed the hometown Cleveland Browns 20–13 in the fourth quarter with less than six minutes left in the game. Time wasn't the problem, but the Broncos' field position was. They started from their two-yard line with Elway mixing short passes and runs. Faced with third and 18 at the Cleveland 48-yard line, Elway zipped a 20-yard completion to Mark Jackson. Five plays later, Jackson caught the five-yard scoring pass that tied the game and sent it into overtime.

Overall, Elway completed five of eight passes for 73 yards in The Drive. In overtime, he added a 60-yard march that set up Rich Karlis for the 33-yard field goal that won the game and stomped the souls of Cleveland's fans and players.

"I think becoming involved with the Super Bowl quest is a lot like falling in love," said Browns' linebacker Clay Matthews. "You dive headfirst and you don't worry about the consequences. It felt so good. But today we broke up."

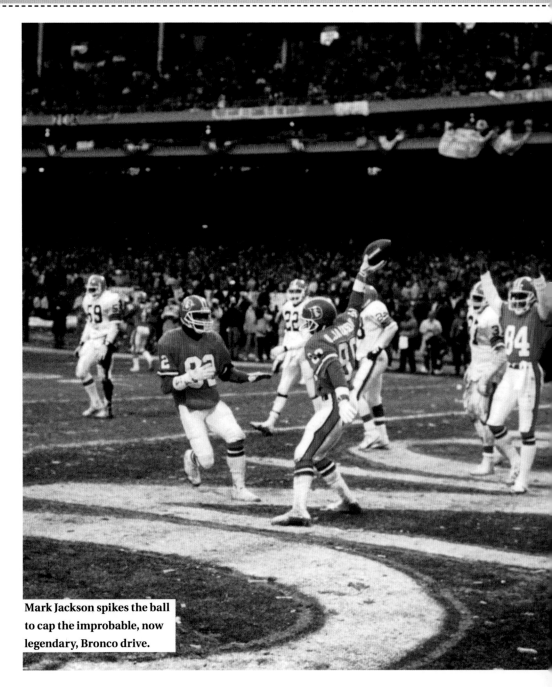

Mark Jackson spikes the ball to cap the improbable, now legendary, Bronco drive.

The Catch

The Catch was San Francisco's joyous version of the Hail Mary. It featured an emerging young star in quarterback Joe Montana, a venerable receiver in Dwight Clark and a 49ers' team that was bursting at the seams with greatness in 1982.

With Dallas leading 27–21, Montana directed his offense to the Cowboys' six-yard line with 58 seconds remaining in regulation time. Rolling to his right, Montana was corralled by three Dallas defenders and, at the last possible second, threw the ball high in the end zone before stepping out of bounds. Clark made a finger-tip grab at the back of the end zone to put San Francisco in front 28–27.

"You just beat America's Team," Dallas defensive end Ed (Too Tall) Jones told Montana.

"Well," answered Montana, "you can watch the Super Bowl on TV with the rest of America."

With 51 seconds left in the same game, Drew Pearson (Remember him?) almost scored for the Cowboys on a long pass reception. Unfortunately for the Cowboys, they fumbled

95

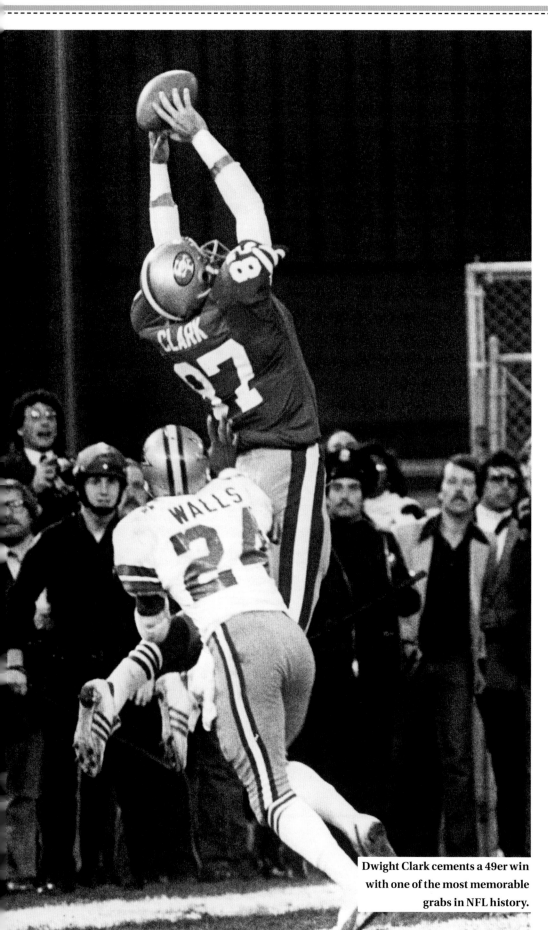

Dwight Clark cements a 49er win with one of the most memorable grabs in NFL history.

two plays later, San Francisco recovered and The Catch was immortalized.

The victory helped the 49ers capture their first Super Bowl title and established them as the NFC's new powerhouse over Dallas. After losing to San Francisco, the Cowboys' fortunes took a turn for the worse. They didn't make it to the Super Bowl once in the 1980s, which meant they got to watch the game on TV an awful lot.

The Comeback

The Comeback started as the Blow-Out on a cold January afternoon in 1993. The Buffalo Bills were hosting the Houston Oilers after having lost to them the week before. In that game, starting quarterback Jim Kelly suffered strained knee ligaments and was subsequently sidelined for the re-match in the AFC wild-card playoff game.

On top of that, the Bills lost their ace running back Thurman Thomas when he hurt his hip in the first half of their play-off battle with Houston. Left with Frank Reich, their backup quarterback, and Kenneth Davis, their backup running back, the Bills promptly went out and fell behind 28–3 by halftime.

The lead had grown to 35–3 when the Oilers intercepted a Reich pass and returned it for a touchdown in the second half. At that point, a Houston radio announcer said, "The lights are on here at Rich Stadium, but you might as well turn them off … this one is over."

Not so. Buffalo scored on its next possession when Davis ran in from the one-yard line. The Bills recovered the ensuing onside kick and scored again, this time on a 38-yard pass from Reich to Don Beebee. On his next series, Reich tossed a 26-yard touchdown pass to Reed, and Buffalo had sliced Houston's lead to nine points, 35–24. Reich went back to Reed again, connecting on a fourth-and-five completion that covered 18 yards for another touchdown. Then it was Reich to Reed for a third touchdown.

Trailing for the first time, the Oilers fashioned a 63-yard drive capped by Al

Del Greco's 26-yard field goal that tied the score at 38–38 forcing overtime. Houston won the toss and went on the attack. On his 50th pass attempt of the game, Oilers' quarterback Warren Moon was intercepted. Adding to the damage was a 15-yard penalty against Houston for face-masking, which gave the Bills a first down at the Houston 20-yard line. Steve Christie calmly kicked a 32-yard field goal giving Buffalo the win and the greatest comeback in NFL history. As a tribute, Christie's kicking shoe was enshrined at the Pro Football Hall of Fame in Canton, Ohio.

Other Amazing Comebacks

Perhaps as payback, the Bills took one off the shins in 2007 by being on other side of an amazing comeback. For much of a Monday night game against Dallas, the Bills had rattled the Cowboys and forced quarterback Tony Romo into throwing five interceptions. The score was 24–16 in favor of Buffalo with 24 seconds left in the game. Romo found Patrick Crayton for a four-yard touchdown pass but the two-point convert attempt was stopped.

The Cowboys successfully recovered an onside kick and appeared to be in excellent position for a game-winning field goal after Terrell Owens caught a 20-yard pass. But the Bills challenged the catch and replays showed that Owens had trapped the ball. That put Dallas back at the Buffalo 47-yard line with 11 seconds to play. Romo completed two passes, setting up rookie kicker Nick Folk for a 53-yard field goal.

Folk's kick was good but the officials standing in the end zone refused to make a signal. At the last possible second, Buffalo had called a time out in a bid to unnerve Folk. On his

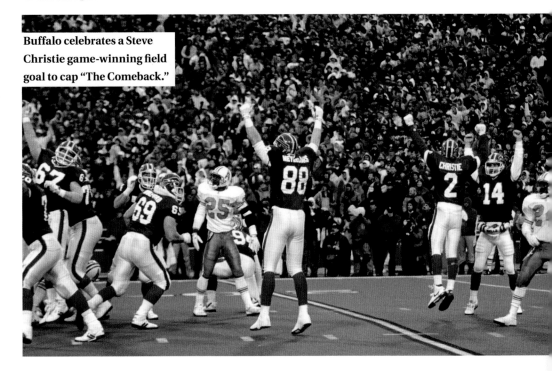

Buffalo celebrates a Steve Christie game-winning field goal to cap "The Comeback."

UNFORGETTABLE
SNAPSHOTS

There have been many unforgettable moments in NFL history. Among them:

• Joe Montana's last-minute Super Bowl XXIII-winning touchdown pass to receiver John Taylor. Trailing the Cincinnati Bengals 16-13 with 3:10 left in the game, Montana marched the San Francisco offense 92 yards. Taylor's 10-yard catch with 34 seconds left gave the 49ers their third Super Bowl title.

• Tony Dorsett's 99-yard touchdown run for Dallas in a *Monday Night Football* game in 1982. Dorsett took a handoff in his own end zone, ran through the left side of the Cowboys'

offensive line, cut right and was off to the races. The best part about Dorsett's record romp? Dallas had only 10 men on the field when it happened.

• Minnesota rookie Adrian Peterson rushing for a record 296 yards in a game in 2007. To underscore just how impressive Peterson was against the San Diego Chargers, he gained the bulk of his yards (253 to be precise) in the second half. His three touchdown runs covered one yard, 64 yards and 46 yards.

• Green Bay receiver Max McGee's relief performance in the first AFL–NFL championship.

McGee had stayed out the night before the game because he figured there was no way in the world he was going to play. When an injury to another receiver rushed him into the game, a thoroughly hungover McGee surprised even himself with seven catches for 138 yards and two touchdowns.

• The 1968 "Heidi Bowl" that saw NBC cut away from the New York Jets–Oakland Raider match-up with 50 seconds left, in order to begin the movie *Heidi* at the top of the hour. The Raiders scored two touchdowns in those last 50 seconds to win 43–32. But they were not seen live on TV.

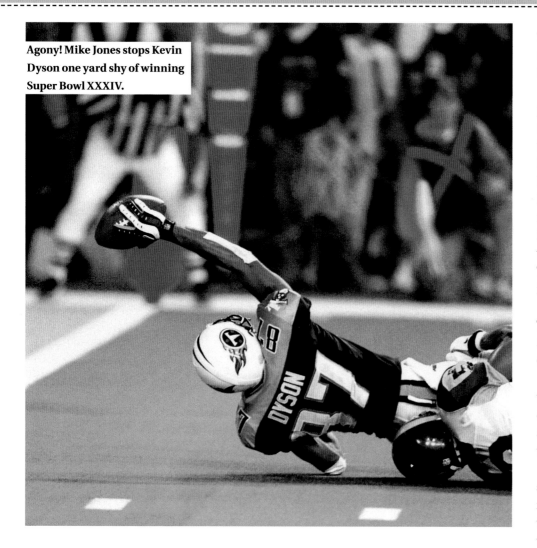

Agony! Mike Jones stops Kevin Dyson one yard shy of winning Super Bowl XXXIV.

second try, the ball sailed straight down the middle. Dallas scored nine points in 20 seconds to win 25–24.

"I haven't been around anything like that," said Dallas head coach Wade Phillips, "and that's 31 years I've been in the league."

Still on the comeback theme, San Francisco pulled a late rabbit out of its helmet in the 2002 NFC wild-card playoff game. The New York Giants were holding a seemingly comfortable 38–14 lead when the second half began at San Francisco's Candlestick Park. But again, things began to change. Jeff Garcia, the 49ers' quarterback, opened the third quarter with a 70-yard drive that included a 26-yard touchdown strike to Terrell Owens, who also added the two-point convert. New York 38, San Francisco 22.

Garcia then scored on a 14-yard run and Owens added another two-point convert to make the score New York 38, San Francisco 30, just seconds into the fourth quarter. San Francisco added a field goal and then went ahead, 39–38, with one minute remaining on a Garcia scoring toss to Tai Streets. The Giants attempted a 40-yard field goal for their shot at the win, but blew it with a bad snap.

Monday Night Football put one into the memory bank when the Indianapolis Colts edged the Tampa Bay Buccaneers 38–35 in 2003. Trailing by 21 points at the half, the Colts scored 35 points — including three touchdowns in the final four minutes — to force overtime before winning the game on a 29–yard field goal by Mike Vanderjagt.

The Tennessee Titans could write a book about their come-from-behind sagas and call it *The Ecstasy and the Agony,* a rearrangement of the title of Irving Stone's great novel. The Titans accomplished the Music City Miracle only to end up One Yard Shy of Glory. First, the Miracle.

With 16 seconds left in their AFC 2000 playoff match-up, the Buffalo Bills kicked a field goal to take a 16–15 lead over the Titans. On the ensuing kickoff, Tennessee's Lorenzo Neal fielded the ball, pitched it to Frank Wychek, who lateraled it to receiver Kevin Dyson, who raced 75 yards for a mind-blowing touchdown. The Bills were incensed and claimed the Wychek lateral was actually a forward pass and illegal. The officials reviewed the play and the ruling stood: touchdown.

That was the ecstasy, especially since the Titans (formerly the Houston Oilers) were able to avenge their loss to Buffalo in The Comeback seven years earlier.

And the good times continued for the Titans, who won two more playoff games and earned their ticket to Super Bowl XXXIV against the St. Louis Rams. But that's where the Titans would experience their agony.

Tennessee fell behind 16–0 before someone broke out the smelling salts and revived its offense. By the time the Titans tied the score, there were little more than two minutes left in the game, but the Rams responded with their most explosive outburst of the day, a 73-yard catch and run for a touchdown by Isaac Bruce. When the Titans got the ball back, they had 1:54 to travel 90 yards for the tying touchdown.

Titans' quarterback Steve McNair passed and dashed his way to the St. Louis 10-yard line, where he used his last time out. There were only six seconds showing on the game clock. This was it. McNair completed a short pass to Dyson, who looked as if he had room to score. Instead, Rams' linebacker Mike Jones made a text-book tackle stopping Dyson, the Music City Miracle Man, one yard short of the end zone.

"You'd rather get beat by 50 [points] than get beat by inches," McNair said afterwards.

The Tour de Force

Kellen Winslow may not have been as

flamboyant as some, but he was very much a character player in a 1982 AFC playoff game between his San Diego Chargers and the Miami Dolphins. To this day, some observers rate Winslow's tour de force as the NFL's finest. Here's what Winslow did: He played the game despite suffering a pinched nerve in his shoulder, severe dehydration, cramps and a sliced lip that required three stitches. He caught 13 passes for 166 yards, scored a touchdown and then, with the game on the line, he blocked a Miami field-goal attempt to force overtime.

Then he helped the Chargers win 41–38 before being helped off the field by two of his teammates, an image that was photographed and preserved for eternity.

"I've never felt so close to death before," Winslow said. "That's what Muhammad Ali said in Manila and that's how I felt out there at the end."

The Kick Heard Around the World

Our last look back has to do with the man who first kicked the longest field goal in NFL history. It came, as you might expect, in the final seconds of a close game in 1970, with the home team losing and having but one chance to win. And if having to make a 63-yard field goal from a mucky field wasn't demanding enough, Tom Dempsey had a significant disadvantage to overcome: his right foot, his kicking foot, wasn't really a foot, but a stump. His right hand was also misshapen by a birth defect. Not that Dempsey was troubled by his limitations.

He had cracked the New Orleans Saints' roster the year before, in 1969, as their full-time placekicker and reserve defensive end. Even his nickname, the horribly inappropriate Stumpy, failed to bother Dempsey, who had developed a thick skin to any kind of taunting while playing football in high school and college.

Dempsey had had a free-agent tryout with the San Diego Chargers in 1968 and at that time was outfitted with a special boot that was cut-off at the toes, giving his foot a flat edge to drive into the ball. In 1969, his first season with the Saints, he hoofed 22

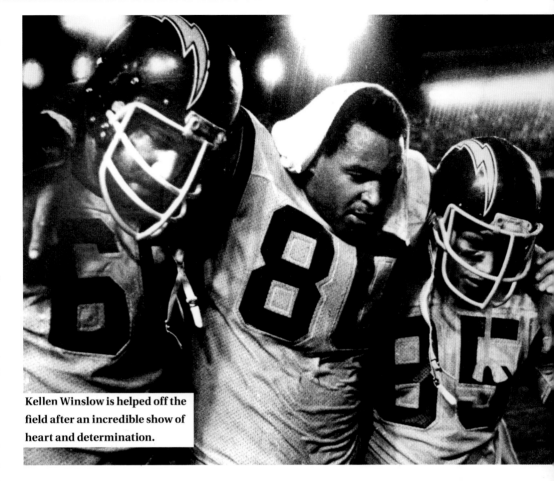

Kellen Winslow is helped off the field after an incredible show of heart and determination.

field goals and scored 99 points. On Nov. 8, 1970, against the visiting Detroit Lions, Dempsey had already made three field goals, but his team trailed 17–16 with only seconds remaining. When the New Orleans field-goal team trotted out onto the field for one last kick, several Detroit players started laughing. "We didn't even rush it," Lions' tackle Alex Karras said later.

But photographs of the kick show Karras desperately reaching out to block a kick that was perfectly snapped, perfectly held and perfectly propelled 63 yards for a 19–17 New Orleans' triumph.

"I thought I kicked it pretty well," Dempsey recalled years later. "I was hoping the winds wouldn't swirl and drive the ball off-course. It seemed like it took forever to get there. I just kept watching it, wondering if it had enough distance. Finally, the referees raised their hands that it was good."

While the kick was good, others around the NFL complained that Dempsey's shoe gave him an unfair advantage. There was even a rumor the boot was reinforced with steel, which allowed him to kick the ball further than anyone else. There was no steel in that boot, and Tex Schramm of the Dallas Cowboys eventually called Dempsey to apologize for implying that being born without a full foot and hand was an unfair advantage.

"I guess if not having any toes is an unfair advantage, I have an advantage," said Dempsey.

Twenty-eight years later in 2007, Jason Elam of the Broncos tied the record, kicking his 63-yarder into Denver's thin air. One of the first people to call Elam was Dempsey.

"I wanted to congratulate Jason because when I set the record, Bert Rechichar (who had previously kicked the longest field goal, 56 yards, for the Baltimore Colts), was very gracious to me," Dempsey said of the man he dislodged from the record book. "I told Jason that if someone breaks our record, it would be up to him to do the same thing."

As a player, Dempsey was 100 percent character, all of it good. ■

THE
BEST
OF THE REST

Troy Aikman
Lance Alworth
Fred Biletnikoff
George Blanda
Mel Blount
Tom Brady
Earl Campbell
Eric Dickerson
Tony Dorsett
Dan Fouts
Darrell Green
Franco Harris
Jack Lambert
Dick Lane
Steve Largent
Ray Lewis
Howie Long
Ronnie Lott
John Mackey
Peyton Manning
Bruce Matthews
Anthony Munoz
Joe Namath
Ray Nitschke
O.J. Simpson
Mike Singletary
Bruce Smith
Bart Starr
Thurman Thomas
Steve Young

8 TROY AIKMAN

QUARTERBACK

BIG IN THE BIG GAMES

Auspicious would hardly be the word to describe Troy Aikman's NFL baptism.

As the Dallas Cowboys surveyed the wreckage of their 1989 season, the prospect of a Hall of Fame career for their rookie field marshal — three Super Bowl rings, half a dozen Pro Bowl appearances and more wins throughout the decade of the '90s than any other quarterback — seemed almost laughable.

Aikman, the boy wonder — their No. 1 pick from the UCLA Bruins, had lost his first 11 games as a starter. The 'Boys flat lined 1–15 that year under a new coach, Jimmy Johnson, who had controversially replaced the legendary and beloved Tom Landry.

The smell of doom hovered over Big D.

"I know how difficult my rookie year in the NFL was," Aikman would say years later, "and I know how competitive the sport is."

But those who wrote off the Cowboys after the horrors of '89 underestimated the ambition of owner Jerry Jones, the savvy of coach Jimmy Johnson and, most foolishly, also underestimated the spirit of Troy Aikman.

In 1990, ignoring the naysayers, Aikman

brought the Cowboys back to respectability and into playoff contention. The next season, despite being injured, he bounced back to start an NFC Divisional postseason game. The Cowboys were beaten 38–6 by the Detroit Lions that day. But the seed of onrushing success had been planted in Irving, Texas.

The golden years of Troy Aikman began in 1992, when the 'Boys won 13 games in the regular season and ran the table come playoff time, brutalizing the Buffalo Bills 52–17 in Super Bowl XXVII in 1993.

The quarterback that the critics had so openly questioned only three years earlier passed for 273 yards and four touchdowns en route to being named the game's Most Valuable Player. No one would ever doubt Aikman again.

Consistency would become his trademark down through the years (he'd finish with a 61.4 percent completion figure, fourth highest in history). He may never have put up the same kinds of passing yardage numbers as, say, Dan Marino. But then Marino never had a running back like Emmitt Smith to hand the ball to.

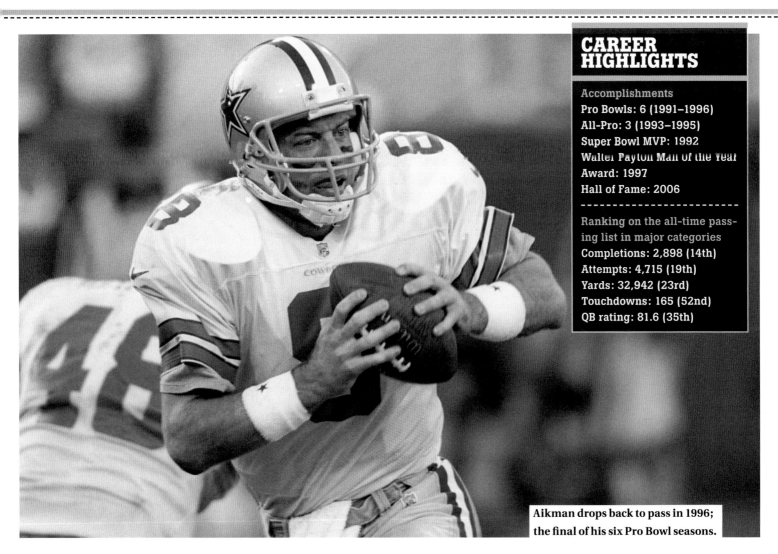

Aikman drops back to pass in 1996; the final of his six Pro Bowl seasons.

For Aikman, running the show, not being the show, was always the priority.

There would be still more Super Bowl glory: in 1994 against the beleaguered Bills again, 30–13, and a 27–17 decision over Pittsburgh in 1996.

By now, Aikman was a star, the toast of Dallas. He exuded a folksy charm. It was impossible not to warm to the man. When asked about being selected as one of *People* magazine's 50 Most Beautiful People, for instance, he was typically self-deprecating: "I thought, 'Well, they don't know that many people.'"

During his final seasons, Aikman absorbed a ferocious physical pounding. In December 2000, while rolling out to throw a pass, Washington linebacker LaVar Arrington drilled the unsuspecting quarterback. That jolt triggered Aikman's 10th concussion, and it would be his final NFL play.

The hit left a dent in his helmet. Its aftermath left a hole in his heart.

Still wanting to play but unable to find a team to take the chance on someone who had given so much, at such great personal cost, Aikman retired the next year.

He left behind him a decade of excellence: 90 wins (more than any QB in a 10-year span), six consecutive Pro Bowl appearances and a place on the Cowboys' Ring of Honor alongside his buddies in the famed Triplets offensive set-up: Emmitt Smith and receiver Michael Irvin.

The once-derided messiah had, in the end, proven a worthy successor to Roger Staubach.

"In my mind," said Jimmy Johnson, "I always judge a quarterback by how he plays in the big games. How does he perform in the playoffs? Troy Aikman always came up big in the big games."

On Feb. 4, 2006, Aikman took his place in the Pro Football Hall of Fame.

Standing at the podium during the induction ceremony, his thoughts must've drifted back to that first season.

"I'd like to share something that a close friend used to tell me back when I was playing," he told the audience. "When times are tough, maybe we'd lost a close game, I'd thrown the deciding interception or the grind and the rigors of the season were beginning to take their toll on me. He would say this: 'Sometimes we have to remind ourselves that these are jobs we've always dreamed of having.'

"For as long as I can remember, all I ever wanted to do was play pro sports. A lot of kids want that, but only a few actually get there. I was able to live a dream. I played pro football." ∎

19 LANCE ALWORTH

WIDE RECEIVER

THAT INDEFINABLE QUALITY

"He runs like a deer," blurted one astonished teammate. And so, Lance Alworth became Bambi.

Possessed of a graceful, almost balletic stride, great leaping skills, sure hands and an ability to cover 100 yards in 9.6 seconds, he would leave an indelible mark on the game in only 11 seasons.

Alworth was only six feet tall and weighed a scant 184 pounds, but that didn't stand in the way of his partnership with San Diego Chargers' quarterback John Hadl, one of the great collaborations of a decade. When the canny Al Davis, then an assistant coach with the Chargers, coaxed Alworth into signing with the AFL club in 1962 rather than the NFL San Francisco 49ers, he knew his franchise had landed more than just a great receiver.

"Lance Alworth," Davis would recall, "was one of the maybe three players in my lifetime who had what I call 'It.' You could see right from the start that he was going to be a superstar."

Smart man, that Al Davis. His prize catch more than justified the hyperbole. He had 'It,' and more.

Fitting perfectly into the west coast, sun-and-surf lifestyle, Alworth flourished. His talents were undeniable, even by those who openly mocked the AFL's overall quality. The slender gazelle from Houston cut across leagues and prejudices.

He was as electrifying as that lightning bolt on the sides of his helmet, and in short order came to symbolize the Chargers' franchise. From an All-America halfback at the University of Arkansas to one of the finest receivers of the '60s, he would be one of the few AFL players to be featured on the cover of *Sports Illustrated*. A decade and a half after he exploded onto the scene, he was the first AFL player inducted into the Pro Football Hall of Fame.

He helped San Diego win an AFL title in 1963, hooking up with Hadl on a 48-yard TD pass-and-run to slay the Boston Patriots. He caught at least one pass in 96 consecutive games and still holds the record for most games (five) with 200 or more yards receiving.

Alworth apparently never did like the nickname Bambi. But even he had to admit that Chargers' fullback Charlie Flow-

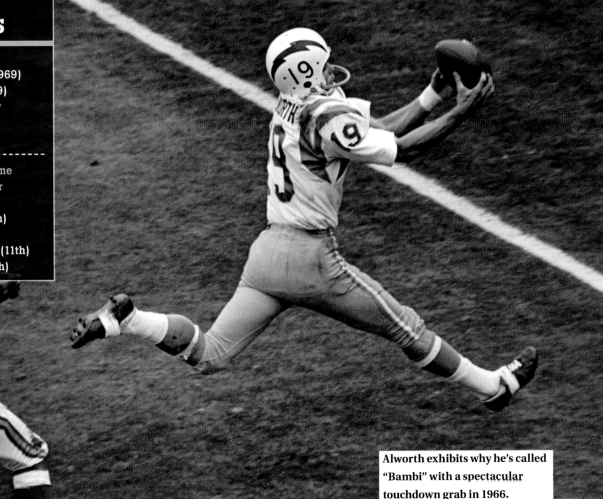

CAREER HIGHLIGHTS

Accomplishments
Pro Bowls: 7 (1963–1969)
All-Pro: 7 (1963–1969)
NFL 75th Anniversary
All-Time Team: 1994
Hall of Fame: 1978

Ranking on the all-time
receiving list in major
categories
Receptions: 542 (77th)
Yards: 10,266 (26th)
Touchdowns: 85 TDs (11th)
Yards/game: 75.5 (8th)

Alworth exhibits why he's called "Bambi" with a spectacular touchdown grab in 1966.

ers caught the essence of his style when he tagged him with the famous moniker. "He looked like a kid of 15," remembered Flowers. "He had real short hair and brown eyes. And he reminded me of a graceful deer when he ran."

Oh, he ran. He ran and ran, superb routes, past opposing secondaries. It seemed as if he never stopped. There was an uninhibited freedom about the way that Alworth flew down a field that caught people's imaginations. Add that to the elegance and the incomparable grace, and his star quality would be difficult to overemphasize.

In 1965, it'd be difficult to argue that he wasn't the best receiver in all of pro football. That season he caught 69 passes for 1,602 yards and 14 touchdowns, averaging an astounding 23.2 yards a catch. There was a home run waiting to be hit on every snap of the ball.

In 11 professional seasons, Alworth snared 542 passes for 10,266 yards and 85 touchdowns. More amazing is an 18.94-yard per-catch average, a testament to his dazzling abilities after making the grab.

Bambi finished out the final two seasons of his career in Dallas, and won a championship ring there, catching the first touchdown pass in the Cowboys' 24–3 conquest of the Miami Dolphins in Super Bowl VI. But he only latched onto 49 passes in two seasons in Big D, and wasn't particularly enthralled with the way coach Tom Landry deployed him. He decided to retire, and did so on top.

He left on his terms, with the admiration of his peers and having given more than a decade of keepsake catches to fans of two leagues. There were, naturally, honors aplenty to come. He would be enshrined in the Breitbard Hall of Fame at the San Diego

Hall of Champions Sports Museum and his No. 19 would be retired by the Chargers (only Air Coryell's quarterback Dan Fouts has been similarly honored since). To this day, he remains one of the most popular Bolts of all time.

Six years after walking away from the game, Lance Alworth was inducted at Canton, the first player from the renegade league so honored by the football Establishment.

But his heart, his legacy, lay in California, not Ohio.

"This is about as good as it gets," he said about the day of honors bestowed on him in San Diego. "It's a humbling experience. Being inducted into the Hall of Fame was special, but being honored at home means even more."

Lance (Bambi) Alworth: Forever a Charger. ▪

25 FRED BILETNIKOFF

WIDE RECEIVER

CHEWING GUM, EYE-BLACK AND STICKUM

Before every game, it was the same fastidious ritual: Fred Biletnikoff would examine his football pants and cut every tiny thread hanging from them, probably so they wouldn't slow him down when he was running. He'd cut the back of the pants behind the knees to allow for more flexibility. He'd tie and re-tie the laces on his football cleats before covering them in white tape. He'd tape a crucifix under his shoulder pads and tape his wrists and douse his fingers in Stickum. Then he'd slip on his jersey and his helmet and adjust (and re-adjust) his chinstrap for as long as it took to feel right.

Finally, when he was ready to play, his teammates on the Oakland Raiders would shout, "Hey Freddy, your uniform looks like crap today." And Biletnikoff would take everything off and start all over.

Such was the depth of Biletnikoff's perfectionist nature. Of course, it all paid off on the field, where the sinewy, eye-black-wearing, sticky-fingered receiver ran pass routes so sharp and precise you could have cut a diamond with them.

Biletnikoff was never the fastest receiver in the game, nor the most gifted, but he got the most out of his abilities through tireless effort. For either quarterback Daryle Lamonica or his good buddy Ken Stabler, Biletnikoff was the Raiders' go-to receiver.

In his career, he tied Raymond Berry of the Baltimore Colts by catching 40 or more passes in 10 consecutive seasons. Most of Biletnikoff's numbers were fashioned in the shorter, 14-game regular seasons, at a time when cornerbacks didn't have to stop bumping the receiver five yards downfield. He also added 70 catches for 1,167 yards and 10 touchdowns in 19 playoff games. Although he had a meager four receptions for 79 yards in Super Bowl XI, three of his grabs led to Oakland scores and the 32–14 win.

After receiving the game's MVP award, a humbled Biletnikoff quipped, "A stick of gum would have been enough."

To suggest Biletnikoff was quirky, both in how he dressed and how he played, is to say Oakland owner Al Davis used just a little dab of Brylcreem in his hair. Biletnikoff was as unusual as Davis remains greasy. No other receiver in the NFL used as much Stickum as Biletnikoff. Eventually, the NFL banned the substance, saying it provided

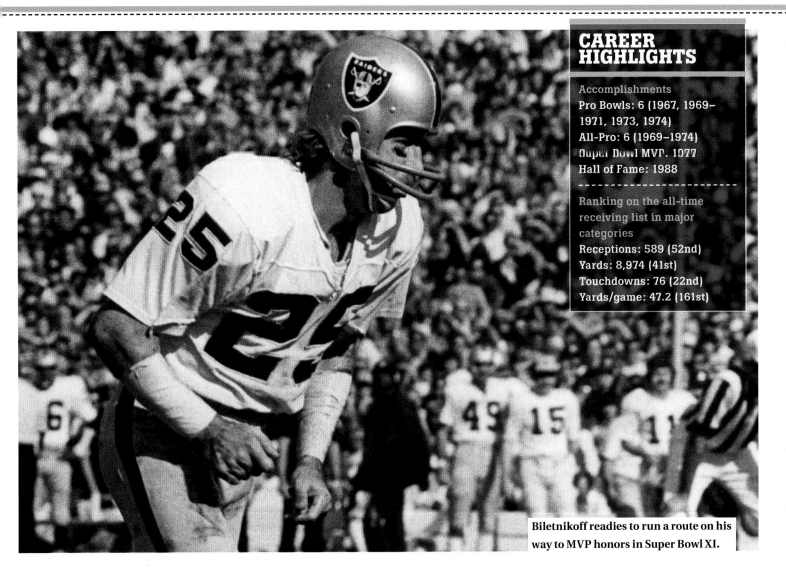

Biletnikoff readies to run a route on his way to MVP honors in Super Bowl XI.

an unfair advantage — not that Biletnikoff needed one, considering how good he was at catching a football.

Along with Stickum, Biletnikoff was addicted to cigarettes. The word was that he smoked heavily while playing for the Raiders and that his socializing, usually with Stabler, was off the charts.

"We lived together for like four years, which really wasn't a great idea," Biletnikoff joked of his friendship with Stabler. "I had a little bar called The Flanker so that's where we were able to eat and go drink and nobody had to pay the tab."

Biletnikoff, whose nicknames were Coyote and Dr. Zhivago due to his Russian heritage, was born into an athletic family. His dad was a regional Golden Glove boxing champion. His younger brother was a quarterback at the University of Miami who left

to sign with baseball's New York Yankees.

In his collegiate days at Florida State, Biletnikoff became his school's first consensus All-America in 1964. That same season, FSU defeated Oklahoma in the Gator Bowl on the strength of Biletnikoff's 13 catches, 192 yards and 4 touchdowns.

Both the AFL and the NFL drafted Biletnikoff, who chose the Raiders and stayed long enough to be named to six Pro Bowls. He spent one year in the CFL with the Montreal Alouettes, and then retired in 1980. Two years later, he began a coaching career that took him from high school to small colleges to the USFL, CFL and back to the Raiders, where he coached their receivers until 2007.

While working for the Raiders, Biletnikoff and his wife Angela suffered a staggering loss. In 1999, their 20-year-old daughter

Tracey was murdered by a man she had met while the two were undergoing drug rehabilitation. The man's arrest created a maelstrom of anger since he was on probation for kidnapping an ex-girlfriend. He was sentenced to 64 years to life in prison for first-degree murder.

Biletnikoff didn't attend the sentencing but a statement was read on his behalf. "You created a hole in my heart and all of Tracey's family's hearts," his daughter's killer heard. "That can never ever be repaired."

The Biletnikoffs established a non-profit foundation for their daughter "dedicated to support young women recovering from substance abuse, and education for the prevention of domestic violence." It's proving to be a new cause for an old perfectionist. ■

16 GEORGE BLANDA

QUARTERBACK/PLACEKICKER

PUNT, PASS AND KICK

Back in 1970, when people were singing "Bridge Over Troubled Waters," watching *Love Story* at the movies and *The Flip Wilson Show* on television, they couldn't help but notice this old guy who kept doing the most amazing things time after time, week after week, for more than a month.

Apparently, the guy was so old that he was born before the Great Depression, in the same year as Charles Lindbergh's historic solo flight across the Atlantic Ocean in 1927.

But for five weekends in the autumn of 1970, 43-year-old George (The Fossil) Blanda was cooler than string art, eight-track players, pet rocks and Led Zeppelin. Well, maybe not *that* cool, but certainly close to it.

He didn't just blow the NFL's mind with his last-minute comebacks as the quarterback/placekicker for the Oakland Raiders — he struck a blow for mid-lifers everywhere. He defied his younger opponents. Scoffed at Father Time. Made people believe in the power of positive thinking.

"Can you imagine even playing at 43, never mind doing what he did in the 1970 season?" Oakland teammate George

Atkinson said of Blanda's heroics.

Blanda was rushed off the bench to replace starting quarterback Daryle Lamonica against the Pittsburgh Steelers and responded by throwing two touchdown passes and kicking a field goal in a 31–14 win. The next week, he nailed a 48-yard field goal with three seconds left in the game to break a 17–17 tie with the Kansas City Chiefs and steal the game. The weekend after, against the Cleveland Browns, Blanda again came off the bench and threw a late touchdown pass that deadlocked the score at 20–20. As time ran out, he hoofed a 53-yard field goal to win the game.

Of his winning boot, Blanda said, "I put a little more rear end into the kick than usual."

And he wasn't done.

A week after beating the Browns, Blanda did in the Denver Broncos. Again, he came off the bench, and again he threw a touchdown pass with less than two-and-a-half minutes left in the fourth quarter, this time for a 24–19 decision. The week after that, he kicked a 16-yard field goal in the dying seconds to clip the San Diego Chargers, 20–17.

Blanda hoofs an overtime winner against Washington in 1975, his last season.

No one else rocked the NFL's cosmos the way Blanda did that season or since.

The son of a Pennsylvania coal miner, Blanda had a storied football career long before he got to Oakland. After his senior year at Kentucky University, he was signed by George Halas, the crusty owner of the Chicago Bears. The year was 1949 and Blanda received a contract for $6,000 plus a $600 signing bonus. He didn't get a raise for four years.

Used mostly as a kicker by the Bears, Blanda eventually got bored and retired after the 1958 season. He worked as a sales manager with a trucking company, a job he held during 22 of his record 26 seasons in professional football.

When the AFL was formed in 1960, the 33-year-old Blanda dusted himself off and joined the Houston Oilers as a quarterback and kicker. He led the team to the league's first two championships and was named the AFL's Player of the Year in 1961. That season he threw 36 touchdown passes, the most ever in a single season. The record stood until Dan Marino of the Miami Dolphins shattered it in 1984.

Having led the Oilers in passing and scoring for seven seasons, Blanda was thought to be spent, and thus he was traded to Oakland, where he kicked and served as a backup quarterback.

And then in 1970, George got his groove back. Every time the Raiders trotted him out, he moved the ball. Every time people cringed because the old guy was going into the game, he completed a pass or kicked a field goal and his team would win. His teammates were in awe of him.

"George was never gentle," said Raiders' linebacker Phil Villapiano.

"There were three people on the Raiders whom you were scared of because you knew if you made a mistake they were really going to get on you —[head coach John] Madden, [center] Jim Otto and George Blanda."

At the end of the 1970 season, after Oakland lost to the eventual Super Bowl champions, the Baltimore Colts, Blanda was presented with the Bert Bell Award as Player of the Year. It was followed by a funny line from Chiefs' owner Lamar Hunt, who said: "Why, this George Blanda is as good as his father, who used to play for Houston."

His second retirement, in 1975, was permanent. The NFL record book lists him as the first player to score more than 2,000 points and the first to score more than 500 points for three teams. He was inducted into the Pro Football Hall of Fame in 1981.

He was 54 then, and probably had another season or two left in him. ∎

47 MEL BLOUNT

DEFENSIVE BACK

THE BUMP AND RUN

Mel Blount had a rule when he played: no free passes. Every receiver he covered had to earn his yards, even when he was running his routes, even if the football hadn't been thrown, especially if the ball hadn't been thrown.

To protect his ground, Blount would "bump" receivers. Bump them like a Central Park mugger. One smack from the 6-foot-3, 205-pound Blount and some pass catchers stopped dead in their tracks. Others went down like a sack of wet towels.

Naturally, the receivers complained, and the NFL put in a rule (the bump-and-run rule), which restricted how far downfield a cornerback could molest a receiver. Offenses were delighted. The Mel Blount rule had saved them from the man who was single-handedly (sometimes two-handedly) rerouting their passing game.

That's how domineering Blount was when he played for the Pittsburgh Steelers. In 1972, his third season in black and gold, Blount played his position to perfection. He intercepted three passes, recovered two fumbles, returned one for a touchdown, and did not give up a single touchdown pass in 14 games.

"When you could nail receivers all over the field before the ball was thrown, pass defenses had a big edge," said former Pro Bowl cornerback Rod Perry, now an NFL assistant coach. "Mel Blount in Pittsburgh was 6-foot-3, and he just planted and killed guys all over the field on the way to the Hall of Fame."

Blount's role in the fabled Steel Curtain defense cannot be understated. If a ball carrier could slip past Mean Joe Greene on the Pittsburgh defense, and then avoid linebacker Jack Lambert, he was bound to run into Blount, who played the running game the same way he covered receivers — with an edge.

In 1975, Blount intercepted a league-leading 11 passes and was named the NFL's Defensive Player of the Year. It was one of many accolades he would receive over his career.

Hundreds of NFL players have come from humble beginnings. Blount came from a place that made humble beginnings look like the Hamptons. He grew up on a farm in Georgia, the youngest of 11 children. The house had no plumbing or electricity. His first job was stacking tobacco on a wagon in the early morning hours, before going to school.

Blount learned to take pride in the hard work and his father's praise. On Sundays, the Blount boys and friends went to church and then played football. In high school, Blount starred in football, basketball, baseball and track and earned a football scholarship at Southern University at Baton Rouge, Louisiana.

Earning Southwestern Athletic Conference all-star status, Blount was chosen by the Steelers in the third round of the 1970 draft (quarterback Terry Bradshaw was taken in the first). Soon after he arrived in Pittsburgh, Blount settled in at right corner and stayed there for 14 seasons, helping the Steelers win four Super Bowls. His biggest championship moment came in Super Bowl XIII in 1979 when his steal of a Roger Staubach pass led to a key Pittsburgh touchdown in its 35–31 win.

Blount's uncanny athleticism is illustrated in the following 1982 story: When the 31-year-old veteran came across a group of scouts at Three Rivers Stadium recording the vertical jumps of a prized prospect, Renaldo Nehemiah, who happened to be the world-record holder in the 110-meter hurdles. There was a mark on a wall. Blount saw it and was told that it represented how high Nehemiah had leaped. Dressed in street clothes, Blount jumped higher and said, "That's the Steelers' mark."

There's also the story of Blount's moral conviction, when, in 1977, he sued his own coach, Pittsburgh's Chuck Noll. It happened after Noll had accused Oakland Raiders' defensive back George Atkinson of being part of the NFL's "criminal element" for using a forearm hit to knock out Steelers' receiver Lynn Swan. Atkinson sued and Noll testified that the criminal element included Blount.

Blount's response was to file a $5 million defamation suit against his coach. It was dropped when Blount ended a 56-day

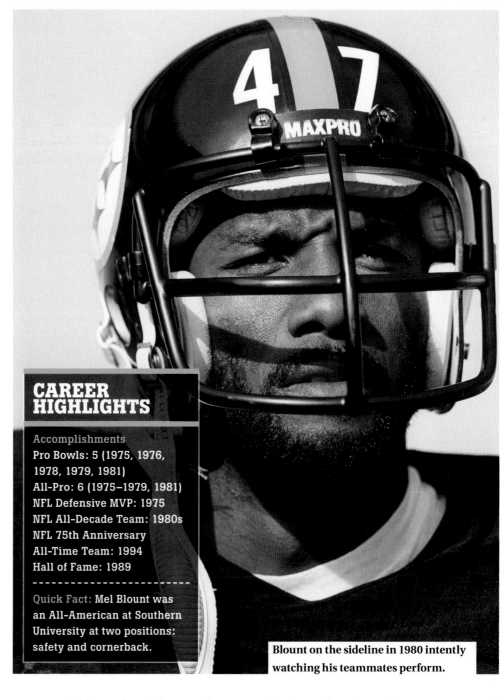

CAREER HIGHLIGHTS

Accomplishments
Pro Bowls: 5 (1975, 1976, 1978, 1979, 1981)
All-Pro: 6 (1975–1979, 1981)
NFL Defensive MVP: 1975
NFL All-Decade Team: 1980s
NFL 75th Anniversary All-Time Team: 1994
Hall of Fame: 1989

Quick Fact: Mel Blount was an All-American at Southern University at two positions: safety and cornerback.

Blount on the sideline in 1980 intently watching his teammates perform.

contract holdout (the Atkinson suit was dismissed). The coach and his cornerback patched up their differences.

"It was never anything personal," Blount told the *Pittsburgh Post-Gazette*. "I showed my character by being the type of player I was after I came back. Chuck showed his character by never holding it against me."

Blount's football accolades came in droves. He was named to the Pro Bowl five times and was MVP in 1976. He was voted to the NFL's 1980s All-Decade Team,

the league's 75th Anniversary Team, and was inducted into the Pro Football Hall of Fame in 1989.

Since retirement, he has immersed himself in charity work and horse breeding and competition. In December 2004, he finished third in the National Cutting Horse Association World Championship in Fort Worth, Texas.

No doubt, he treats his horses better than he ever treated the opposition's receivers. ▪

12 Tom BRADY

QUARTERBACK

THE CONSUMMATE PERFECTIONIST

It makes perfect sense that Tom Brady — who, as the late Bill Walsh stated, was the closest thing to a Joe Montana clone he'd ever seen — grew up in San Mateo, California, attending San Francisco 49ers games and idolizing No. 16 in red and gold. Neither man fit the prototype NFL quarterback model, and coming out of college neither man was considered a surefire No. 1.

"Don't let other people tell you what you're capable of," is a favorite saying of Brady's — and for good reason.

From unheralded NFL beginnings — he was the 199th overall pick in the 2000 draft — a fortuitous blending of the right talent, the right coach (Bill Belichick) and the right team has combined in the NFL's most recent dynasty.

In four Super Bowl appearances for the New England Patriots, Brady has driven his team to three titles and collected two game MVPs. While the individual awards are nice, it's the collective accomplishment that means the most to Brady:

"This," he said the year receiver Dion Branch ousted him for MVP honors, "is a team full of guys who cheer for one an-

other. The MVP is nice, but that's not why you play. I'm playing for that diamond ring that's as big as a belt buckle."

Brady isn't so much the NFL's poster boy as its cover boy, gracing the glossy of *Sports Illustrated*, *GQ* and *VMAN*, to name a few. He is in the company of such icons as Muhammad Ali, Johnny Depp, "Shaken, not stirred" Sean Connery and Air Jordan. He's been profiled on *60 Minutes*, featured on *The Simpsons*, *Family Guy* and hosted *Saturday Night Live.*

But peel back that layer of fame a moment, and understand it's as much about substance as it is about style. There are ample reasons for all the fuss.

Brady thinks the game better than any quarterback today — just like Joe in his time. It's Brady's businesslike manner, his utter efficiency; the sheer control with which he runs his offense, that has impressed those of stature within the sport.

"I look at the demeanor of a quarterback, and there is such a calm and a confidence about him," marveled Hall of Famer Warren Moon. "It's the look of a guy who knows he is prepared."

Brady reads the defense in a 37–16 wild-card victory over the Jets in 2007.

His almost obsessive desire to succeed, to push for more, can be traced back to childhood in San Mateo.

"I had the worst temper when I was little," he once said. "I could never stand to lose in anything. I kicked through glass windows and threw video game controllers at the TV and broke more tennis rackets than I could count. You never really grow out of it, I guess. It got to where nobody ever wanted to play with me."

Now it's gotten to where nobody would want to play against him. There isn't a coach in the game who wouldn't want Brady at the controls with the game on the line; a player anywhere who wouldn't want to line up beside him; a fan anywhere who wouldn't want to be just like him.

When he engineered the Pats to that first Super Bowl in 2001, a huge upset of the heavily favored St. Louis Rams, the one question on the lips of all but the most diehard football fan was: *Who* on earth is Tom Brady? Only a few years later, you'd be hard-pressed to find anyone in North America who doesn't know his name or recognize his face.

Ironically, Brady's finest individual year, highlighted by an NFL record 50 TD passes, and the Patriots' pursuit of 2008 perfection ended in defeat in Phoenix to Eli Manning and the upstart NY Giants in Super Bowl XLII.

Harried and hounded by a relentless Giants' defense, Brady and a New England offense that had put up a record, pinball-wizard number of points (589) in going 16–0 during the regular season, were shackled and suffocated in the biggest game of the year.

Brady did hook up with Randy Moss for a go-ahead touchdown with 2:42 left on the clock, but Eli Manning engineered a comeback of his own to trigger one of the biggest upsets in Super Bowl history: Giants 17, Patriots, 14.

"You score 14 points," muttered Brady afterwards, "that's not going to do it."

You can wager large that Tom Brady and the nearly perfect Pats won't sit and sulk. They'll be in the thick of the hunt again, gunning for more Super Bowl titles.

"I don't care about three years ago," Brady once said. "I don't care about two years ago. I don't care about last year. The only thing I care about is this week."

Satisfaction and fulfillment, he has always understood, lies ahead of you, not behind. ∎

34 EARL CAMPBELL

RUNNING BACK

IN A CLASS BY HIMSELF

Only four men have ever been named an Official State Hero of Texas: Davy Crockett, Stephen F. Austin and Sam Houston, for obvious political and historical reasons. The fourth is a football player, and not just any football player.

Earl Campbell was a star even in high school when he led John Tyler High to the Texas 4A state championship. He was a bigger star at the University of Texas, where he was nicknamed the Tyler Rose and led the NCAA in rushing, en route to winning the Heisman Trophy as the best player in collegiate football. Then he signed with the NFL's Houston Oilers and became an even bigger star. As Oilers' coach Bum Phillips liked to say of his 232-pound battering ram, "He may not be in a class by himself, but whatever class he's in, it doesn't take long to call roll."

Squat and muscular, with legs that belonged to a Clydesdale, Campbell was a tough load to topple. His approach to running was straight on, straight ahead. He liked to run into tacklers instead of avoiding them. That was his trademark. That and the fact it usually took two or three men to stop him.

"I always thought if I let one or two guys tackle me, I wasn't doing something right," he said of his wrecking-ball style. "I mean, I didn't think I was part of a game unless I had the ball in my hands 20 or 30 times. I had to get lathered up, you know? And right when the game was over was when I felt like really gettin' it on. Not that I didn't get it on in the middle. But I always thought if there was a fifth quarter, I could really show 'em something, you know?" Campbell showed plenty when he first got to the NFL. In 1978, in a *Monday Night Football* game against the Miami Dolphins, he carried his team to a 35–30 victory by gaining 199 yards and scoring four touchdowns. He was named the league's Rookie of the Year and its Most Valuable Player after rushing for 1,450 yards.

He was again hailed as the NFL's MVP in 1979 and 1980, which proved to be the high-water mark of his career. In that 1980 season, Campbell rolled to four 200-yard rushing games and finished with 1,934, second only to O.J. Simpson's 2,003 yards, which was set in 1973. By the time Campbell said farewell to football in the summer of 1986, he had totaled 9,407 yards and 74 touchdowns in eight seasons and appeared in five Pro Bowls.

In 1991, he was inducted into the Pro Football Hall of Fame, where fans and former players alike regaled others with stories of how Campbell would purposely look for the largest collection of defenders, then charge headlong into them. Campbell's success had NFL coaches searching for bigger, bolder runners or, as *Sports Illustrated* once described them, "beefy, big-butted backs who could both bowl over and blow past the opposition." Consider the likes of Jerome Bettis, Eddie George, Jamal Anderson and Craig (Ironhead) Heyward as those whose styles were allowed to rumble down a path blazed by Campbell.

"One time," said former Dallas Cowboys' running back Tony Dorsett, "I asked Earl, 'Why don't you let one man bring you down sometimes?' He said, 'I got to get them. They're talking that noise.'"

Soon after he retired, Campbell insisted all the pounding had been worth it. Born the 6th of 11 children to a working-class family, one of his early wishes as a pro football player was to earn enough money to buy his mother Ann a new house, which he did. Sadly, though, all those on-field collisions and noisemakers wreaked havoc on Campbell, not so initially, but later on in life.

Now in his early 50s, Campbell has trouble walking. Sometimes the pain is so bad he has to get around in a wheelchair. He recently underwent back surgery to remove the bone spurs from his spinal column that had prevented him from sleeping in a bed. Instead, he would sleep in a recliner to ease the discomfort. "Earl was the biggest, baddest player in the game," said Dorsett. "But no matter how big or strong you are, the game ultimately wins."

If you ever want to get a sense of what Campbell was like as a young, powerful football player, go to the southwest entrance of Darrell K. Royal-Texas Memorial Stadium in Austin and look for the statue of Campbell, wearing his Longhorns jersey No. 20. The statue is made of bronze and stands 9-feet tall. Ask a lot of those 175-pound NFL defensive backs Campbell plowed through, and they'll probably tell you his statue would be easier to bring down. ▪

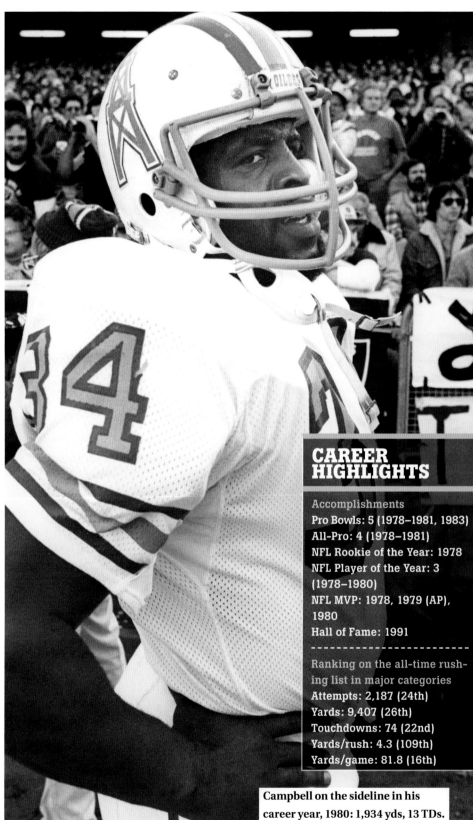

CAREER HIGHLIGHTS

Accomplishments
Pro Bowls: 5 (1978–1981, 1983)
All-Pro: 4 (1978–1981)
NFL Rookie of the Year: 1978
NFL Player of the Year: 3 (1978–1980)
NFL MVP: 1978, 1979 (AP), 1980
Hall of Fame: 1991

Ranking on the all-time rushing list in major categories
Attempts: 2,187 (24th)
Yards: 9,407 (26th)
Touchdowns: 74 (22nd)
Yards/rush: 4.3 (109th)
Yards/game: 81.8 (16th)

Campbell on the sideline in his career year, 1980: 1,934 yds, 13 TDs.

20 ERIC DICKERSON

RUNNING BACK

THE STRAIGHT UP GOODS

Long before he totaled an astonishing 2,105 yards in a single season, before his 13,259 career yards earned him a place in the Pro Football Hall of Fame, NFL general managers and coaches looked at Eric Demetric Dickerson and wondered, "How can he run like that? He's so rigid, so straight up and down he looks like an exclamation mark. One big hit and he'll be carried off the field on two stretchers."

Dickerson's style was nothing like Jim Brown's or Earl Campbell's, which is to say he wasn't bent at the waist just waiting to lower his shoulder into an oncoming tackler. Instead, Dickerson had the perfect posture of a butler. He carried his head high, as if he were looking over downtown traffic for an empty cab.

But what seemed dangerous for Dickerson turned out to be more so for the guys trying to cut him in half. Dickerson was 6-foot-3, 220 pounds, as fast as any receiver, and could move, this way or that, in the blink of an eye.

"I believe if I stay tall and run high, I can see better," Dickerson explained. And when Dickerson saw people coming to-

wards him, he could do his thing and give them the slip. "I don't give players a chance to hit me," he added.

Dickerson's NFL career began in the September of 1983, and to the delight of his we-told-you-so critics, the big exclamation mark fumbled six times in his first three games with the Rams. One fumble led to a game-winning field goal by the opposition. In his fourth game, he snapped off an 85-yard touchdown run and got himself on track. At season's end, he had rushed for 1,808 yards and 18 touchdowns and was named the league's top rookie.

What would he do in his sophomore season? Even more, it turned out.

Enabled by the Rams' superior run-blocking techniques, Dickerson went wild. He ran for more than 100 yards in 11 games breaking the previous record of 10 set by O.J. Simpson in 1973. He set his sights on Simpson's single-season record of 2,003 yards and, as he got closer, Dickerson obsessed about his pursuit and often dreamed he would finish short of his goal.

He need not have worried. He bettered Simpson's record by 102 yards. To be com-

Accomplishments
Pro Bowls: 6 (1983, 1984,
1986–1989)
All Pro: 6 (1983, 1984,
1986–1989)
NFL Rookie of the Year: 1983
NFL Player of the Year: 1983
Hall of Fame: 1999

Ranking on the all-time rush-
ing list in major categories
Attempts: 2,996 (7th)
Yards: 13,259 (6th)
Touchdowns: 90 (12th)
Yards/rush: 4.4 (87th)
Yards/game: 90.8 (6th)

The well-protected Dickerson hurdles a
49er on his way to a substantial gain.

pletely fair and accurate, Dickerson did it in 16 games while Simpson played in 14.

There is no doubting Dickerson was a bona fide star, a virtuoso. But in his five years with the Rams and a second five seasons with the Indianapolis Colts, Dickerson was often described as disgruntled. He got into several contract disputes. Sometimes he held out and was suspended. Sometimes he got what he wanted. Through it all, he earned a reputation for being "arrogant, inconsiderate, greedy, self-centered, a malcontent," he said. "I could go on and on."

With the Rams, Dickerson uttered a quote that finished him in L.A. Knowing head coach John Robinson's salary was slightly less than his own, Dickerson remarked, "Let him run 47 Gap," the Rams bread-and-butter play. Less than two weeks later, Dickerson was traded to Indianapolis in a three-way deal that included the Buffalo Bills. And for a time, things were good in Indianapolis.

Eventually, he said the game had lost its appeal for him and that he was going to retire. Then he asked for more money and began chastising the Colts in a bid to be traded. The Colts signed him to a four-year, $10.65 million deal. And again, for a time, things were good. In 1991, he missed three games for supposedly refusing to practice. He asked to be traded. The Colts happily obliged and shipped him to the Los Angeles Raiders.

One year later, he was traded to the Atlanta Falcons, where he was traded to the Green Bay Packers and retired after failing a physical.

"Some of the things I've done, I've been wrong in doing," he admitted. "I've been hasty. You lose your cool and say things you don't really mean. I think mine was out of frustration. It's not fun losing a lot of games."

Along with his aptitude and attitude, Dickerson amused his teammates by donning every piece of protective gear he could find. He wore elbow pads, sometimes gloves, a neck collar and even goggles. There were jokes he would have strapped old tires to himself, the way they do on tugboats, if he could have gotten away with it.

No matter. Dickerson proved he could run his way and no one could slow him for long. At retirement, he owned the record for needing only 91 games to surpass 10,000 yards in his career. He picked up a telling compliment along the way, too.

"If you were blind," Robinson, his former coach, said, "he could run right by you, and you wouldn't know it unless you felt the wind. He's the smoothest runner I've ever seen." ▪

33 TONY DORSETT

RUNNING BACK

THE LITTLE BIG MAN

When Tony Dorsett was young, he dreaded the night and going to sleep. Sleeping meant dreaming, and dreaming meant going to the dark places he wanted to avoid. The worst ones were about living inside the soulless, soot-covered confines of a Pittsburgh steel mill, the kind his father endured for 30 years so he could support a wife and seven children.

Wes Dorsett was a hard-working man. Sometimes he came home so dirty his family couldn't recognize him. Always, he told his children they should concentrate on getting an education and finding a job they loved. Tony Dorsett took those words to heart. He would become a football player. Somehow, he would go to university, get his degree, then play professionally. It would be his ticket out.

From star running back to superstar running back, from college hero to NFL All-Pro, Tony Dorsett made good on his promise. He won an NCAA national championship at the University of Pittsburgh one season (1976), then a Super Bowl with the Dallas Cowboys the next. He was a Heisman Trophy-winning standout, a sought-after first-round draft pick, and the NFL's Rookie of the Year, with just over 1,000 yards rushing and 12 touchdowns. He exceeded everyone's expectations, even his own.

"Coming out of college, everyone said I would be too small to play professional football at 188 pounds," Dorsett recalled. "To be honest with you, I figured maybe I would play four or five years [in the NFL] and that would be it. I never dreamed I would play 12 seasons."

In those dozen seasons, Dorsett ran for 12,739 yards and 77 touchdowns and gave tacklers third-degree burns with his searing speed. His 99-yard scoring run against the Minnesota Vikings on January 3, 1983, is an NFL staple. He became the league's first player to surpass the 1,000-yard mark in each of his first five seasons. In 1981, he rambled for 1,646 yards, narrowly missing out on the NFL rushing title — all remarkable feats considering how things could have turned out.

Having convinced himself that football was the key to his future, Dorsett almost quit after agreeing to attend Pittsburgh. He was shy and lonely, and the school's preseason

Accomplishments
Pro Bowls: 4 (1978, 1981–1983)
All-Pro: 5 (1978, 1979, 1981–1983)
NFL Rookie of the Year: 1977
NFC Rushing Champion: 1982
Hall of Fame: 1994

Ranking on the all-time rushing list in major categories
Attempts: 2,936 (9th)
Yards: 12,739 (7th)
Touchdowns: 77 (19th)
Yards/rush: 4.3 (109th)
Yards/game: 73.6 (28th)

Dorsett runs in 1983; the third consecutive year he was both a Pro-Bowler and an All-Pro.

practices were taking their toll. At one point, Dorsett called his mother, Myrtle, and talked about coming home. His mom told him to stay strong; that things would get better. Things would work out. They did.

As a 155-pound freshman, Dorsett led the NCAA in rushing with 1,586 yards and carried Pittsburgh to the 1973 Fiesta Bowl. He added 30 pounds of muscle and two more 1,000-yard seasons before his senior year, which began with a 181-yard performance in an easy win over Notre Dame.

When his college days ended, Dorsett had become the first player to rush for more than 6,000 yards in four seasons. The NFL beckoned, and that's when things once again worked in Dorsett's favor, as if fate had taken a liking to the young man with the big dreams.

Tex Schramm played the pivotal role this time. The Dallas general manager wanted Dorsett's speed and pass-catching skills in the Cowboys' multiple-formation offense. Unfortunately for Dallas, the Seattle Seahawks had the second pick overall in the 1977 draft and were keen to select the Pittsburgh prize. So Schramm made a deal. He packaged the Cowboys' first-round pick with three second-round choices and exchanged them for Seattle's No. 2 pick, which Schramm used to take Dorsett.

Had he gone to Seattle, would Dorsett have been as prominent a player in the NFL? Not likely. The Seahawks had just completed their debut season and were very much a work in progress. Dorsett would have played behind so-so blockers in an offense that had quarterback Jim Zorn, receiver Steve Largent and little else.

Dallas was the right fit for Dorsett and Dorsett was right for Dallas. Granted, the Cowboys could have given him the ball more, but how they used Dorsett proved to be as effective as how often they used him.

"If I wanted to risk Tony, I think he could gain as many yards as [Walter] Payton and [Earl] Campbell," Dallas coach Tom Landry once explained. "But Tony is much different from Earl, who is so big. Payton is probably the strongest little man I've ever seen. Then there is Wilbert Montgomery, who did get used a lot and got hurt. I don't want that to happen to Tony."

Eventually, the injuries came and Dorsett had to retire. At his induction to the Pro Football Hall of Fame in 1994 he talked of his father and the desires forged by a working man's life.

"He taught me an awful lot about common sense, about street sense," said Dorsett. "He never forced me to do anything. He always told me, 'Son, if you're going to accomplish anything in life, do it yourself.'"

Tony Dorsett did, and he rarely had trouble sleeping again. ∎

14 Dan FOUTS

QUARTERBACK

JUST THROW IT

With the San Diego Chargers of the Air Coryell years, when footballs filled the air in Jack Murphy Stadium like golf balls whizzing over a crowded driving range, one man, and one man only, was in charge. His word was sacrosanct. So was the way he threw the ball — at any time, under any circumstance, on any down.

"It was a real joy to be able to operate in that system," said Fouts years later. "I've been out of the game a long time now, but it's nice when people come up to you and say they really enjoyed the way we played the game in those years."

Daniel Francis Fouts was seemingly born to play pro. His father, Bob, called the San Francisco 49ers' games for years. Young Dan worked as a ball boy for the Bay Area team.

Fouts and the Chargers proved to be a fortuitous combination — a happy collaboration of man and moment. Selected in the third round, 84th overall, out of Oregon, he at first struggled to find his identity.

The hiring of Don Coryell as head coach in 1978 changed all that. Future 49ers' legend Bill Walsh (an assistant with the Char-

gers in 1976) and Washington Redskins' architect Joe Gibbs (San Diego's offensive coordinator for 1979–80) certainly can be credited with having a hand in the nurturing of Fouts, but Coryell's master plan, and his reading of the innate qualities of his strapping young field general, were inspired and decisive.

The Chargers surrounded their strong-armed, strong-willed quarterback with a huge force field of an offensive line and a cast of exceptional pass-catching talents from the likes of Charlie Joiner and All-Pro tight end Kellen Winslow, to John Jefferson and Wes Chandler.

The results were electrifying: In 1980 and 1981, Fouts, nicknamed the Bearded Bomber, registered unheard of numbers. He threw for a combined 9,517 yards (including a league record 4,802 in '81) and 66 touchdowns. In the pocket, he was absolutely fearless, and ruthlessly single-minded. He simply could not be rattled. Throw an interception? He could've cared less. He knew where his strength lay. He'd be up gunning on the next series.

"He's like E.F. Fouts," Winslow said in

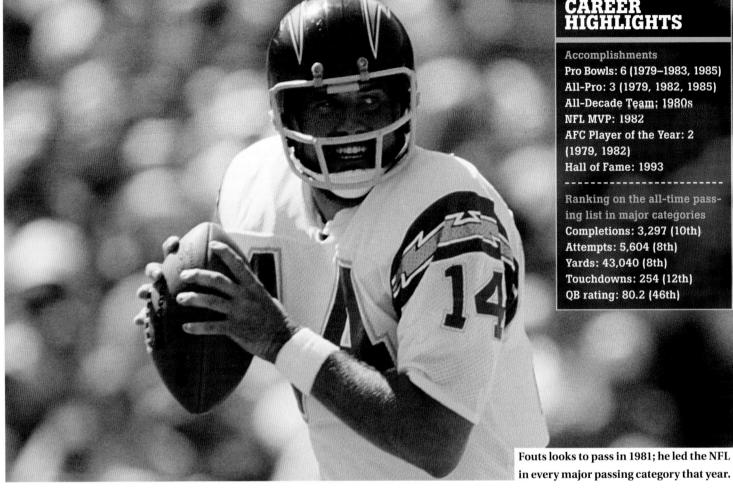

Fouts looks to pass in 1981; he led the NFL in every major passing category that year.

reference to the E.F. Hutton television commercials of the day. "When he talks, people listen."

As his offensive line aged and crumbled in the twilight of his career, Fouts absorbed a tremendous amount of physical punishment. His toughness was legendary.

In fact, for years in the Chargers' offices, a particular photo of Fouts held prominence. His nose, broken by a Ted Hendricks forearm, stuck out at an awkward angle, a swatch of tape holding it together. Blood spattered on the front of his white jersey. His left shoulder, dislocated by another hit, hung limply under center, forcing him to take the snap with only his right arm.

"Darn fool, that guy," muttered Fouts, when reminded of the photo.

He remained a Charger his entire career, from 1973 through 1987. Perhaps his, and the team's, greatest moment came in the 1982 AFC Divisional playoff game against the Dolphins, Jan. 2, at the Orange Bowl. *Sports Illustrated* called it "The Game No One Should Have Lost," a wild 41–38 overtime San Diego victory.

Fouts finished the afternoon that stretched into evening with 33 completions on 53 attempts for 433 yards and three touchdowns, all NFL postseason records at the time. He led the Chargers on a 74-yard drive to set up the decisive 29-yard Rolf Benirschke field goal.

But the euphoria was to be short-lived.

An Associated Press photo from San Diego's subsequent 27–7 loss to the Bengals at Riverfront Stadium — the steam of Fouts' breath in the arctic chill all but obscuring his head — remains a heart-wrenching symbol of lost opportunity to frustrated Bolts' fans of the era.

So the Fouts years never produced what many had expected — a Super Bowl triumph. An over-reliance on the pass and a middling defense are generally accused of being co-conspirators in the failure.

But neither Dan Marino nor Fran Tarkenton won a Super Bowl, which puts Fouts in pretty fine company. What he did, superlatively, was entertain a generation, set off fireworks for a decade, and leave a lasting image of a commanding presence hanging in the pocket, oblivious to the chaos around him, scanning downfield.

He exited the game as a three-time All-Pro with six Pro Bowl appearances, and as only the third man to throw for over 40,000 yards. His famous No. 14 is one of only two numbers that have been retired by the Chargers.

The only thing missing? A ring.

"I'm over it," Fouts said the day he was enshrined among the game's immortals in Canton. "You strive to win a Super Bowl and you do everything you can to get there.

"But being in the Hall of Fame, you never play for that honor. It's incredible." ▪

28

DARRELL
GREEN

CORNERBACK

SPEED, SPEED AND MORE SPEED

Watching the play over and over, it's as if everyone else on the field is running in slow motion, except for Washington's Darrell Green. He is moving in an effortless, purposeful way. A shark drawn to its prey. Tony Dorsett, the prime running back for the Dallas Cowboys is in the midst of a 77-yard gain with only six yards to go for a touchdown.

No one has ever caught Dorsett from behind when he is out in front, headed for the end zone.

Most fans watching know little about Green, who is starting the game as a rookie cornerback, only because veteran Jeris White has yet to sign a contract.

But there's Green, running past two of his teammates and tackling Dorsett from behind to prevent a Dallas touchdown.

It was a "Did-you-see-that?" moment, replayed throughout the NFL in the fall of 1983 and for years beyond. Darrell Green had arrived, and Jeris White's career with the Washington Redskins was over.

For 20 years, no one played cornerback like the mercurial Green. How could they? The man was a speeding bullet. He stood only 5-foot-9 and weighed 184 pounds,

but every receiver who thought they could out-muscle, out-jump and out-run Green thought wrong. No one could out-run Green.

Once, he clocked a 40-yard dash in 4.125 seconds. In 1986, he unofficially covered 40 yards in 4.09 seconds. Four times, he won the NFL's fastest man competition. When he attended Washington's training camp in 2000, he was still the fastest player on the team — at age 40.

Green was so adept at covering and tackling, that opposition quarterbacks would avoid his side of the field and throw elsewhere. Still, he finished his career with 54 interceptions for 621 yards, six touchdowns and seven Pro Bowl selections, earning enduring accolades.

It didn't start out that way.

Green was laughed at in Grade 11 when he first tried out for his high school football team. He attended Texas A&I University (now Texas A&M-Kingsville) and was invited to try out for the NFL's scouting combine as it prepared for the 1983 draft.

"Going to the combine in my Texas A&I jersey, they didn't know me from a chicken.

Green helps lead Washington to a play-off win against Atlanta on Jan. 4, 1992.

They didn't even know our school," said Green. "[Redskins' general manager] Bobby Beathard said, 'If you're there, we're going to draft you.' In the back of my mind, I was, 'Yeah, okay. Thanks.'"

The Redskins did draft Green, in the first round, which mystified and angered some of their fans. Who was this guy, anyway? After his celebrated tackle on Dorsett, everyone took notice and Green's career was off and running.

Another of his highlights came in a 1987 NFC playoff game in Chicago against the Bears. On fourth down from deep in their own territory, the Bears punted to Green, who was an occasional punt return specialist, and a good one at that. Catching the ball at his 48-yard line, Green headed down the sideline, hurdled over a Chicago tackler and made a hard cut that tore cartilage in his ribs. He ran the last 25 yards into the end zone clutching his right side with his left arm.

The touchdown finished the Bears and Green's afternoon, too.

A week later, Green wasn't sure he'd be ready for the NFC championship game against the Minnesota Vikings. His ribs were still sore, but as Bostic and others suggested, "You need to be out there."

Green didn't want to take a needle's worth of pain killer but eventually did. He later said that six minutes into the opening quarter the painkiller wore off. Green stayed in and made the play of the game.

The Minnesota Vikings were at the Washington six-yard line, fourth down, last play of the game. Trailing 17–10, Minnesota quarterback Wade Wilson threw a pass that looked like it was going to be caught at the goal line. Green, who was covering Anthony Carter, came off his man and hit the intended receiver Darrin Nelson so hard

the pass fell incomplete. The Redskins were off to Super Bowl XXII, where they'd defeat the Denver Broncos.

When he retired in 2002, Green was still playing corner at age 42. In 19 of his 20 years with Washington, he recorded at least one interception, an NFL record. No wonder his teammates admired his commitment and dubbed him the Ageless Wonder.

In the years following football, Green has worked at his Youth Life Foundation, which he started in 1988. His program is aimed at helping young students stay in school. Green has been involved in several charitable causes, including the NFL/NFL-PA's Sept. 11 Relief.

"I worked and I got a check," Green said of his time in the NFL. "[Working after football] is a totally different feeling because it deals with a person's life … it has no equal."

Ageless wonder, indeed. ■

32 F RANCO HARRIS

RUNNING BACK

OF HUSTLE AND SHOE TOPS

The eerie life-size likeness, situated near the escalators leading to the baggage carousel at Pittsburgh International Airport, is in mighty good company.

There, leaning down to snatch the football, maybe a foot from the ground, is the spitting image of Franco Harris, the famous No. 32 in Pittsburgh Steelers black. Directly beside, stands a statue of another fairly recognizable American hero, George Washington. That's how much Franco Harris means to the city breast-fed on pig iron. That's how much one play can linger in memory, decades later — the Immaculate Reception.

Even had Harris not rushed for 12,120 yards over 13 seasons, eight times for 1,000 or better; even if he had not played in nine Pro Bowls, or piled up 14,622 all-purpose yards. Even if he had not been part of four Super Bowl championship teams, or been named MVP of Super Bowl IX, or eventually been enshrined among the immortals in Canton, even then, Franco Harris would still be a part of NFL history.

"I've played football since the second grade," marveled Steelers quarterback Terry Bradshaw in the aftermath of arguably the NFL's most famous single play. "And nothing like that ever happened. It'll never happen again."

The details are familiar to all football fans across North America: 22 seconds remaining, the hometown Steelers trailing the Oakland Raiders 7–6 in the AFC divisional playoff game, Dec. 23, 1972. Bradshaw was flushed out of the pocket on fourth and 10, then pushed back inside. His desperation throw, too far for the intended receiver, caromed off Raider safety Jack Tatum and/or Pittsburgh wideout John "Frenchy" Fuqua. And there, to pluck the ball off his shoe tops on the ricochet was Franco Harris. Forty-five yards later, Harris crossed the goal line, and the entire city of Pittsburgh went absolutely nuts.

"When I see the film," Harris told ESPN years later, "that's like proof that it happened. But it still seems like a dream."

If the ball did — as the Raiders of that day insist — hit Fuqua at all, the play should've been ruled invalid as it had touched two offensive players. If it only struck Tatum, the catch and the touchdown were

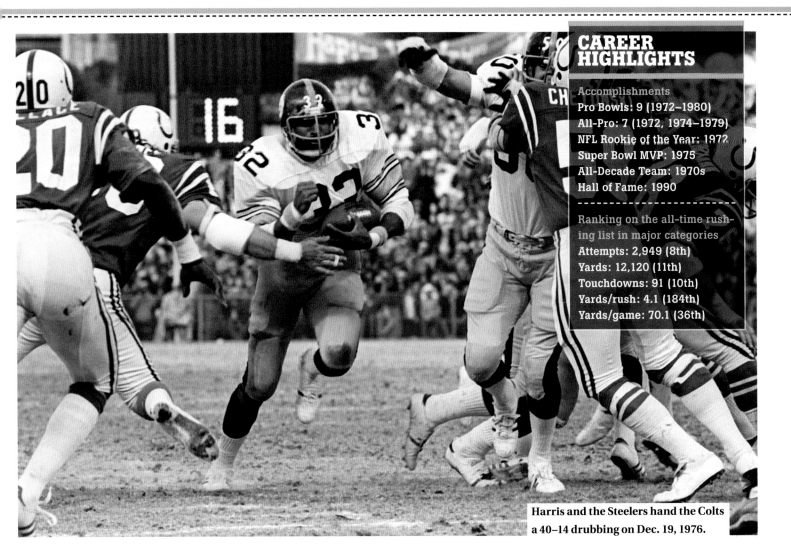

Harris and the Steelers hand the Colts a 40–14 drubbing on Dec. 19, 1976.

legitimate. The debate rages on. Replays seem inconclusive.

Steelers' coach Chuck Noll praised his prize rookie's attitude in the controversial aftermath.

"Franco made that play because he never quit on the play," he said. "He kept running. He kept hustling. Good things happen to those who hustle."

To remember one of the NFL's most versatile, durable backs for that piece of drama alone would be a disservice to the man, an injustice to his legacy.

They all became a legendary lot. Bradshaw. The balletic Lynn Swann. The menacing Jack Lambert and Jack Ham at linebacker. Center Tom Webster. And, of course, the Steel Curtain defensive front of Mean Joe Greene, L.C. Greenwood, Dwight White and Ernie Holmes — the four horsemen of any quarterback's apocalypse.

"Halfway through the decade [1970s]," recalled Harris, "we realized that we had a great team and could do great things, that we could probably have something here that we believed had a chance to reach greatness."

Coach Chuck Noll's Steelers reached greatness, and then kept topping it. They had swagger. They had style. And they had Harris, the perfect complement to Bradshaw's aerial game. At 6-foot-2 and 230 pounds, he had size enough to run over people, and enough spring in his legs to slide past them.

Besides his Hall of Fame career rushing totals (he ran for 100 or more yards on 47 occasions), the 13th overall pick in the 1972 NFL draft also caught 307 passes for 2,287 yards and nine touchdowns. When he retired, his combined yardage of 14,622 was the third highest total ever. Sparking

Pittsburgh's first Super Bowl triumph in 1975, Harris rushed 34 times for 158 yards, breaking Larry Csonka's record of the year before to earn MVP honors.

He spent his final year in Seattle as a Seahawk, but never looked right in anything other than vintage Steeler black.

During his dozen seasons in the Steel City, the man who inspired Franco's Italian Army in the stands at Three Rivers, who developed into one of the most dependable backs of his era, could run away from the most punishing, the most pursuant, of NFL defenses.

What he can never run away from is that incredible, improbable play, and Franco Harris will never be able to shake that.

One play forever frozen in time, beside the escalators leading down to the baggage carousel at Pittsburgh International Airport — right beside George Washington. ∎

58 JACK LAMBERT

LINEBACKER

A STEELER TO THE END

John Elway was a rookie quarterback for the Denver Broncos when he looked across the line of scrimmage and almost wet his football pants. There, in the cold heart of the Pittsburgh Steelers defense, was the scariest man he had ever seen. Count Dracula from Pittsburgh, Transylvania. Jack Lambert.

With his pronounced bicuspids and snarling mood, Lambert played middle linebacker like a lion tearing into a fallen gazelle, and just the look of him was enough to send a trickle of fear through the young quarterback.

"He had no [front] teeth, and he was slobbering all over himself," recalled Elway. "I'm thinking, 'You can have your money back, just get me out of here. Let me go be an accountant.' I can't tell you how badly I wanted out of there."

Elway couldn't have been alone in his fear of Lambert, who would sometimes play up his evil image by saying, "I am very aggressive and very physical. On the field I guess I am just plain mean."

Lambert was a brutal hitter. He'd drive himself into the ball carrier, then sort through the pieces to find the ball. In his second season in Pittsburgh, in the Super Bowl no less, Lambert went after Dallas Cowboys' defensive back Cliff Harris, who had tapped Steelers' kicker Roy Gerela on the helmet after a missed 33-yard field goal and said, "Way to go." Lambert took offense, tossed Harris to the ground, and then had to talk his way out of being ejected by the officials.

Lambert also had a trio of run-ins with the Cleveland Browns after flattening their quarterback Brian Sipe. He was penalized three times for a late hit on Sipe, ejected twice and fined by the league. All three times, Lambert was mobbed by Cleveland players who took exception to his actions. A week later, Lambert told Howard Cosell on *Monday Night Football*, "Quarterbacks should wear dresses."

The Steelers drafted Lambert from Kent State, where he had played a rambunctious game at linebacker despite weighing only 204 pounds. While it was assumed Lambert lost his teeth playing football, he actually had them knocked loose by a teammate during a high school basketball practice. (Was he a good basketball player? He av-

Lambert, the 1976 Defensive MVP,
makes a playoff tackle on December 19.

eraged 17.9 points and 13 rebounds per game.) Still, Lambert's image as a menacing predator was already well established. On the eve of training camp in 1974, Steelers' defensive line coach George Perles told one of his players, "We've got a rookie who's so mean he doesn't even like himself."

Being drafted by the Steelers afforded Lambert two early opportunities. Pittsburgh was a two-and-a-half-hour drive from where he was born in Mantua, Ohio, so Lambert was able to drive to the team's office every weekend to watch game film before training camp opened. Then, starting middle linebacker Henry Davis got hurt in the preseason. Lambert moved into the position and never stepped out. The Steelers won their first Super Bowl in 1975 in Lambert's rookie season and four in a six-year period.

The Steelers' defense of 1976 was one of the best in league history. Led by Lambert, it allowed just two touchdowns in a nine-game span, recorded five shutouts, and finished first in almost every defensive statistic kept by the NFL. Overall, the Steelers gave up just 9.9 points per game over a 14-game schedule while 8 of their 11 defensive starters were selected to the Pro Bowl. Lambert was named Defensive Player of the Year.

"Jack had the image of a wild man, but he killed opponents with his perfection," said linebacking partner Andy Russell. "His greatness has nothing to do with his popular image."

The blood-sucking, wild-man persona was awfully tough to get past, though. Lambert was as fiercely private away from the game as he was punishing during it, which simply added to his myth. He didn't like to talk much. His teammates recalled how Lambert would cringe when recognized in public. Once, when spotted by some young fans, he was asked, "What's your sign, Jack? You know, astrology."

"Feces," he said.

Lambert once joked that he was from Buzzard's Breath, Wyoming. Some people took him seriously.

In the end, the man who almost turned John Elway into an accountant finished with more than 1,400 tackles, 23.5 sacks and 28 interceptions. He was voted to the 1970s All-Decade Team as well as the 1980s All-Decade Team, and played in nine consecutive Pro Bowls.

In 1990, Lambert achieved the ultimate recognition when he was inducted into the Pro Football Hall of Fame. His acceptance speech was delivered with the passion and purpose that punctuated the way he played his position.

"If I could start my life all over again, I'd be a professional football player," he said, "and you damn well better believe I would be a Pittsburgh Steeler." ▮

81

DICK
LANE

CORNERBACK

THE MIDNIGHT EXPRESS

If you pitched a movie script based on the life and professional football career of Dick (Night Train) Lane, even the most agreeable Hollywood producer would have a hard time buying it.

"Let me see if I've got this straight," the producer would say. "Our star is found in a dumpster at the age of three months by a woman who decides to raise him as one of her own. The kid loves sports but later joins the Army and serves in World War II and Korea. One day, he walks into the office of the Los Angeles Rams and asks for a contract. He never went to college, and all he has with him is a scrapbook full of clippings from his high school days. Somehow, the Rams go for it. Our hero wants to play receiver, but the Rams are loaded with receivers so they say, 'Try cornerback.' He does, and not only does he make the team, he intercepts a record 14 passes in 12 games in his first NFL season and goes on to become a Hall of Famer."

"Right," the producer would add, "and maybe we should do a movie about a palooka fighter who gets a shot at the title and call it *Rocky*."

The story of Night Train Lane is two parts improbable, one part incredible. Everything mentioned happened. Lane was left in a dumpster in Austin, Texas. His mother was a prostitute, his dad a pimp. The woman who discovered him in the dumpster, Ella Lane, was a widow, who mothered young Night Train along with her two other children.

Lane had risen to the rank of Lt. Colonel before leaving the Army. And in 1952, after duty in two wars, the 24-year-old was working at a dead-end factory job when he decided to take his high school scrapbook with him and ask the Rams for a tryout.

Head coach Joe Stydahar had two future Hall of Fame receivers in Tom Fears and Elroy (Crazy Legs) Hirsch, but he loved Lane's speed and size (6-foot-2, 200 pounds) so he made him a cornerback. Little did anyone know Lane was about to set the standard for a position he had never played before.

"Train will always be the Godfather of cornerbacks," said former Detroit Lions' defensive back Lem Barney. "He was as large as some linemen of his era. He also was agile and very fast. His tackling was awesome. He did the clothesline and other tackles that just devastated the ball carrier."

Most everything about Lane was a contradiction. He played corner but kept the number he'd been assigned as a receiver, 81. He initially hated the nickname Night Train, since it was taken from a hip tune of the day. Lane changed his mind when he saw his moniker used in a headline that read, Rookie Dick "Night Train" Lane derails Charlie "Choo Choo" Justice. If it was good enough for the newspapers, it was good enough for Lane.

Cornerbacks aren't supposed to frighten their opponents but Night Train did. He had a habit of tackling receivers high around their head and neck. Back in those days it was called a horse collar. Later, it became known as a clothesline. With Lane, it was dubbed the Night Train Necktie, and it was a punishing move that injured several players.

"I've never seen a defensive back like him," said Green Bay Packers' Hall of Fame cornerback Herb Adderley. "I mean, take *them* down, whether it be Jim Brown or Jim Taylor."

Lane was so effective at neck-tying ball carriers that the NFL banned its practice. In 14 seasons, Night Train also played for the Chicago Cardinals and Detroit. He was selected to seven Pro Bowls and was voted to the 1950s All-Decade Team. His final statistics included 68 interceptions for 1,207 yards, five touchdowns, 11 fumble recoveries and another touchdown. And to top things off, he added eight pass receptions for 253 yards and a touchdown.

"I was a small, very wiry kid so therefore

CAREER HIGHLIGHTS

Accomplishments
Pro Bowls: 7 (1954–1956, 1958, 1960–1962)
All-Pro: 10 (1954–1963)
All-Decade Team: 1950s
NFL 75th Anniversary
All-Time Team: 1994
Hall of Fame: 1974

NFL records held
Most interceptions in a season: 14 (1952)
Most interceptions in a season by a rookie: 14 (1952)
Most seasons leading the league in interception return yards (tied): 2 (1952, 1954)

The veteran Night Train spent his last six seasons in Detroit Lions blue.

nobody gave me a ghost of a chance of making it," Lane said. "But I had a big heart."

Lane was such a physical presence he is credited with inventing the bump-and-run technique. The cornerback jams the receiver as he leaves the line of scrimmage, then runs with him downfield. Lane's bumps were strong enough to knock some receivers to the ground.

"My object is to stop the guy with the ball

before he gains another inch," said Lane, who revised his plan and stopped guys before they even got the ball.

In 1969, four years after he retired from the Lions, Lane was voted the best cornerback in the NFL's first 50 years. He was inducted into the Pro Football Hall of Fame in 1974. He died at age 73 after fashioning an inspirational life and a most improbable tale. ■

80 STEVE LARGENT

WIDE RECEIVER

187 POUNDS OF PURE HEART

Four preseason games into Steve Largent's NFL dream, the bottom seemed to drop out. Largent was deemed surplus by the Houston Oilers — over before it had even had the chance to begin,

Fate, obviously a football fan, then intervened in the shape of a trade to the Seattle Seahawks. For an eighth-round draft pick, yet.

Seems absurd now, traded for an eighth-round pick, since for the next 14 years, Largent caught more footballs than anyone who had gone before him. But because of the mediocre teams he played on during his years in Seattle, Steve Largent has been largely overlooked by the casual fan when listing the greatest receivers in NFL history. But he rates. He definitely rates.

From the perspective of the defensive backs assigned to cover him, the clean-cut, religious kid out of Tulsa wasn't super-fast like a Bob Hayes. Or built as if he'd been chiseled from a block of Carrara marble like a Kellen Winslow. He was ... just... : Just fast enough. Just slippery enough. Just tough enough. Just flat-out good enough to beat you just about every time he wanted to.

We're all so quick to measure things when judging an athlete — height and weight, speed in the 40, how much weight someone is able to bench press. What remains elusive, what cannot ever be measured or quantified, is heart. There has never been, will never be, an instrument capable of calibrating that.

The No. 80 in blue and silver who would go on to the Hall of Fame is further proof of that.

Seems amazing now, but pro scouts weren't all that impressed with Largent, despite the All-America status at the University of Tulsa and despite leading the nation in touchdown catches his final two seasons. He wasn't selected until the fourth round of the 1976 draft, 117th overall.

How good was Largent?

So good that Jerry Rice, who would eventually shatter all of Largent's receiving records, admitted studying the way he ran pass routes, picking up pointers to incorporate into his own game. Sort of comparable to Orson Welles running John Ford's iconic western *Stagecoach* over a hundred times in preparation for *Citizen Kane*.

Oct. 21, 1984, Largent grabs one of 12 touchdowns on the season, a career high.

So good that when he retired, the guy who wasn't big enough, strong enough or fast enough, who only missed four games due to injury in his first 13 NFL seasons, had latched onto every major receiving record available: receptions (819), yards (13,089), TD catches (100) and games-with-a-reception (177).

He caught 50 or more passes for 10 seasons. He caught 70 or more in six seasons. A tireless worker for community and charity, he was voted the NFL's Man of the Year in 1988.

Not bad for a guy the Houston Oilers, in all their wisdom, were convinced didn't have the right stuff to be in the NFL.

He might've been only 5-foot-11 and 187 pounds, but Seahawk fans still recall with relish the afternoon he chased down Denver Bronco defensive back Mike Harden on the return of an intercepted pass thrown by Seahawk quarterback Dave Kreig. Largent not only tracked him down, but leveled his prey, knocking the ball loose and then recovering the fumble.

Sweet justice, in that Harden had almost ended Largent's career earlier in the season, hitting him with such viciousness that the Seahawks' All-Pro, as legend has it, lost two teeth and wound up with a dented helmet.

A quiet, humble person and exemplary pro, Largent wouldn't crow about his payback, a play that has now entered franchise lore. Well, not much, anyway. "It wasn't meant to be a vindictive thing," he is quoted on the Spirit of the Seahawks website as saying, "but it sure felt good."

His final two years represented a significant drop-off in production. He caught only 39 and 28 passes for five touchdowns. But nothing could diminish the glories of what had gone before.

In his post-football life, Largent entered politics, serving in the U.S. House of Representatives for Oklahoma from 1994 to 2002 as a Republican. He was once asked which press corps was tougher: beat writers who cover the NFL or the political writers who cover Capital Hill? Largent laughed and replied: "Let's put it this way. On Capital Hill, I still need a helmet."

Largent later moved to the business world, as president and CEO of the CTIA Wireless Association, after losing in a three-way dogfight for the governorship of his home state.

Perhaps his mistake was in where he decided to run. Maybe he should've just shifted over to the State of Washington. In Seattle, as one of a handful of athletes who has attained iconic status, it goes without saying, he could've gotten elected to anything he wanted. Anything at all. ∎

52 RAY LEWIS

LINEBACKER

A LION IN SHEEP'S CLOTHING

Football coaches don't want saints at middle linebacker. They want hell-raisers. They want men who would peddle their souls to make a tackle or better yet a tackle for a loss of yardage. They want a player with menace in his eyes, brimming with aggression.

Would they take Ray Lewis for such a job? In a heartbeat they would.

Lewis is the NFL's most daunting middle linebacker — tough as week-old meatloaf, intimidating, able to elude blockers and overpower running backs. From his 1996 rookie season, which saw him lead the Baltimore Ravens with 142 tackles, to 2007, Lewis has been exceptionally adept at wreaking havoc, pillaging offenses, plundering stadiums, all the while convincing people he is one scary dude. And make no mistake — Lewis can be scary on a football field. Boastful, too.

"I already believe I am the best linebacker in the game," he has said. "Now I have to show one more thing: that I am the most dominating, influential person in the game and the best football player to ever put on a pair of cleats."

Even in 2007, when it was suggested he was losing a step at age 32, Lewis managed 120 tackles, 10 pass deflections, two sacks, two interceptions and a touchdown to earn his ninth Pro Bowl selection. If that's what losing a step means there are plenty of NFL linebackers longing for a decline in speed.

Lewis is so established, so acknowledged at his position, that his spin-off perks include his own radio show and being featured on the box of the Madden NFL 2005 video game. Why, in 2006, he was even featured on the cover of *Sports Illustrated* magazine looking skyward and praying with a headline that read, "God's Linebacker" — a reference to Lewis's proclaimed Christianity.

The cover struck a nerve since Lewis was implicated in the murders of Jacinth Baker and Richard Lollar, who were stabbed to death outside an Atlanta nightclub on Jan. 31, 2000.

Lewis and two friends were questioned by the police, who later indicted the three for murder and aggravated assault. Lewis agreed to plead guilty to a lesser charge of obstruction of justice in exchange for his testimony against his two friends. For that, Lewis was sentenced to a year's probation.

Lewis collects one of his 46 tackles in a six-game injury shortened 2005 season.

His two friends were eventually acquitted of the murder charges.

While the NFL fined Lewis $250,000, it did not suspend him, which produced a most incongruous turn of events. Almost one year after the double stabbings in Atlanta, the Ravens advanced to the Super Bowl, clobbered the New York Giants, and Lewis was named the game's MVP. At his postgame news conference, he addressed the media, saying, "If the world wants to see me stumble now," he said, "I'll stumble with a [Super Bowl] ring on my finger."

Lewis has upset countless people with his comments, yet his supporters say his charitable acts belie his image as a 250-pound brawler. He has been active not only in Baltimore, where he has staged celebrity auctions, bowling tournaments, food drives and youth camps, but in Angola and Ethiopia, where he helped war victims and championed their need for help, all the way

to the U.S. Congress.

So the question is: Who is Ray Lewis — hell-raiser or God's linebacker?

Lewis was born in Lakeland, Florida. He went on to the University of Miami in 1993 but left after his junior year to play in the NFL, where he was an instant success.

Between 1996 and 2000, Lewis won dozens of awards, while the Baltimore defense set a league record for fewest points allowed. But his arrest and plea bargaining in 2000 damaged his reputation, even among other players in the NFL.

Philadelphia Eagles' receiver Terrell Owens escalated his public feud with Lewis by copying the linebacker's celebration dance in a 2004 game between the two teams. Lewis and the Ravens were miffed when Owens shunned Baltimore to sign with Philadelphia.

After mocking Lewis in the Eagles' 15–10 victory over the Ravens, Owens wondered

aloud why Lewis was able to re-cast himself as a noble humanitarian while Owens has drawn repeated criticism for his on-field antics.

"You have a guy like Ray Lewis who I thought was pretty much my friend," said Owens. "This is a guy, double-murder case, and he could have been in jail, but it seems the league embraces a guy like that, but I'm going out scoring touchdowns and having fun and I'm the bad guy."

The truth of the matter is Lewis will be enshrined in the Pro Football Hall of Fame once eligible. Those who sing his praises note it is not called Pro Football's Most Humble Hall of Fame or the Never Been Arrested Hall of Fame. It's a Hall of Fame that honors only the best to have ever put on a pair of cleats, and on that count Ray Lewis has a place waiting for him as one of the game's most commanding middle linebackers. ▪

75

HOWIE LONG

DEFENSIVE END

FROM BEANTOWN TO HOLLYWOOD

For the longest time, Howie Long was a massive contradiction. He played a prickly game for the NFL's nastiest team, the Oakland/Los Angeles Raiders. Yet he was funny and engaging out of uniform, a media darling who used his charm to get into acting and broadcasting.

As a kid, Long didn't care for school. Yet his high school tutor was surprised to hear Long speak with perfect grammar, a gift from his grandmother, who raised Long in one of Boston's working-class neighborhoods.

When younger, Long secretly wanted to play hockey like Bobby Orr, but he enjoyed football as well. The problem was, he hated playing it in front of big crowds with people watching and counting on him to produce. He loathed that kind of pressure. "I had no confidence," he said of himself as a teenager and rookie professional. "None."

Still, Long matured into a good high school football player, a better college player, and one of the NFL's most formidable defensive linemen, easily able to separate his football actions and transgressions from his desire to be just a regular, everyday normal guy, with good grammar.

It was that fully developed, fully secure 6-foot-5, 270-pound Long who became a Raiders' mainstay and terrorized offenses to the point where he once walked into an opposing team's huddle during a time-out and yelled at the trainer, "Give me that water. They don't need it. They're not doing anything."

Then there was the game against Chicago where Long screamed at a Bears' offensive lineman, "I'm going to get you in the parking lot after the game and beat you up in front of your family!"

This guy could be prickly.

"I think the moment you're content is the moment you're heading backwards," said Long, who was never content with his level of play. "It's the proverbial quest for perfection, which is unattainable, and therein lies the dilemma."

Long's childhood was rife with hardship. He was turned over to his grandmother after his parents separated and later divorced. He was 12. His future seemed destined for thankless work in anonymous jobs, although he had to overcome some early ailments.

Accomplishments

Pro Bowls: 8 (1983–1987, 1989, 1992, 1993)

All Pro: 6 (1983–1986, 1989, 1990)

NFL Alumni Defensive Lineman of the Year: 1984

Hall of Fame: 2000

Quick Fact: During the Raiders' Super Bowl run in 1983, Long met journalist Hunter S. Thompson who was visiting the team. Thompson later stated "Howie is the manliest man on the planet earth."

Long rushes the pass in 1983; he posted a career-high 13 sacks that season.

"I was sick a lot, and doctors told my grandmother I'd never grow up to be big and strong. Isn't that ironic?" Long recalled.

Long was shipped to an uncle who lived in the suburbs and was fortunate to meet a high school football coach who not only believed in him but had him tutored by his wife, a math and English teacher. Long responded by becoming a Scholastic Coach All-America defensive player in his senior year, 1977. He was spotted by a coach from Villanova and offered a scholarship. In the 1980 Blue-Gray All-Star game, Long was named Defensive MVP. A year later he was drafted by the Raiders in the second round.

Not having played at a major Division 1 school, Long's inexperience became obvious when he arrived at the Raiders' training camp. In no time, he was taken to the woodshed by the Raiders' veteran offensive linemen and later by rival offensive linemen, who thwarted his every rush. Aware

that he had much to learn, Long convinced himself he could play in the NFL if he prepared himself better than anyone else.

He took a VCR with him on the road and watched game tape while staying in hotels. He started the last five games of the 1982 NFL season and became a regular in 1983, when he went to the Pro Bowl for the first time after recording what would be a career-high 13 quarterback sacks. There would be seven more such visits in a career that included 84 official sacks, two interceptions, 10 fumble recoveries, and a 1980s' All-Decade Team nomination.

Long and the Raiders made it to Super Bowl XVIII against the Washington Redskins and won handily, 38–9. In that game, Long recorded five tackles as the Raiders forced two interceptions, a fumble, and allowed just 90 yards rushing.

Two seasons later Long turned in a distinguished campaign using his patented rip move, an uppercut-like blow that sepa-

rated him from his blocker. He was voted the 1985 George Halas Trophy winner as Defensive Player of the Year. By the time he retired in 1993, Long had earned the admiration of his NFL peers and coaches, particularly Raiders' defensive line coach Earl Leggett, who said, "In those 13 years, I thought that he became the most disruptive force in pro football."

Once finished as a player, Long jumped into acting. He became an action hero starring in the movies *Firestorm*, *Broken Arrow* and *3000 Miles to Graceland*. Most recently, he has been an NFL analyst for the FOX Network, where every year he picks his Howie Long's Tough Guys team.

At his induction into the Pro Football Hall of Fame in 2000, Long thanked his family, friends, coaches and teammates, and then his grandmother, Ma Mullan, who "is up there somewhere saying, 'See, I told you you'd be somebody special.'"

Turned out she was right on the mark. ∎

42

RONNIE
LOTT

SAFETY

TRUTH LIES IN THE DIGITS

The story of Ronnie Lott and his left pinky finger has become as mangled as the defensive back's damaged digit.

Some say the finger was so badly fractured during a game that doctors cut it off at halftime, and let Lott return to action. Others insist Lott hacked it off when doctors told him his finger was a goner.

"It's like Babe Ruth pointing to center field," Lott said of his legendary tale. "That's the kind of story it's turned out to be."

It's a telling saga, even if the facts have been mutilated over the years. What is without any doubt is Lott's deserved reputation as a fearless, ball-seeking missile who played it rough as a Pro Bowl cornerback and even rougher as a Pro Bowl safety. He was as vital to the San Francisco 49ers' four Super Bowl wins as Joe Montana and Jerry Rice. He would do anything, make any hit, intercept passes, create fumbles, and score touchdowns to ensure the 49ers' success.

Even lop off a finger? The acknowledged version of events goes like this:

In San Francisco's last game of the 1985 regular season, the baby finger on Lott's left hand was crushed in a full-bore collision with Dallas Cowboys' running back Tim Newsome. Lott's hand was caught between his chest and Newsome's helmet and "exploded," according to Lott. A piece of his finger was left on the field as Lott was taken to the dressing room, done for the day.

He refused to miss the following week's playoff game and played with his hand taped up. The 49ers lost to the New York Giants and, in the offseason, doctors gave Lott the choice of undergoing an intricate surgical procedure involving pins and skin grafts or having the tip of the finger removed.

"The doctors thought it would be better for me to [have part of the baby finger amputated] since I was continuing to play," said Lott, who was told the surgery would require months of recovery and rehabilitation. "It wasn't like I was going to have a good-looking finger, because it was pretty much destroyed."

By agreeing to have his finger pruned, Lott was ready for the start of the 1986 season, one that would see him snare a career-

CAREER HIGHLIGHTS

Accomplishments
Pro Bowls: 10 (1981–1984, 1986-1991)
All-Pro: 9 (1981, 1983, 1984, 1986-1991)
All-Decade Team: 1980s
All-Decade Team: 1990s
NFL 75th Anniversary
All-Time Team: 1994
Hall of Fame: 2000

Ranking on the all-time defensive list in major categories
Interceptions: 63 (6th)
Fumbles recovered: 17 (144th)
Interceptions returned for touchdowns: 5 (19th)
Interception return yards: 730 (40th)

Lott snags an interception in 1989; his fifth consecutive season with five or more.

high 10 interceptions, make 77 tackles, force three fumbles and record two sacks, despite missing the final two games of the regular season with a leg injury.

"That shows [Lott's] dedication to the game," said Dennis Thurman, who played for the Cowboys and was Lott's teammate at the University of Southern California. "I think it's a tremendous story about courage, determination and grit, and how important football was to Ronnie, and still is. I'm sure if he could still play, he would."

Lott arrived at USC as a potential running back. He lost out to Marcus Allen and was asked to play safety, which turned out to be a good thing for the Trojans. Lott helped his school garner enough votes to win a share of the 1978 national championship alongside Alabama. He played in two Rose Bowls, was a team captain and a unanimous All-America selection.

Drafted in the first round by the 49ers,

he stepped in as a rookie cornerback and made seven interceptions, returning three for touchdowns — tying an NFL record for a rookie defender. In 1985, he switched to safety and was able to punish receivers and running backs from his new vantage point.

One of his best mood-altering hits took place Jan. 27, 1989, in Super Bowl XXIII. Cincinnati Bengals' runner Ickey Woods was gaining significant yardage early in the game when Lott promised his teammates that was about to stop. The tackle he put on Woods was so nasty it should have come with a warning, "Viewer discretion is advised."

"It just knocked Ickey's spark right out of him," said 49ers' defensive coordinator Ray Rhodes. "The game turned right then because Ickey just didn't run with the same authority after that."

Lott did the same thing to a number of other players over the years, but was also

quick and heady enough to intercept 63 passes in his career. He was even better in big games, notching 89 tackles, nine interceptions, a fumble recovery and two touchdowns in 20 playoff games.

"He's like a middle linebacker playing safety," Dallas head coach Tom Landry once said. "He's devastating. He may dominate the secondary better than anyone I've seen."

Lott was showered with awards and honors. He was voted to both the 1980s and 1990s All-Decade Teams and elected to the Pro Football Hall of Fame in 2000.

Asked if he had made the right decision about his left pinky being shortened, Lott replied, "All in all, yes. I don't have any regrets. You do that because you just love playing the game of football ... That's the ultimate compliment to pay to your teammates, to play hurt."

With nine-and-a-half fingers, no less. ■

88 JOHN MACKEY

TIGHT END

LEAD BY EXAMPLE

He was the proverbial bull in a china shop. The man they couldn't bring down with ropes or a tranquilizer gun. He did more than reinvent the tight end position — he made football fans forget anyone had ever played it before he came along.

Watching John Mackey catch a pass and shrug off tacklers was like watching a rhinoceros shake off a batch of pestering egrets. You marveled at the ease, the power, the way he raced downfield — and he could run.

In 1966, his fourth season with the Baltimore Colts, Mackey caught nine touchdown passes, six of which were 50 yards or more in length. That was unheard of at the time. Tight ends were supposed to be accomplished run blockers, extra offensive tackles that could occasionally slip out of their yokes to catch a pass or two. Never for 50 yards, though. That was the wide receiver's job.

But there was no controlling Mackey. In college at Syracuse, he had been a 220-pound fullback and had learned how to challenge tacklers. When he got to the Colts, head coach Don Shula wasn't sure where to play the 6-foot-2 Mackey. Shula watched him overpower smaller defensive backs and out-maneuver linebackers in practice and decided, "Tight end it will be."

Mackey started every game in his rookie year (he also ran back kickoffs for a 30.7-yard average) and became a Pro Bowl fixture in the 1960s, being named three years in a row. Twice, he averaged more than 20 yards per catch in a season. His career average after 10 years was 15.8 yards. When the NFL voted on its All-1960s team, Mackey was picked at tight end, by a landslide.

He played in two Super Bowls. The first was the Colts stunningly wretched 1969 loss to the New York Jets in Super Bowl III. In that game, the Colts were supposed to leave their hoofprints all over the Jets. They didn't. Two years later, the Colts beat the Dallas Cowboys in Super Bowl V on Jim O'Brien's late field goal. The game was a Marx Brothers movie of goofs, gaffes and comedic blunders except for one play. Quarterback Johnny Unitas threw a pass for Eddie Hinton that was off the mark. The ball deflected off Hinton's hands, off the

CAREER HIGHLIGHTS

Accomplishments
Pro Bowls: 5 (1963, 1965–1968)
All Pro: 3 (1966–1968)
All-Decade Team: 1960s
NFL All League Tight End: 3 (1966–1968)
Hall of Fame: 1992

Quick Fact: John Mackey has a collegiate award named in his honor. The John Mackey Award is given to the top tight end in Division 1A football.

Mackey running a route against the 49ers in Kezar Stadium on Nov. 16, 1969.

hands of Dallas defensive back Mel Renfro and into the hands of Mackey, who ran untouched for a 75-yard touchdown. The Cowboys complained, noting that a ball can't be tipped from one receiver to another. Replays showed Renfro had touched the ball in between the two Colts and the touchdown stood.

Mackey left the Colts in 1972 and signed with the San Diego Chargers, where he was bothered by a knee injury and retired. His career statistics were 331 catches for 5,236 yards and 38 touchdowns. As soon as he was out of the game, Mackey was back in the thick of things. He had been named president of the NFL Players' Association and sued the NFL for its restrictive policies regarding free agency.

"They gave us what they wanted to give us," Mackey said of the NFL owners, "made us smile and say 'thank you.' But from that day forward we decided to build a legitimate union."

Mackey saw to it the NFLPA hired its first executive director, attorney Ed Garvey. The union's headquarters was established in Washington. D.C. Mackey fought the NFL's free agency policy and today's players, who can move at will when their contracts expire, owe a debt of gratitude to Mackey's tenacity.

"John revolutionized the tight end position," said Shula. "[But] as much as he made an impact on the field, he did the same off the field. He was a leader of men of all colors at a time when that was not an easy thing to do."

Mackey wasn't the first true tight end to be inducted into the Pro Football Hall of Fame. Mike Ditka was and even he asked, "Why wasn't John in first?" Eventually, the petty politics that branded Mackey a militant union man were put aside and he joined the Hall in 1992. Eight years later, the NCAA commissioned the John Mackey Award to be presented to the best tight end in college football. That same year, Mackey received something else, something unwanted. He was told he was suffering from frontotemporal dementia. He can remember Super Bowl V, but he can't remember last week.

The illness has made him protective of personal possessions, and Mackey was arrested at the Baltimore-Washington International Airport for refusing to take off his Super Bowl ring before going through a metal detector. Mackey shrugged off security guards. It took four of them to bring him down and handcuff him. Mackey was 64 at the time of the incident.

Still looking to over-power people. Still eager to run. ▪

18 PEYTON MANNING

QUARTERBACK

LIKE FATHER LIKE SON

Peyton Manning likes to say, "Pressure is something you feel when you don't know what the hell you're doing."

Manning has always known what to do with a football in his hand and a defense unfolding in front of him like a road map. It's been that way since he was old enough to watch his dad play quarterback on television; since he passed for 92 touchdowns in three years of high school football; since he started at the University of Tennessee as an 18-year-old freshman; since he joined the Indianapolis Colts as the first pick overall in the 1998 NFL draft.

Through all those stages in his life and career, Manning has known when to throw, where to throw, how to set records and how to win a lot of games. But being impervious to pressure didn't come easily. Imagine what it must have been like always being targeted as Archie Manning's son: the one with the blood lines and newspaper headlines.

Some people are born great, the expression goes. Some have greatness thrust upon them. Peyton Manning had both.

Because his father was a Pro Football Hall of Fame quarterback, Peyton was supposed to be something special too, as if blessed in the womb. When he played well, it was all because of his dad. When he played poorly or "lost it," it was because he couldn't handle the stress and wasn't nearly as gifted as everyone thought.

By comparison, Tom Brady of the New England Patriots traveled under a cloak of invisibility. As the 199th pick in the 2000 draft, Brady pretty much snuck into the Patriots' camp, learned from his mistakes and quietly waited for his chance to play. Whereas Manning, the first overall pick in the 1998 draft, was expected to step into the Colts' offense that season and perform spontaneous acts of glory. He did amazingly well, passing for 3,739 yards and 26 touchdowns while setting five NFL rookie records. The problem was the Colts' inexperience, coupled with a hole-in-the-wall defense. At season's end, Indianapolis had won just three of 16 games.

In 1999, Manning lifted the Colts to a 13–3 record, the 10-game turnaround from the year before setting an NFL record. But when the team lost 19–16 to the Tennessee

Manning calls the play in the Colts' Super Bowl XLI victory over the Bears.

Titans in the playoffs, Manning drew criticism for not living up to his promise. People began to openly wonder if the prodigy could win the big ones.

The wondering took on mythical proportions after each postseason loss, including a pair to New England by a combined score of 44–17. In those two AFC title games, Manning threw five interceptions and only one touchdown pass. Was it all too much for the kid who grew up having to be great because that was his calling — to be better than everyone else?

Manning never saw his heritage as a burden. He grew up not just with a celebrity dad, but with two brothers who competed at everything. Their battles on the basketball court were fiercely fought. The loser had to drag the family garbage cans from the house, down a long bumpy dirt path to

the road, often having to stop to pick up the smelly droppings that plopped out.

Manning's older brother, Connor, went on to play at Archie's alma mater, the University of Mississippi, not at quarterback but as a receiver. Unfortunately for Connor, he needed surgery to correct a spinal problem and had to quit football. Younger brother Eli Manning played quarterback at Ole Miss, was the first pick overall in the 2004 NFL draft and became the New York Giants' No. 1 pivot midway through his rookie season. He would continue to progress all the way to Super Bowl XLII, where he won MVP honors for guiding the Giants to an upset of New England.

The way Peyton saw it, being counted on to win and being a Manning was a good thing, something to cherish, and he reveled in it.

"I'm proud to be Archie's son," he said. "Being a quarterback, I had my mentor and hero living in the same house."

Still, it wasn't until Manning led the Colts to a victory in Super Bowl XLI that his supremacy was assured. Against the Chicago Bears in a rain-soaked Dolphin Stadium in 2007, Manning completed 25 of 38 passes for 247 yards and a touchdown.

All those NFL records and touchdown tosses, all those 4,000-yard seasons, were wonderful, but not nearly as magnificent until placed alongside the glow of a championship. On that day, everyone was in agreement: Peyton Manning had achieved greatness on all counts.

"He did what he did all season," stated Colts' president Bill Polian. "He overcomes adversity. Whatever people throw at him, he handles it." ▪

74

BRUCE
MATTHEWS

OFFENSIVE GUARD

IRON MAN ON THE OIL FIELD

Someone once wrote of Bruce Matthews, he "is so old school he's log cabin." It's a wonderful line and positively true.

Matthews played a working man's position and worked it hard. For 19 years, he was the offensive line of the Houston Oilers (later the Tennessee Titans). He started a full season at every position, from tackle to guard to center. He played in a record 296 career games, the most by a non-kicker. He appeared in 14 consecutive Pro Bowls, tying him with Los Angeles Rams' defensive lineman Merlin Olsen for the most appearances.The difference between Matthews and Olsen was that Matthews made the Pro Bowl at two positions — nine times at guard, five at center — and thought nothing of it. No big deal. Just doing his job.

"I have seen Bruce injure a [medial collateral knee ligament] on Sunday," said former Oilers' general manager Floyd Reese, "walk on crutches Monday through Wednesday, participate in limited practices on Thursday and Friday and play at an All-Pro level on Sunday."

Rarely missing a game and giving his all was a point of honor for Matthews, a matter of family pride.

Clay Matthews Sr. (Bruce's father) was an All-America at Georgia Tech, playing two positions: offensive tackle and defensive end. He went on to become a defensive lineman with the San Francisco 49ers in the 1950s. Clay Matthews Jr. (Bruce's brother) spent 19 years (and 278 games) in the NFL as a linebacker with the Cleveland Browns and Atlanta Falcons. When Matthews Jr. retired in 1996, the father and the two brothers stood on the 50-yard line at the Georgia Dome and soaked up the adulation of the crowd."I had a set of rules I could use on all of my kids," Matthews Sr. told ESPN.com. "I told them all, 'You can do whatever you want to. You can go and play any sport you want to … But there are two rules you can't ignore. One of them is, 'I don't care if you're on the last string and sitting on the bench all of the time and are the worst guy out there, you can't quit.' And No. 2 is, 'If I ever see you play or practice and you're not giving 120 percent, I'll yank you out of there myself.' I think they all pretty much got the message."

Matthews at center in Pittsburgh, 1994: his seventh of 14 consecutive years with 16 starts.

Bruce Matthews settled on football and enrolled at the University of Southern California, where he played every position along the offensive line and made All-America in his senior year. He was drafted by Houston in the first round in 1983 and was soon blocking for Earl Campbell, the bone-crushing running back who laid waste to tacklers.

Those early seasons in Houston were wretched for Matthews, who experienced just 13 wins in his first three years. But by 1987, the Oilers would begin a string of seven consecutive trips to the postseason. The team's offense was changed to more of a passing game with the emergence of quarterback Warren Moon, the former CFL star who would establish himself as one of the NFL's top passers. The Oilers, with Moon, would challenge, but never make it to the Super Bowl. One of their most inexplicable playoff losses came against the Buffalo Bills when they blew a 35–3 lead and lost 41–38 in overtime. "The 35–3, that was such a freak thing," said Matthews, who would suffer additional tough losses in the years ahead.

One such loss was in Super Bowl XXXIV in 2000, when the Oilers (who, by this time, had been transformed into the Tennessee Titans) lost to the St. Louis Rams. Receiver Kevin Dyson was stopped one-yard short of a game-tying touchdown. The other came the year after the Super Bowl, when the Titans lost to the Baltimore Ravens in the AFC championship game.

"I was so tired," Matthews said of his only Super Bowl showing. "I saw [Dyson] was tackled and said, 'It's over.' I walked straight into the dressing room … Next year, we lost to the Ravens. Losing that game was the most difficult playoff loss I ever endured."

His spirit may have been sapped, but it always recovered when the next game or season rolled around. That's how Matthews was taught and that's what he did until he retired after the 2001 season. He was voted onto the NFL's 1990s All-Decade Team and he had his No. 74 retired by the Titans, he was also inducted into the Pro Football Hall of Fame. He recalled how, in his third NFL season when the Oilers played the New York Giants in a preseason game at Canton, Ohio, he watched the inductees arrive at the shrine by motorcade. "I shook Joe Namath's hand. That was a huge thrill," Matthews said. "I've always appreciated the history of the game … I never contemplated that's where I belonged. It seemed too big to me."

But him there, among the greats of the NFL, seems just right, for the old-school lineman. ■

78 ANTHONY MUNOZ

OFFENSIVE TACKLE

FROM THE WRONG SIDE OF THE TRACKS

A split-second after Anthony Munoz had knocked NFL Hall of Famer Forrest Gregg to the ground, he thought, "Oh no. I'm in trouble now."

Gregg was the head coach of the Cincinnati Bengals and a gridiron immortal, who had played for the Green Bay Packers and Vince Lombardi. Munoz had just finished his university career at Southern California, playing in only one game at offensive tackle. His knees had been operated on three times in four years and the book on him was "talented but a medical risk."

Gregg had come to Los Angeles to worout Munoz and see if he was really damaged goods. Here's how Munoz remembered the session: "He put me through some drills and I moved along and all of sudden he decided to pass rush me. I wasn't sure how to react but I reacted like any offensive lineman would react. He made a move inside, made a move outside. Just as he made them, I stuck both hands right into his chest and jammed him to the ground.

"You better believe I was scared," Munoz said. "I extended a hand, I apologized, and he said, 'No problem.' He smiled, he goes,

'That's okay.'"

It was better than okay. On that day, Munoz proved he had the footwork and strength to be a good player, perhaps a great one in the NFL. With Gregg's recommendation, the Bengals selected Munoz with their first-round choice in the 1980 draft, making him the third pick overall, behind Billy Sims of the Detroit Lions and Johnny (Lam) Jones of the New York Jets.

With the 6-foot-6, 278-pound Munoz manning the all-important left tackle position — for right-handed quarterbacks, at least — the Bengals experienced instant results. In 1979, the offensive line had been an off-ramp to the quarterback, giving up 63 sacks. In Munoz's rookie season, that number dropped to 37. A year later, it dropped to 35, and Munoz won his first of three NFL Offensive Lineman of the Year awards.

Like many star NFL players, Munoz's childhood was not an easy one. He never knew his father, who bolted and left Esther Munoz to raise five children by herself. Munoz's neighborhood in Ontario, California, was poor and laced with gangs, drugs and hostility. The Munoz family had no car.

Munoz helps lead the Bengals to a 33–27 overtime win over the Steelers in 1991.

Anthony went everywhere on his bicycle.

Munoz played flag football because he grew to be too big for Pop Warner's kids' football program. He played a lot of baseball and liked to pitch. When he earned a scholarship to USC, Munoz pitched for the Trojans' 1978 national championship baseball team before settling on football. That same year he was named All-America at tackle.

In his final season at USC, Munoz vowed to recover from his third knee operation and play in the 1980 Rose Bowl against Ohio State. He made that pledge while still wearing a cast. He told his coach, John Robinson, he'd be back for the Rose Bowl. Robinson said sure, he'd put Munoz in for a play or two at wide receiver, just to reward his senior lineman.

Munoz wanted no such pity. He wanted to play and he did, helping USC to a 17–16 win for the national championship, while winning the Lombardi Trophy as college football's best lineman.

"[Munoz] is one of the greatest players at any position I ever saw," Robinson said later. Cincinnati head coach Sam Wyche would say the same after coaching Munoz in the NFL.

For 11 straight years, Munoz was voted to the Pro Bowl. During that time, the Bengals won three AFC Central Division titles and two AFC championships. The first came in 1992 when they hosted the San Diego Chargers in what became known as the Freezer Bowl. The temperature at Riverfront Stadium was minus 13 Fahrenheit, but with the wind chill it was a lung-shattering minus 59.

"You've never seen anything until you've seen Anthony Munoz and our offensive line trying to get into Hanes queen-sized panty hose," former Bengals' receiver Cris Collinsworth said of his teammates' desire to wear anything to stay warm.

The Bengals won the game 27–7 to earn their first trip to the Super Bowl. There would be another such trip in Munoz's career, in 1989, but Cincinnati would lose to the San Francisco 49ers (both times) by a total of just nine points.

Nowadays, Munoz does his best to knock down poverty and intolerance. He has his own foundation that sponsors student athletes and teaches leadership. In addition, he runs a football camp that teams inner-city kids with those from the suburbs.

"As someone who comes from a diverse environment in Southern California, I grew up that way," said Munoz. "Having played athletics for as long as I have, the primary goal was to win games. It didn't matter where you were from. You did it as a unit. I think it works that way in life." ■

12 JOE NAMATH

QUARTERBACK

SASS, SWAGGER, SAVIOR

At some time or other, every male in North America of a certain generation would've sold his soul to spend a week as Broadway Joe.

The guy who'd called his shot before Super Bowl III — "We'll win. I guarantee it" — just like the Babe. He owned Manhattan's trendiest club, Bachelors III, and could be spotted on the bench wearing a full-length mink coat.

"I like my Johnnie Walker red and my women blonde," he said, and everyone lapped it up.

Joe Willie Namath, the slope-shoulder kid with the lopsided grin from Beaver Falls, Pennsylvania, did more over the years than become a great quarterback, although arguably the finest pure passer in history. He came to symbolize a moment in time, the way author F. Scott Fitzgerald had.

He threw more interceptions than touchdowns over his career, finishing with a 50 percent completion rating. And yet, to this day, remains one of the game's most famous quarterbacks.

Why, this guy could pitch pantyhose and get away with it. He didn't look ridiculous in a Fu Manchu moustache (which he later shaved in a Remington commercial for a fee of $10,000). He wore white shoes. If he wasn't autopsying defenses with chilling precision, he was off starring in a chopper flick, cozying up to sex kitten Ann Margaret.

Those knees may have been held in place by ruinous ligaments. But that pass release? Ohhhh, heaven-sent.

"He was like a cause," former teammate John Dockery told ESPN Classic. "It was like traveling with a rock star. He just was a magnet. Talk about energy and excitement. Wow!"

The time was ripe for an anti-hero, a rebel, and Joe Namath fit the bill brilliantly. The '60s were a decade of musical and political upheaval. The young believed in dissent, thumbed their noses at the status quo and sought their heroes through the classic anti-hero. The Johnny Unitas crew-cut and Bart Starr's bible studies didn't wash anymore. But Joe Willie did.

Namath broke rules and ruffled the establishment. His hedonistic lifestyle drove the old guard crazy. In hospital, battling the cancer that would claim his life, the ultimate rules/establishment coach, Vince Lombardi, vented his displeasure. His widow, Marie, would later recall "He talked once in his sleep about Namath. I just heard his end of the conversation. He was shouting at Namath, telling him to sit down and yelling about how he was a disgrace to football."

Lombardi might've hotly disagreed with the methods and the style. But no one could dispute Joe Namath's gift.

Lost in the fact that Namath was a state of mind, as much as a quarterback, are the accomplishments. He is, never forget, the only man to throw for 4,000 yards in a 14-game season — his third year in the league, first as starter, in 1967. Three times he led the league in passing.

In addition to that sublime right arm and a great football intellect, he possessed a tremendous will to win. When Joe Namath talked, people around him listened, and believed.

"To be a leader, you have to make people want to follow you," he said. "And nobody wants to follow someone who doesn't know where he's going."

Where Joe Willie planned on going was right to the top against Don Shula's seemingly unbeatable Baltimore Colts in the 1969 Super Bowl III.

His signing by the AFL Jets for a reported $400,000 a season in 1965 was a huge coup for the fledgling league, determined to rival the clout and star-wattage of the established NFL. Namath had been selected 12th overall by the NFL's St. Louis Cardinals, first by the Jets. Typically, Joe made the risky choice. Now the moment had arrived to back up the hype.

The lead-in surrounding "the guarantee" of victory is a bit hazy. He made his bold — some would claim insane — promise in response to a heckler at the Miami Touchdown Club dinner three days before the Jets were predicted to be wiped out by the NFL's monster truck from Baltimore. It made for headline-grabbing fodder.

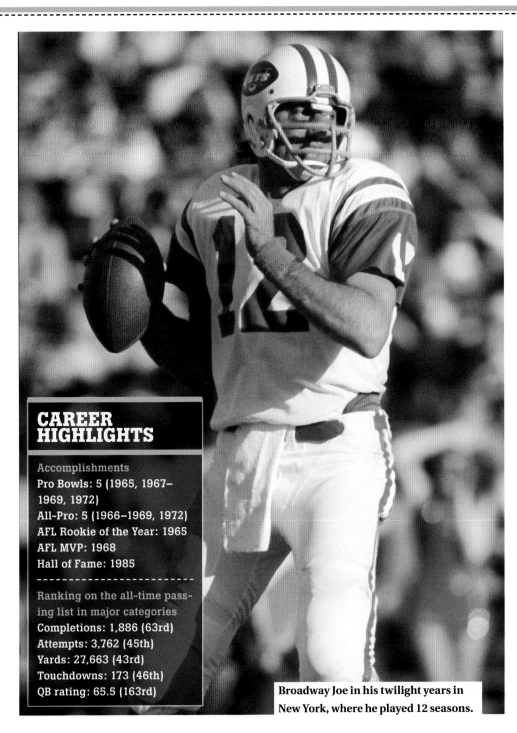

CAREER HIGHLIGHTS

Accomplishments
Pro Bowls: 5 (1965, 1967–1969, 1972)
All-Pro: 5 (1966–1969, 1972)
AFL Rookie of the Year: 1965
AFL MVP: 1968
Hall of Fame: 1985

Ranking on the all-time passing list in major categories
Completions: 1,886 (63rd)
Attempts: 3,762 (45th)
Yards: 27,663 (43rd)
Touchdowns: 173 (46th)
QB rating: 65.5 (163rd)

Broadway Joe in his twilight years in New York, where he played 12 seasons.

Then Namath went out and backed up the talk, completing 17 of 26 passes for 206 yards to snare MVP honors, as the upstart AFL cemented its legitimacy in the neon glow of a 16–7 New York victory. It may not be the most memorable Super Bowl ever, but it remains the most famous.

"When we won the league championship," quipped Namath, "all the married guys on the club had to thank their wives for putting up with all the stress and strain all season. I had to thank all the single broads in New York."

Pure, undistilled, 100-proof Joe.

The knee injuries that compromised his brilliance and cut short his career dated back to his senior year at Alabama. We are only left to ponder what he would've been like on two healthy pins. What we saw, however, was more than enough. For his swagger and sass, boldness and daring, Broadway Joe remains timeless.

66 RAY NITSCHKE

LINEBACKER

THE GRIDIRON IMMORTAL

Born in Elmwood Park, Illinois, in 1936, Ray Nitschke lost his father at age three, was orphaned when his mother died at 13 and was raised by an older brother.

Add to that growing up in a rough-and-tumble Chicago neighborhood, and it's a small wonder he turned out to be as tough as his last name. Nitschke. Just the sound of it, the hardness of the syllables, the spit-in-your-eye indomitable ethnicity of it, provided an understanding into the man. For the rest, you simply had to watch him at work. Balding, wild-eyed, missing his four front teeth and apparently some of his mind, Nitschke became the beating heart, the obstinate backbone, of Green Bay's underappreciated defense during the glory decade of the '60s.

Legend has it that a metal tower on the Packers' practice field fell over on top of Ray Nitschke. Coach Vince Lombardi ran over to see what was going on. Informed that it was Nitschke underneath the structure, Lombardi barked, "He'll be fine. Get back to work." Nitschke's biography states that the tower actually drove a stake into his helmet, but he went unharmed. The helmet (complete with hole) is on display in the Packer Hall of Fame in Green Bay.

A caring man with a hard shell, Nitschke went from being a notorious hell-raiser to happy family man, working the off-season in a bank. His is one of the great success stories of football. Perhaps not as famous today as his linebacking contemporary, Dick Butkus of the Chicago Bears, he was nonetheless every bit as visceral, as violent, and as uncompromising between the lines on a football field.

Drafted by the Packers instead of his beloved Bears, Nitschke took $300 of his $500 signing bonus, bought a used Pontiac and drove to Green Bay. He spent the next 15 seasons in Packer green and gold. "Oh, that Nitschke was crazy as hell," said defensive back Emlen Tunnell of the early years. "He had the locker right next to mine. Tom Bettis was the middle linebacker then, so Nitschke didn't play much. And Ray used to get on Vinnie [Lombardi] about it. He'd say, real loud in the locker room, 'Just call me the judge. Just call me the judge. 'Cause I'm always on the bench.' Oooh, that would make Vinnie mad."

Accomplishments
Pro Bowl: 1964
All-Pro: 7 (1962–1967, 1969)
NFL Title Game MVP: 1962
NFL All-time Top Linebacker:
1969
All-Decade Team: 1960s
NFL 75th Anniversary
All-Time Team: 1994
Hall of Fame: 1978
- -
Quick Fact: In 1997, the
Packers' east practice field,
across Oneida Street from
Lambeau Field, was named in
Nitschke's honor.

Nitschke on the sideline in 1965; his
fourth of seven Pro Bowl seasons.

Under Lombardi's tough-love guidance, though, Nitschke channeled his rage and energy into football. The coach knew what he had in the raw, untamed beast prowling the middle of the field: one of the most competitive people ever to grace that highly competitive business.

Paul Hornung gleefully recounted a memorable nutcracker drill during practice one day. Future Hall of Fame fullback Jim Taylor was the ball carrier. "There was very little running room," said Hornung, "because the [blocking] dummies were up there tight and the blocker — some rookie — just screened Nitschke while Taylor slid by." Lombardi stopped the drill, walked over to Nitschke and said, "Mr. Nitschke, I have read that you are the best linebacker in the NFL, but after watching you just then I find it hard to believe. Now, do it again!" This time, continued Hornung, "Ray grabbed the rookie by the shoulder pads, literally lifted him up and threw him into Jimmy. All Vince said was, 'Next group.' It took them two minutes to get the rookie to come to."

Nitschke the indomitable met his match in his wife-to-be, Jackie. She provided balance and meaning to his life. "Getting married, settling down, getting responsibility for someone beside myself, having someone to love and later adopting the children — all those things were enough motivation for me to quit making a fool of myself," he wrote in his autobiography, *Mean On Sunday*.

Of all the great Packer players of that era, arguably the most loved in Green Bay was, and is, Nitschke. When he died unexpectedly at 61 in 1998 — the heart, of all things, giving out — the whole of Wisconsin mourned.

The brawler who used to pitch people through windows of bars when the mood struck him would doubtless be astounded to learn that a six-inch NFL Legends action figure, No. 66, has been modeled in his image, and that both a bridge in Green Bay and the luncheon prior to induction at the Pro Football Hall of Fame are named in his honor. In 1999, *Sports Illustrated* named him the third greatest linebacker in history, behind only Dick Butkus and Lawrence Taylor. But people in Titletown, U.S.A., know better.

Ray Nitschke didn't just leave his imprint on anyone daft enough to dare to run between the tackles. He left it on the game. ■

32 O.J. SIMPSON

RUNNING BACK

THE GLORY YEARS

Long before the lurid headlines and the courtrooms and the late-night talk show punch lines and the police mug shots and the posted bail and the almost cartoonish-buffoonish persona. Orenthal James Simpson was known far and wide as a running back.

A running back different from any seen before — The Juice. No. 32 of the Buffalo Bills: a sublime concoction of speed, power and misdirection that ran through NFL defenses as easily as he dashed through airports in Hertz Rent A Car commercials.

Simpson was the first rusher ever to top 2,000 yards in a season. And in only 14 games, at that. He was a man who established records for yards along the ground in a game (273), and touchdowns during a season (23); a three-time UPI Player of the Year, four-time leading rusher, All-AFC and All-Pro for five consecutive years, he participated in six Pro Bowls and was the NFL's MVP in 1973.

Here was an athlete so extraordinary, so unique, that legendary University of Southern California coach John McKay declared, "Simpson was not only the greatest player I

ever had — he was the greatest player *anyone* ever had."

Watching videos of Simpson now still has the power to amaze and delight. He provides viewers with the same sort of goose bumps that Gale Sayers had before him: the dramatic, seemingly impossible changes in direction, that rare inexplicable ability to make opponents miss, as if he alone were enacting a dance of joy.

"The fear of losing is what makes competitors so great," he said of the game he came to dominate. "Show me a gracious loser and I'll show you a permanent loser."

For the length of his stay there, O.J. Simpson turned frigid Buffalo into Broadway on Sunday afternoons or Monday nights, providing the greatest theatre in the state outside of the Great White Way.

Because of the benevolent, charming façade Simpson studiously built during his decade as a superstar with the Bills, people forgot, or never knew, that he grew up in the rough Potrero Hill section of San Francisco, and was raised by his mother Eunice after his dad walked out on the family. Early on, Simpson hardly seemed a candidate

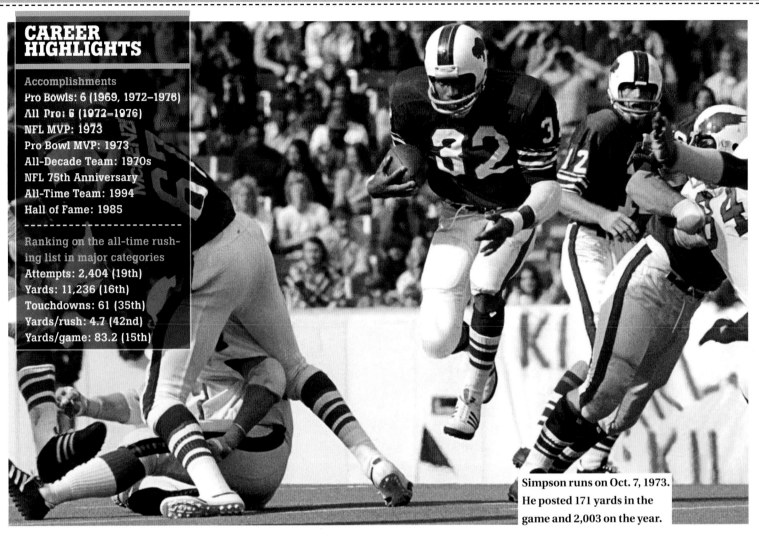

CAREER HIGHLIGHTS

Accomplishments
Pro Bowls: 6 (1969, 1972–1976)
All Pro: 6 (1972–1976)
NFL MVP: 1973
Pro Bowl MVP: 1973
All-Decade Team: 1970s
NFL 75th Anniversary
All-Time Team: 1994
Hall of Fame: 1985

Ranking on the all-time rushing list in major categories
Attempts: 2,404 (19th)
Yards: 11,236 (16th)
Touchdowns: 61 (35th)
Yards/rush: 4.7 (42nd)
Yards/game: 83.2 (15th)

Simpson runs on Oct. 7, 1973. He posted 171 yards in the game and 2,003 on the year.

for football immortality. At just two years old, he developed rickets, leaving his legs skinny and bowed. He joined his first gang at 13, and at 15, Simpson landed in a Youth Guidance Center for a week after one of many fights. There had always been a dark side to O.J. Simpson — the kid-from-the-shabby-side-of-the-tracks side.

But football ability, the great equalizer, was his ticket out of the squalor and into the limelight of mainstream American culture. He only ever wanted to play collegiately, for the Trojans, at USC. And it was there his legend began to take shape. During his phenomenal Heisman Trophy-winning senior season, Simpson set NCAA records for most rushing yards in a season (1,709) and most carries (355). USC won the Rose Bowl that year. In 17 of his 21 career games for the Trojans, he ran for over 100 yards, in five of them, for over 200.

Chosen first in the 1969 college draft, Simpson languished for three seasons in Buffalo, unhappy with how he was being used. When Lou Saban took over as head coach in 1972, though, he built his offense around the workhorse back and was rewarded with 1,251 yards, the NFL high that year.

In 1973, Simpson exploded into the national consciousness. He had 1,000 yards by the midway point of the season, and people began to speak openly about his chances of hitting 2,000. In Buffalo's next-to-last start, he rambled for 219 yards, leaving him 197 short of the mythical mark. On a bitter, snowy, windswept New York day at Shea Stadium, The Juice bulled, slalomed and slashed for 200, giving him 2,003 on the season. He was carried off the field on the shoulders of his teammates.

During his 11 NFL seasons, Simpson ran for over 11,000 yards and, while he never brought the Super Bowl title to Buffalo, his accomplishments were many and lauded. He was inducted into the Pro Football Hall of Fame in 1985, and he remained an amiable and familiar presence on TV and in film. Until, that is, June 12, 1994, when his wife Nicole Brown Simpson and friend Ron Goldman were found dead outside her condominium.

The football icon was charged with the double murder. Following a yearlong trial that gripped a nation and divided public opinion, he was acquitted. What's certain, is that forever more, Orenthal James Simpson will be primarily remembered for the so-called Trial of the Century and its controversial outcome.

His legacy as one of the game's great running backs, at least, remains wistfully uncompromised. ▪

50 MIKE SINGLETARY

LINEBACKER

A CRAZY-EYED WONDER

The eyes of Mike Singletary were indeed the window to his soul. They looked as if they were going to pop right out of his head. Right out of his helmet, too. They burned with intensity. One look from Singletary and wild animals would have run for cover.

Singletary's soul was no less passionate. He wanted to be the best middle linebacker in the game. The best teammate. The best husband. The best father. Everything worth doing was worth doing to its fullest — that was Singletary's guiding principle.

"If you want to be the best, if you want to be the best at something, you will not be denied," he said. "You're not going to quit. You're not going to stop. You're going to keep fighting."

Singletary was a never-quit fighter who overcame his lack of size (6-foot, 230 pounds) with a crackling disposition. His tackles bordered on assault and battery. One of his all-time favorite targets was Los Angeles Rams' running back Eric Dickerson. In a 1985 playoff showdown in Chicago, Dickerson took a handoff on third and one and looked to have room running through the right side of the Bears' defense. Single-tary charged in, stopped Dickerson dead in his tracks, then threw him for a loss. To celebrate, Singletary began barking like a dog.

A bemused linebacker, Wilbur Marshall, said after Chicago's 24–0 win, "Dickerson didn't know where he was at."

Chicago head coach Mike Ditka had a better story about that playoff game. The day before, he was talking to the offense while Singletary was addressing the defense in a room next door. As Ditka tells it, what started out as a calm and rational speech quickly turned into a Knute Rockne rant, complete with Singletary screaming and his defensive mates turning over tables and trashing chairs.

With his determination and his smarts, Singletary was the defensive catalyst of the Bears' 1985 season, which saw them go 15–1. In the ensuing playoffs, Chicago dominated from start to finish, ravaging the New England Patriots in Super Bowl XX. That season, Singletary recorded 109 solo tackles, three sacks, one interception, three fumble recoveries and knocked down 10 passes. He was named the NFL's Defensive Player of the Year.

Accomplishments
Pro Bowls: 10 (1983–1992)
All Pro: 8 (1988–1991)
NFL Defensive Player of the Year: 2 (1985, 1988)
All-Decade Team: 1980s
Hall of Fame: 1998

Chicago defensive team records (1981–1992)
Led the league in fewest points allowed: 3 (1985, 1986, 1988)
Most sacks in a season: 72 (1984)
Led league in fewest yards allowed: 3 (1984–1986)

A rookie Singletary in 1981 displays the ferocity for which he became famous.

Singletary's need to be the best was forged in childhood. He was born the last of 10 children in Houston, Texas. When he was five years old, his brother Dale died. When he was 12, his parents divorced and his dad, a Pentecostal pastor, left. That same year, another brother, Brady, was killed in a car crash.

Singletary was lost, with "no confidence … no self-esteem," he said. His mother sat him down and told him he could accomplish anything he wanted because there was greatness in him. She told Singletary to trust in his faith and believe in its values. Singletary said as soon as his mom finished her talk he went to his room and wrote down his goals: "Find a way to get a scholarship to go to college; become an All-American in college; get my degree; go to the NFL; and buy my mom a house and take care of her for the rest of my life."

Singletary went to Baylor University and was a two-time All-America. The Bears drafted him in the second round in 1981 and, by the seventh game of his rookie season, Singletary was giving opponents fits with his crazy-eyed look and Samurai warrior attacks.

In 12 seasons in Chicago, the voracious defender appeared in 10 Pro Bowls, made 1,488 tackles and was voted to both the Pro Football and College Football Halls of Fame. And when it came to being the best husband and dad, Singletary has worked hard on that front, too.

He has helped raise his seven children, one of whom, Matt, enrolled at his dad's alma mater in 2007. His wife, Kim, who met Singletary while they were attending Baylor in the late 1970s, was the presenter who introduced him as a Pro Football Hall of Fame inductee. He called her his best friend.

"A lot of people think I'm corny," Singletary told the *Chicago Tribune*. "I want it that way, and I like it that way. You watch me as close as you can, and I'll do my best to teach you something. You follow me anywhere, into any closet, and you won't see something else."

Corny, keen, a natural leader, those qualities have held Singletary in good stead as a coach. He worked as an assistant with the Baltimore Ravens, where he tutored Ray Lewis. He joined the San Francisco 49ers in 2005 and since then has been mentioned as a viable candidate for several head-coaching jobs.

While no one is certain how Singletary would fare as a head coach, this much is guaranteed: He will strive to be the best. He will not quit. He will bring it all.

Eyes and soul. ∎

78

BRUCE
SMITH
DEFENSIVE END

THE ALL-TIME HUNTER

Tommy Kramer was the first to go down in 1985. Jesse Palmer became the record-breaker in 2003. In between, the list of victims included John Elway, Joe Montana, Phil Simms, Dan Marino, Steve Young and 70 others, including Ken O'Brien, who was hunted down and bagged more than a dozen times by Bruce Smith.

It's a wonder that O'Brien, a Pro Bowl quarterback for the New York Jets, didn't jump like a startled cat at the mention of Smith's name. The Buffalo Bills' defensive end had that effect on quarterbacks.

He had the same effect on his teammates.

With the Bills trailing the Kansas City Chiefs in a key AFC match-up, Smith stomped into the offensive meeting at halftime and yelled at his teammates, "Gosh darn it, stop turning over the football." (Okay, he didn't say gosh darn it.) Aware Smith would be even angrier if the game ended the same way it began, the Buffalo offense held onto the ball, scored 17 points and easily defeated Kansas City.

"I'm not a very outspoken person until the time comes," Smith said afterward. "If I step on somebody's toes, I'm not sorry about it because it's the truth and it hurts."

Smith stepped on toes, rammed helmets and did whatever he could to make quarterbacks worry and wince. He chased lesser-knowns such as Browning Nagle and Dave Brown as unremittingly as he hounded Drew Bledsoe and Donovan McNabb. As a harasser of quarterbacks, Smith was an equal opportunist.

"I watched my first NFL game in Detroit in 1934 when I was a kid," Bills' owner Ralph Wilson once said, "and I think Bruce Smith is the best defensive lineman I have ever seen. I'm not saying that because he's a Buffalo Bill. I'm saying that because I have seen all the great ones and I don't think anyone was ever better."

Statistically, Smith holds the overall sack record with 200. It took him 19 seasons, including four with the Washington Redskins, to put up that number, which may stand for some time. But Smith's pursuit of the record was not well received in all corners.

Several sports columnists and NFL commentators criticized him for staying in the game longer than he should have and for taking a roster spot that should have gone to a younger player. He was called selfish and record hungry. And when he was benched by Washington coach Steve Spurrier, Smith spoke out, saying he was still the team's best pass rusher, even at age 40.

One newspaper quoted an unnamed NFL scout as saying, "Bruce Smith is just limping toward that sack record. The first four games [of his final season] he seemed to be pumped up, but the last two weeks he looks bad."

No one ever thought Smith looked bad when he played for the Bills. Buffalo's first-round selection in the 1985 draft, he was the team's all-time sack leader by 1989 (with 52) and one of the Bills' undisputed leaders. With Jim Kelly, Andre Reed and Thurman Thomas holding onto the ball on offense, Smith inspired a defense that back-stopped Buffalo to a record four consecutive Super Bowl appearances.

In 13 of his 19 seasons, Smith recorded 10 or more sacks. His best showing came in 1990, when he got to the quarterback 19 times and earned his first of two NFL Defensive Player of the Year awards. The same year, he was voted to the Pro Bowl, an honor he would receive 11 times. Virtually each time the ball was snapped, he was double-teamed by offensive linemen and blocking backs.

"There are five players in this league who can take a team on their shoulders and make a difference," Jets' quarterback Boomer Esiason said. "Barry Sanders, Jerry Rice, Emmitt Smith, Thurman Thomas and Bruce Smith."

Buffalo fans wanted Smith to retire as a Bill but it was not to be. In 1999, he was released to free up salary-cap room for the Bills and, two days later, he signed with

CAREER HIGHLIGHTS

Accomplishments
Pro Bowls: 11 times (1987–1990, 1992–1998)
All-Pro: 12 times (1986–1990, 1992–1998)
NFL Defensive MVP: 2 (1990, 1996)
1987 Pro Bowl MVP: 1987
All-Decade Team: 1980s
All-Decade Team: 1990s

Quick Fact: Although Bruce Smith hinted about returning to the NFL in 2004, the Washington Redskins cut him from the roster to save $6.5 million in cap space.

All-time sack leader Smith celebrates sack 133.5 against Miami on Oct. 13, 1996.

Washington, which was close to his hometown of Virginia Beach.

With the Redskins, Smith was not the player he once was. And yet, he managed 29 sacks in four seasons, including the 199th of his career, the sack that lifted him ahead of Reggie White and his record count of 198.

It happened Dec. 7, 2003, at Giants Stadium. Smith had knocked New York's starting quarterback Kerry Collins out of the game and, in the fourth quarter, was able to

tackle Collins' replacement, the Canadian-born Jesse Palmer, for a seven-yard loss.

The Redskins' players rushed onto the field to congratulate Smith, who was given the game ball. Later in the Washington dressing room, he opened a gift that had been given to him by his tailor. It was a burgundy-colored robe with the Redskins' logo on the back and "All Time" written across the front.

He wore it with pride; the all-time hunter content at last. ■

15

BART STARR

QUARTERBACK

FROM SIDELINES TO HEADLINES

Controlled. Precise. Economical. Humble. Cerebral. Efficient.

Bryan Bartlett Starr came to embody the perfect Vince Lombardi quarterback: the ultimate game-manager. He was the brain center of those legendary Packers' teams of the 1960s that had folks in tiny Green Bay answering their telephones with "Hello, Titletown U.S.A.!"

Ironically, at the beginning, Lombardi was far from convinced. Largely lost in the mists of the time and the almost mythic reverence in which that Packer era is held by football fans of two generations is the moment during the 1960 title game, which the emerging Pack lost 17–13 to the Philadelphia Eagles: Starr failed to spot a wide-open Max McGee at a critical point in the game. The missed opportunity gnawed away at Lombardi long after Eagles' linebacker Chuck Bednarik stuffed running back Jim Taylor at the Philadelphia nine-yard-line to end Green Bay's bid.

"Yeah, some guys see them and some guys don't," Lombardi groused to NFL executive director Jim Kensil during dinner early in 1961. "Then," recalled Kensil,

"he told me 'I'd really like to get that guy [Don] Meredith.' He told me he'd offered the Cowboys, who had just played their first season, any two players on the Packers' roster. I said 'Any two?' He said, 'Any two.' He really didn't think that Bart Starr was what he wanted in a quarterback. I thought that was very interesting when Starr started seeing *every* receiver. I always meant to ask Vinnie what happened to that two-for-one deal."

Over the course of a 15-year career, Bart Starr threw for more than 24,000 yards, won the 1966 NFL MVP, played in four Pro Bowls, and, here is the most telling testament to the man and his capabilities, captured five championships, including the first two Super Bowls. No one else — not Joe Montana, not Terry Bradshaw, not nobody — can make that claim.

He arrived in Green Bay a 17th round draft choice, chosen 200th overall. He signed for $6,500. It's no wonder Lombardi didn't know whether he wanted Bart Starr or not — pretty much no one did. He languished on the bench his first season, shared playing time the next. In 1958, he started. The Packers went 1–10–1. During his first five seasons, Starr threw 41 interceptions and only 23 touchdowns. Then Lombardi arrived from the New York Giants, and so began the good times.

"Earlier in my career, many fans misinterpreted my calm demeanor for lack of imagination," Starr wrote in his autobiography.

No imagination?

The most famous single play of Starr's career, arguably in all of Packer lore, can be put down to his imagination: the famous third-down sneak at Lambeau Field in the "Ice Bowl" on Dec. 31, 1967. In almost inhuman conditions — a minus 45 Fahrenheit with wind chill that prompted Cowboys' owner Clint Murchison to quip, "If I owned Green Bay, I'd dome the whole town." — with 13 seconds left, and the Pack down by three points with zero timeouts remaining, positioned two feet from the Cowboy end zone, Bart Starr dove into history. Cowboys' coach Tom Landry felt certain the Packers would throw the ball. Halfback Donny Anderson had slipped on the two previous plays and an incomplete pass would at least give Starr time to run a final play.

Instead, Starr pitched the idea of a quarterback keeper to his coach on the sidelines, a simple dive right over offensive tackle Jerry Kramer (the basis of which would become Kramer's 1968 best-selling book *Instant Replay*). "I told Coach Lombardi there was nothing wrong with the plays we had run," Starr recalled afterwards. "It's just that the backs couldn't keep their footing. I said, 'Why don't I just keep it?' All he said was 'let's run it and get the hell out of here.' That's all he said."

They ran it and got the hell out of there. All the way to Miami two weeks later where the Packers paddled the Oakland Raiders to claim their second straight Super Bowl.

In retirement, the success he enjoyed as a player proved elusive. Starr's nine years as head coach in Green Bay netted only

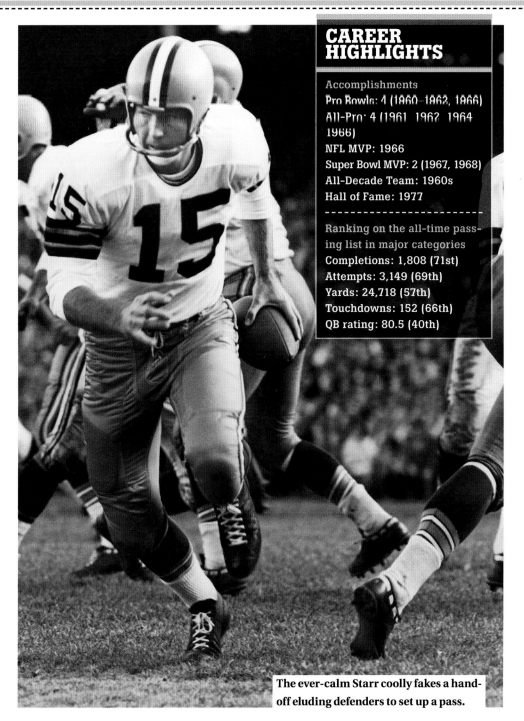

The ever-calm Starr coolly fakes a hand-off eluding defenders to set up a pass.

one playoff game, and he was fired after an 8–8 season in 1983. Off the field, he suffered tragedy. In 1988, his oldest son, Bret, battling cocaine addiction, died of a heart attack that doctors felt was brought on by drug use.

Often, life leaves us no control. On the field, though, with Taylor and Hornung in the backfield, with Boyd Dowler and the madcap McGee split wide, and with Forrest Gregg, Jerry Kramer and Jim Ringo providing protection, Starr was in complete control.

"Bart Starr," said Lombardi once in tribute, "stands for what the game of football stands for: courage, stamina and co-ordinated efficiency. You instill desire by creating a superlative example. The noblest form of leadership is by example and that is what Bart Starr is all about."

All talk of Dandy Don Meredith had by then been long forgotten. The best two-for-one deal Vince Lombardi never made. ▪

34 THURMAN THOMAS

RUNNING BACK

THE TRIPLE THREAT

Few players smoldered the way Thurman Thomas did. He could bristle during practices. He glowed red hot during games. His intensity was a three-alarm blaze waiting for a strong wind to make it uncontrollable.

It didn't matter if you were friend or foe, teammate or media type, if you got near Thomas's blast furnace you got scorched. Even Jim Kelly, the Buffalo Bills' star quarterback, felt the sting of Thomas's ire if he didn't play up to his potential.

"He brings an edge to the team because he's not afraid to get in anybody's face," Buffalo linebacker Darryl Talley once said of Thomas, "In my opinion, he was the best back I've ever seen at being able to catch the ball out of the backfield and being able to run the ball at the same time."

He could run, he could catch and he bubbled with a desire that matched his versatility. Thomas is the only player in NFL history to lead the league in total yards from scrimmage for four consecutive seasons, and also the only player to have scored a touchdown in four consecutive Super Bowls.

He is one of four running backs to date to have rushed for more than 1,000 yards in eight consecutive seasons. (The others are Emmitt Smith, Barry Sanders and Curtis Martin.) And he is one of six running backs to have rushed for more than 10,000 yards and caught 400 passes. (The others are Walter Payton, Marshall Faulk, Marcus Allen, Tiki Barber and LaDainian Tomlinson.)

"I don't believe there has ever been a more complete player at his position than Thurman," Bills' coach Marv Levy said when he delivered Thomas's induction speech at the Pro Football Hall of Fame in 2007.

Branded the Thurminator, Thomas was such a complete competitor that his teammates marveled at everything he did on a football field, including the way he blocked.

"I swear to God, I watched film of it at times to remind myself of the proper way to do things," said Buffalo center Kent Hull. "If Thurman had been bigger, he would have made a heck of an offensive lineman."

Thomas was such an outstanding running back at Oklahoma State University he kept Barry Sanders glued to the bench,

CAREER HIGHLIGHTS

Accomplishments
Pro Bowls: 5 (1989–1993)
All-Pro: 6 (1989–1994)
NFL MVP: 1991
All-Decade Team: 1990s
Hall of Fame: 2007

Ranking on the all-time rushing list in major categories
Attempts: 2,877 (11th)
Yards: 12,074 (12th)
Touchdowns: 65 (30th)
Yards/rush: 4.2 (148th)
Yards/game: 66.3 (45th)

Quick Fact: In 21 postseason games Thomas recorded 21 postseason touchdowns, one behind all-time leader Jerry Rice.

Thomas rumbles past the Dolphin defense to his 21st playoff touchdown on Jan. 2, 1999.

a pretty neat trick considering how good Sanders was.

In four seasons at OSU, Thomas ran for 4,595 yards and 43 touchdowns. He had 21 100-yard games but caught just two passes for 15 yards. By the time he left for the NFL, Thomas was his school's all-time leading rusher and a likely first-round draft pick in 1988. But a knee injury sent Thomas's stock plummeting. He was taken in the second round, 40th overall, by a Buffalo team that was eager to add a skilled running back to its budding offensive arsenal.

With Thomas locked in, the Bills revamped their attack to take advantage of his skills. They became the masters of the hurry-up offense and used it, not just as time was winding down late in the second and fourth quarter, but as a change-of-pace tactic that caught opponents flat-footed.

"One [game] that really started the no-huddle was when he caught a playoff record against the Cleveland Browns, like 13 catches or something," recalled Kelly. "Defensive coordinators really didn't know how to guard against what we had."

Not being able to stop Buffalo's multi-faceted offense was a common problem in the AFC. The Bills won four conference titles in a row to earn four consecutive trips to the Super Bowl, a feat no team has managed since.

Unfortunately for the Bills, their first Super Bowl appearance in 1991 was their best, and it was still a loss. Thomas totaled 190 yards rushing and receiving, and scored a touchdown, but the Bills were left heartbroken when kicker Scott Norwood's 47–yard field goal sailed wide right, sealing their 20–19 loss to the New York Giants.

A year later in Super Bowl XXVI, everything went wrong for the Bills. At the start of the game, Thomas couldn't find his helmet and had to miss two plays. He didn't touch the ball until 12 minutes had been played. That set the tone for the game, as the Bills lost to the Washington Redskins, 37–24. In their next two Super Bowl appearances in 1993 and 1994, the Bills would be drubbed by the Dallas Cowboys by a combined score of 82–30. It was a bitter experience for Thomas, who would, years later, joke about the case of the missing helmet:

"You always sent me out well-equipped," Thomas told Levy at the Hall of Fame ceremony, "except for that one time when you played tricks on me with my helmet."

When it came to giving his best in a number of ways, from performing to keeping his teammates honest, few players in NFL history were better equipped than Thomas. He gave the Bills their spark.

And he burned brightly doing it. ∎

8 STEVE YOUNG
QUARTERBACK

IN THE FOOTSTEPS OF THE GODS

Someone has to follow in the footsteps of the gods. Someone had to be the heavyweight boxing champ after Muhammad Ali was stripped of the title. Someone had to be the Chicago Bulls' shooting guard after Michael Jordan retired. Someone had to coach in Green Bay after Vince Lombardi moved on.

And someone had to play quarterback after Joe Montana was traded away by the San Francisco 49ers. Steve Young was that someone. He was the follower who bore the brunt of comparative greatness. Montana was king — a four-time Super Bowl champion of mythical proportions. Young came after: a good player who never seemed to measure up when it counted.

It stayed that way until 1995 when Young finally won a Super Bowl, won Super Bowl MVP honors, and set a Super Bowl record by throwing six touchdowns (nosing out the previous record holder, the unparalleled Montana, who had tossed five touchdown passes). In that glorious moment in Young's career, the comparisons ended, and the true appreciation commenced. Theoretically, it should have started sooner.

Young was jaw-droppingly good with the 49ers before his win in Super Bowl XXIX. He could run like a fullback and deke like a halfback. He could throw off the run or from deep in the pocket. Either way, he was utterly proficient, always completing a high percentage of his passes.

"Steve is doing things no other quarterback has ever done," 49ers tight end Brent Jones said. "But there are still people who think they can only like Joe. Steve can't please all the people in the world. There's never going to be another Joe, and Steve knows that. What more can he do? … People have to realize that if they want to follow us, then their favorite quarterback ought to be Steve Young."

Young certainly waited for his chance to succeed Montana. After spending two seasons in the USFL, then another two with the Tampa Bay Buccaneers, Young was traded to the 49ers where he waited another four years before becoming a starter. He got his chance when Montana was sidelined with an elbow injury. Unfortunately, Young suffered a knee injury that limited his playing time.

Accomplishments
Pro Bowls: 7 (1992–1998)
All-Pro: 7 (1992–1998)
NFL MVP: 2 (1992, 1994)
Super Bowl MVP: 1995
Hall of Fame: 2005
- -
Ranking on the all-time pass-
ing list in major categories
Completions: 2,667 (21st)
Attempts: 4,149 (35th)
Yards: 33,124 (21st)
Touchdowns: 232 (20th)
QB rating: 96.8 (1st)

Young in the 1992 playoffs; he led the regular season with 25 touchdown passes.

Still, there were signs that Young was the one to eventually replace Montana. In 1992, despite a serious concussion, Young passed for 3,456 yards and 25 touchdowns and won the NFL's MVP award. The King was dead. Long live the King.

Montana was traded to the Kansas City Chiefs in 1993, clearing the way for Young, who overcame a sluggish start to finish the year with 4,023 passing yards and 29 touchdowns. Losing to the Dallas Cowboys in the playoffs for the second year in a row revved up the critics who thought of Young as a flawed substitute to you-know-who. It didn't help that when Montana's Chiefs played Young's 49ers in September 1994, the Chiefs won 24–17, while Young was sacked and harried all afternoon.

"I really feel like, in being after Joe, I've learned how to be a great quarterback and now I have a chance to go prove it," Young said of his situation. "I think a lot of people feel they have untapped potential in their bodies and don't get a chance to bring it out. In San Francisco, with the pressure, I have a chance to see how good I really can get."

The Chiefs game was the last tough loss San Francisco endured that season. Young threw for 35 touchdowns, led his team past Dallas in the playoffs and would need just one minute and 24 seconds to begin his Super Bowl rout of the San Diego Chargers. He hit receiver Jerry Rice for a 44-yard touchdown, and then found running back Ricky Watters for a 51-yard touchdown on the 49ers' second possession. The game's final stats showed San Francisco with 28 first downs and 455 yards in offense with Young as the game's leading passer and rusher.

"All along, I felt I was playing against the past," Young said afterward. "Honestly, I have distanced myself from all [the Mon-tana comparisons]. I did so a couple of years ago. I want my performance to stand for myself and my teammates."

That it did. Although several more concussions forced Young into early retirement, his numbers stood tall, throwing for more than 3,000 yards in a season six times and for 20 or more touchdowns five times. He holds the NFL record for the highest career passer rating (96.8), and the record for most rushing touchdowns by a quarterback (43).

In 2005, Young was inducted into the Pro Football Hall of Fame — the first left-handed quarterback to be so honored. Arguably, the reward that was just as meaningful was the 49ers decision to retire his No. 8 jersey.

Like the man before him, Young left behind some mighty good footsteps for the next guy to follow. ■

LEGENDS
IN THE MAKING

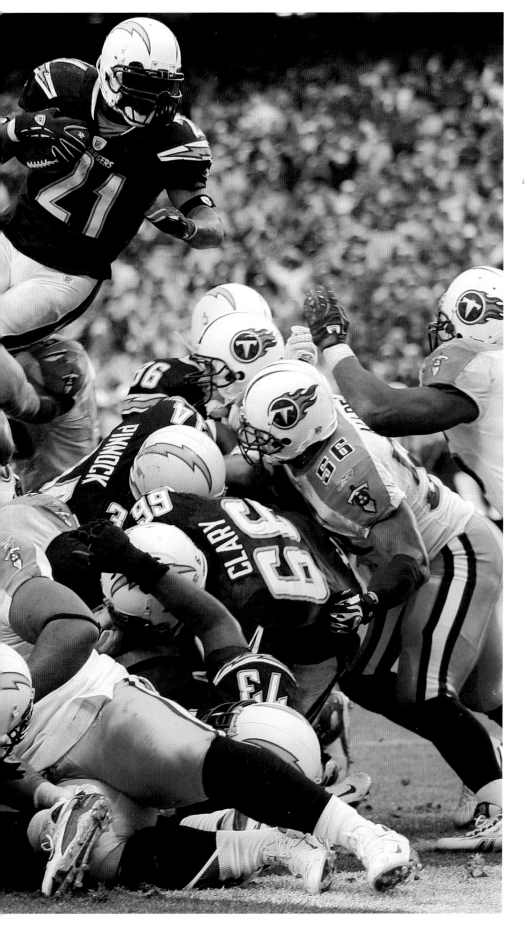

"I should have gone to the Hall of Fame before I stepped on a football field of any kind. It would have given me that much more appreciation for the game."

– Michael Irvin,
Receiver, Dallas Cowboys

Art Monk figured the call would never come. For eight years he had been eligible for induction into the Pro Football Hall of Fame, and for eight years he had been dutifully ignored by the voters.

His receiving statistics with the Washington Redskins were good enough to warrant his inclusion, but as the years flew by Monk suspected his time had passed and that his name and accomplishments would eventually be forgotten.

So when a Hall of Fame official called him in 2008 and said, "Congratulations, you've been elected," Monk, a quiet man by nature, was stunned. As he told friends and family, "Never in my wildest dreams as a little boy did I ever imagine getting to this point."

No football player begins his career dreaming of being in the Hall of Fame. There are too many other things to accomplish first, such as making the team, becoming a starter, an All-Pro and, most importantly, becoming a champion. But when the time is right and their career is done, the Hall of Fame is where every player wants to be.

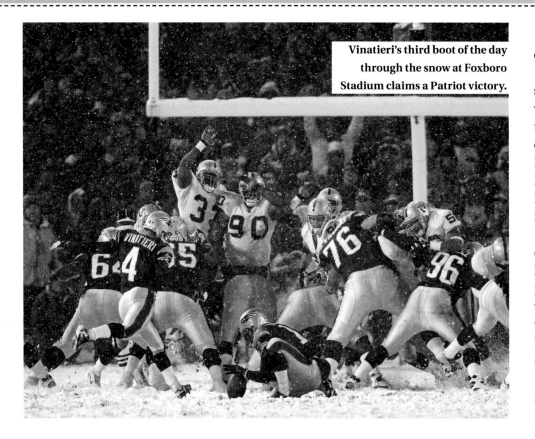

Vinatieri's third boot of the day through the snow at Foxboro Stadium claims a Patriot victory.

It is where greatness is measured, and in different ways; from the star player on the Super Bowl-winning team to the star player on the team that rarely made the playoffs. If they made a difference, if they earned the respect of their peers, the Hall of Fame was their calling, their reward — and no one has ever refused the honor.

Among the 1,500-plus active players in the NFL, only a select few will make the cut and receive the same gold-colored suit jacket given to the likes of Doug Atkins, Raymond Berry and Jack Christiansen. Looking back over the past four decades, ESPN.com has estimated that at least 50 players who participated in the 2005 season will eventually be enshrined at Canton, Ohio.

Among those who retired prior to the 2007 campaign, two men stand out as heavy favorites to be inducted: Jerome (The Bus) Bettis of the Pittsburgh Steelers and Curtis Martin of the New York Jets. Bettis was a six-time Pro Bowl player who rumbled for 13,662 yards and 94 touchdowns. Martin rushed for 14,101 yards, the fourth-highest total in NFL history, and scored 102 touchdowns. Like all Hall of Fame candidates, both backs have to wait five years before being eligible.

It's also reasonable to assume that three quarterbacks will make the grade: Brett Favre, who has thrown for more touchdowns and yards than anyone else in the game; Peyton Manning, who systematically dissects defenses; and Tom Brady, who has routinely won Super Bowls while barely breaking a sweat.

As for who will be joining these men, the possibilities aren't endless, only impressive.

OFFENSIVE CANDIDATES

Adam Vinatieri

We begin our look at the future greats by suggesting that if one is the loneliest number, as Three Dog Night sang, then Jan Stenerud of the Kansas City Chiefs could use some companionship as the only kicker in the Pro Football Hall of Fame.

Adam Vinatieri would make for good company.

Vinatieri is an average-sized kicker who spent four years at South Dakota State University, from which he graduated in 1994 as the school's leading scorer. No NFL team drafted him, so he signed with the World League of American Football and played in Europe for Amsterdam. The New England Patriots made him a free-agent offer and invited him to training camp in 1996.

Vinatieri remembers how Patriots' head coach Bill Parcells did his best to unnerve his kickers in practice so they'd be better prepared for having to boot a game-winning field goal. He'd scuff up the turf where the holder had planned to place the ball. He'd try to distract the kicker as he stepped into the ball.

Just before the Patriots third preseason game, Parcells told Vinatieri, "I want to see if you got what it takes, or pack up your ass and go home." Vinatieri kicked three field goals that day. The Patriots cut veteran kicker Matt Bahr. Was this the birth of a legend? Not immediately.

Vinatieri opened the regular season kicking one field goal. The following week, he missed three out of four. The week after that, he missed an extra point. He eventually turned things around and, near the end of the season in a game against the Dallas Cowboys, Vinatieri arrived, not with a game-winning kick, but with a touchdown-saving tackle.

Herschel Walker of the Cowboys was returning the kickoff deep into New England territory when, out of the blue, Vinatieri tracked him down and made the tackle. To see a kicker, football's least physical athlete, tackle the fleeing Walker sent the game's color commentator over the moon.

"Closing speed," said the commentator. "I never thought I'd use that word for a kicker."

Vinatieri told the *New York Times* that after the game Parcells came up to him and said, "You're more than a field-goal kicker to this team now. You'll see — the way the guys will treat you will be different now." Parcells was right. "All of a sudden I wasn't that snot-nose kicker who no one wanted to talk to," said Vinatieri.

Things were just beginning to heat up for Vinatieri. By the 2001 season, Vinatieri had fine-tuned his swing and was delivering his kicks straight and true. Then came the first big one of his career, in an AFC playoff game against the Oakland Raiders. With New England trailing 13–10, Vinatieri attempted a 45-yard field goal in blizzard conditions and made it. In overtime, he then nailed a 23-yard kick to win the game.

"I still laugh about that [45-yard] kick because it was such a low-percentage kick," he said. "My main thought was, 'Don't fall down.'"

In Super Bowl XXXVI against the St. Louis Rams, Vinatieri was presented with a 48-yard field goal attempt to win the game. On the final play, as time ran out, he made the kick that made him immortal, to give New England its first NFL championship.

Two years later in 2004 at Super Bowl XXXVIII, the Patriots decided things had worked so well the first time they'd try it again. This time they gave Vinatieri a whole four seconds to work with and, on cue, he made a 41-yard field goal against the Carolina Panthers to give New England its second NFL championship. Now Vinatieri was more renowned than ever. The king of the immortals.

For a follow-up, he led the league in scoring in 2004 with 141 points, hitting on 31 of 32 field goals and 48 of 48 extra points. In one game that season, against the flummoxed Rams, Vinatieri kicked four field goals, four extra points and threw a touchdown pass off a fake field goal. When the Patriots reached Super Bowl XXXIX against the Philadelphia Eagles, Vinatieri pretty much had the day off, kicking only one field goal and a trio of converts. Again, New England won.

When free agency came, Vinatieri got a call from the Indianapolis Colts, a team the Patriots had often beaten on the strength of its reliable kicker. The five-year, $12 million contract, complete with a $3.5 million signing bonus, was too good to turn down

and Vinatieri signed. In his first regular-season game with the Colts, he recorded four field goals and Indy beat the New York Giants by five points. Three weeks later in Denver against the Broncos, "Mr. Clutch" drove home a 37-yarder with two seconds on the clock in a 34–31 Colts' victory.

"When [Vinatieri] goes out there, you always feel like he's not going to miss," said Indianapolis head coach Tony Dungy. "That was our whole goal when he was at New England, that you couldn't let him get close enough in a situation where a field goal was going to do it. I don't remember him missing against me in four or five years."

Vinatieri kept making kicks, including five in a playoff game against the Baltimore Ravens, to help Indianapolis win Super Bowl XLI, 29–27, over Chicago. He has scored more than 1,400 points, made 20 game-winning field goals with less than 60 seconds on the clock, and his four Super Bowl wins places him one behind the all-time leader, defensive lineman Charles Haley, who won five in his career. With numbers like that, Vinatieri is duly bound for Canton.

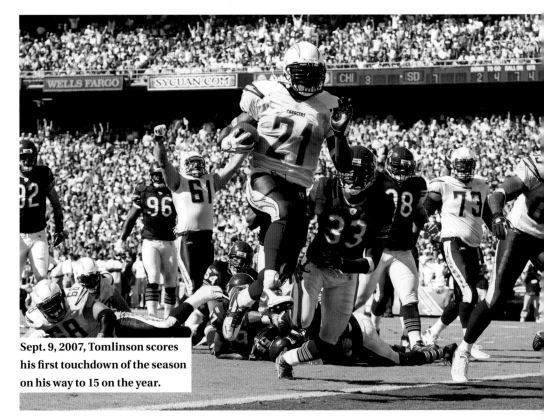

Sept. 9, 2007, Tomlinson scores his first touchdown of the season on his way to 15 on the year.

LaDainian Tomlinson

Tomlinson is in the prime of a career that is purring along like a Ferrari F430. In just seven seasons at running back, all for San Diego, he has surpassed the 10,000-yard plateau and scored 115 touchdowns. Consider these numbers: Since first setting foot on an NFL field, Tomlinson has averaged 1,437 yards and 16 touchdowns a season for seven consecutive seasons — as sure as the swallows return to San Juan Capistrano.

In 2006, the 5-foot-10, 221-pound powerhouse ran for a career-high 1,815 yards and scored a record 28 times. He added three more touchdowns off 56 pass receptions. The downpour of touchdowns led to a flood of NFL records. In a six-game span, he scored an unprecedented 19 times. He became the first player to score three touchdowns per game for three consecutive games. He reached the 100-touchdown mark quicker than any other player, needing just 89 games to do it. Jim Brown and Emmitt Smith reached the century

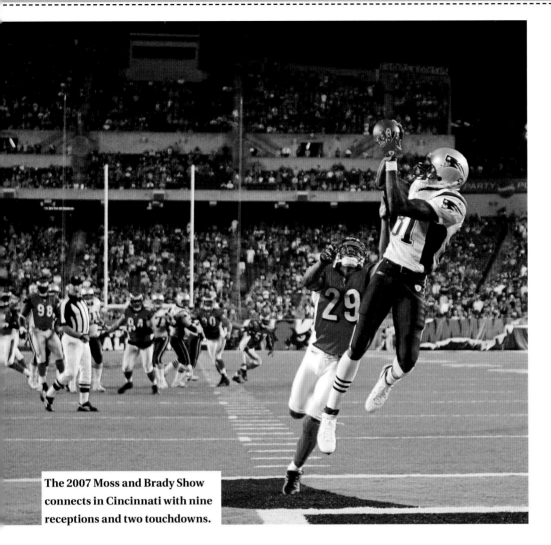

The 2007 Moss and Brady Show connects in Cincinnati with nine receptions and two touchdowns.

Randy Moss

Any defender seeing the back of Moss, the Patriots prime receiver, is also too late and a touchdown short. Then again, seeing the back of Moss is better than seeing his back side. Any Green Bay Packer fan can tell you that.

When Moss was playing for the Minnesota Vikings, he and the Packers would meet twice a season and Green Bay fans were only too glad to maintain their time-held tradition of mooning the opposing team's bus as it pulled away from the stadium. But after scoring a touchdown in a 2005 playoff game at Lambeau Field, Moss decided to get even. He pretended to unbuckle his belt and drop his pants before bending over, two cheeks to the wind. The Green Bay faithful were not amused; neither was TV announcer Jack Buck, who called the display "a disgusting act." Moss was fined $10,000 for unsportsmanlike conduct.

On a similar theme, Moss admitted in a TV interview with Bryant Gumbel that he smoked marijuana "every blue moon." He caught the ire of Viking fans by saying his inconsistent play had to do with the fact that he wasn't happy, and if he wasn't happy he wasn't going to produce. "I play when I want to play," he proclaimed, which went over like a stink bomb in a classroom.

But when Moss wants to play, as he has with the Patriots, his acrobatic stylings have been some of the best ever seen in the NFL. With his angular form, long arms and serpentine fingers, Moss has the ability to go up, over and around a defender, and catch the ball as if plucking an apple off a tree. In his career, he has caught 774 passes for 12,193 yards and 124 touchdowns. In 2007, he snared a record 23 touchdown passes and made a lot of them look breathtakingly easy.

"There have been times when I've forced it and he caught it and it's a great play," said Tom Brady, the Patriots' artful quarterback. "He's always a big part of the plan. I'm always trying to find ways to get him the ball … You want to give him opportunities to make those plays."

club in 93 games. Brown and Smith had been Tomlinson's childhood idols, the players he dreamed about while sleeping with a football tucked under his arms.

Like his gridiron heroes, Tomlinson believes in being the strong, silent type. He's not one for trash talking and post-touchdown gyrations. He did let his emotions bubble up in 2006 after the Chargers lost to New England in their playoff match-up in San Diego. At game's end, a handful of Patriots did their version of the Light Out, a dance created by San Diego linebacker Shawne Merriman. Tomlinson bulled his way into the celebrations and gave the Patriots a piece of his mind. Afterward, he snapped, "I would never, never react in that way. They showed no class, absolutely no class, and maybe that comes from their head coach."

Tomlinson later made peace with New England coach Bill Belichick when the two represented the AFC at the annual Pro Bowl. Still, Tomlinson stuck to his anti-dance stance insisting, "At some point, there are little kids who are wishing to be us and who'll go out and act like that."

Tomlinson's on-field persona has only one showy statement. On his football helmet, he wears a visor so dark no one can see his eyes. The reason for that is twofold: to cut down on the sun's glare and to look cool. "It adds to my personality," he said. "I'm kind of a mask guy. I don't brag; I do."

And he does it exceedingly well. As his fullback Lorenzo Neal has explained: "I know that if I can just get a piece of a block and get him into the secondary with two safeties, I'll just roll over and look at the Jumbotron or listen for the roar. I tell opponents, 'If you're seeing the back of 21, it's too late.'"

Terrell Owens

Owens is another receiver with the kind of game (882 catches, 13,070 yards, 129 TDs) that beckons Hall of Fame acceptance.

Owens played at a small university (Tennessee-Chattanooga) and was only a third-round draft pick of the San Francisco 49ers, the team where his boyhood hero Jerry Rice was playing. When he joined the 49ers, he was in awe and acted extraordinarily shy. He didn't play much at first, but instead was relegated to special teams. But during his sophomore season in 1996, Owens benefited from an injury to Rice and became the team's go-to receiver.

Soon after, Owens was en route to stardom. In 1998, he scored the winning touchdown in a playoff game against Green Bay. With San Francisco trailing 27–23, quarterback Steve Young flung a 25-yard pass to Owens, who caught the ball at the goal line, was rocked by a big hit but held on to secure a come-from-behind victory for the 49ers.

Owens was off and running after that. In Rice's last game with the 49ers in December 2000, he caught an NFL record 20 passes for 283 yards. Chicago coach Dick Jauron joked that it seemed as if Owens caught 81 passes that game, matching his jersey number. The Bears' defensive coordinator Greg Blache framed the significance of Owens' outburst.

"They were showing people the changing of the guard," said Blache. "We happened to be the team that was there … We went in with a switchblade and fought Zorro."

Owens' athletic gifts don't come without some consternation. He wore out his welcome in San Francisco, went to Philadelphia and wore out his welcome there, both times garnering impressive stats while feuding publicly with management and teammates. In two seasons with Dallas he has continued to speak his mind while catching 166 passes and scoring 28 touchdowns. He has shown little, if any, sign of slowing down. When he gets to Canton, try and imagine what Owens might do as a celebration. Pull a pen out of a sock and autograph his gold-colored jacket? Don't be surprised, whatever he does.

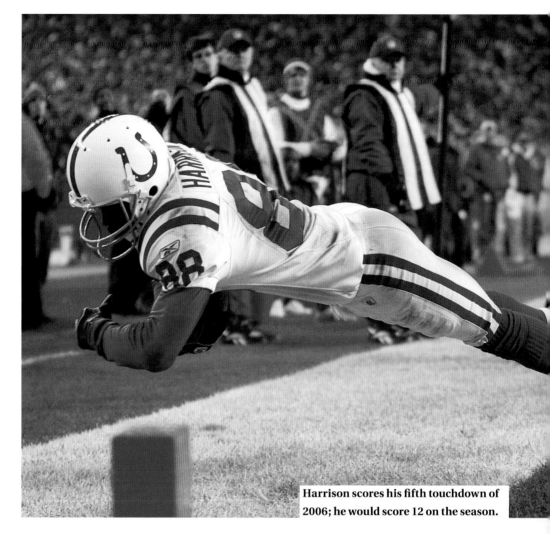

Harrison scores his fifth touchdown of 2006; he would score 12 on the season.

Marvin Harrison

You may not know it, because Harrison doesn't talk like Randy Moss, doesn't showboat like Terrell Owens, but he does catch the ball as well. Truth be told, his statistics are better than both of his more publicized peers.

In 12 seasons, the same number Owens has played, Harrison has caught 1,042 passes for 13,944 yards and 123 touchdowns for the Indianapolis Colts. Four times, Harrison has caught more than 100 passes in a season, including 143 catches in 2002, an NFL record. Six times, he's gained more than 1,200 yards. Eight times, he's scored 10 touchdowns or more and eight times he's been selected to play in the Pro Bowl. In terms of praise, no one has better acknowledged Harrison's skills than former Buffalo Bills' general manager Marv Levy, who said, "Terrell Owens is a guy that has to go out there and get recognized for his antics and celebrations, while a guy like Marvin Harrison wants to be recognized for his play on the field, not his antics or his celebrations. That's the kind of receiver you want on your team."

Harrison and Peyton Manning have teamed up for 107 touchdown passes, making them the most prolific passing duo in the annals of the NFL. That has prompted a curious question: Who made who? Was Harrison the key to unlocking Manning's potential, or did the strong-armed quarterback turn Harrison into a lethal weapon? The most likely answer is that the two raised one another's game. Manning could count on Harrison running precise routes, while Harrison knew the ball would be on target when he made his cuts.

"I think experience has definitely helped," Colts' tight end Dallas Clark said of the

Manning-Harrison partnership. "They've been around each other for so long. I think if any team or duo gets to be on a team that long, which doesn't happen a lot in this league with free agency and everything like that, for guys to be able to stay together and keep that chemistry, it helps a lot … Those guys, they just have a knack — they don't have to talk much to get on the same page."

Harrison used to play quarterback in high school, which meant he knew his way around a game plan and how to watch defenses. With little more than a glance from Manning, Harrison can adjust his route to get open, knowing that his quarterback will get him the ball. And when that happens, he can make plays and win games. If he was any more workman-like, he'd be wearing a tool belt as part of his uniform.

"Talking doesn't get you anywhere in football," Harrison said, "although a lot of people at my position do. I know we're the prima donna position, but I don't know how it got that way."

Chad Johnson

Johnson has proven himself to be a quick-six solution for the Cincinnati Bengals. Since 2003, he has averaged 92 catches, 1,374 yards and eight touchdowns. He's as productive through the air as LaDainian Tomlinson is on the ground, but if there's a shred of modesty in the man it remains to be found.

The Bengals' bombastic receiver has worn a blonde Mohawk, been fined by the NFL for wearing Ocho Cinco (his jersey number in Spanish) on the back of his jersey instead of his name. He's even been fined for showing a sign during a game that read, Dear NFL, please don't fine me again.

"Cornerbacks fear being embarrassed by me," said Johnson, who once wore a gold jacket on the sidelines with Future H.O.F. 20?? written on the back. "I want the spotlight on me."

Larry Allen

The spotlight is something Larry Allen has rarely seen in his 14 seasons in the NFL and that's saying something, since Allen stands at an imposing 6-foot-3 and weighs 325 pounds. Then again, being an offensive lineman, even an exceptionally good one, is not a job for those who crave adulation. As Jim Murray, the *Los Angeles Times* columnist, wrote: "The interior line must be where guys on the lam from the police hide out. They're as anonymous as telephone operators."

While there are few statistics by which to measure an offensive lineman, Allen can match anyone who's ever thrown a block or opened a hole for an appreciative running back. With Dallas, Allen sprang Emmitt

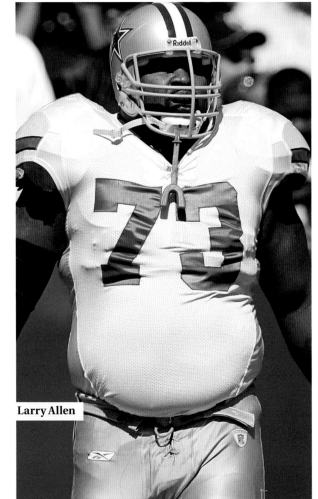

Larry Allen

Smith for enough yards to help him become the NFL's all-time leading rusher. Allen was selected to the Pro Bowl 11 times and twice (2006, 2007) he won ESPN's Strongest Man title held during Pro Bowl week. To earn the crown, all Allen had to do was lift 225 pounds 43 times in succession.

As well as lift weights, Allen has shown he can run, too. In a 1994 game between Dallas and New Orleans, Saints' cornerback Robert Massey intercepted a Troy Aikman pass and looked to be off and running for a touchdown. Seemingly from nowhere, a then rookie Allen tracked Massey down and tackled him before he got to the end zone. Closing speed? Who would have thought of using that phrase to describe an offensive lineman?

Allen won a Super Bowl with the Cowboys, played three different positions in the Pro Bowl (right guard, left guard, left tackle) and was named to the NFL's all-1990s team.

"We call him the legalized killer," New York Giants' pass rusher Michael Strahan once said of Allen. "He doesn't just block people, he hurts people … He's probably the only guy who you watch on film who makes you cringe."

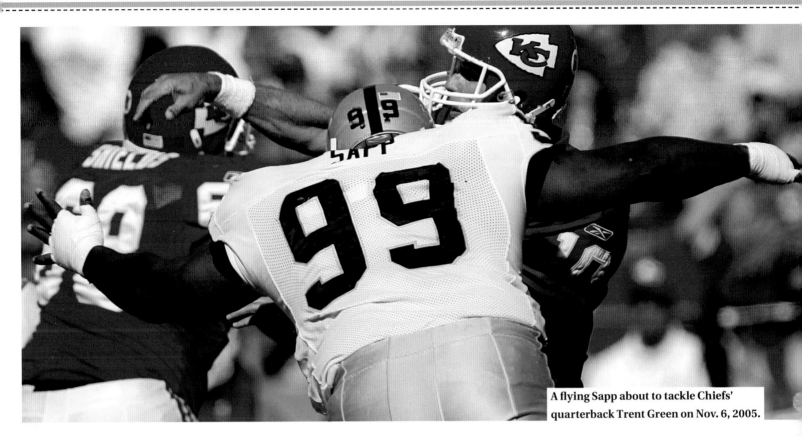

A flying Sapp about to tackle Chiefs' quarterback Trent Green on Nov. 6, 2005.

DEFENSIVE CANDIDATES

Switching to the other side of the ball, if the trenches are where games are won or lost, as conventional football wisdom states, then the pass rushers and run stoppers deserve their recognition in the Hall of Fame.

Warren Sapp

Among the down-and-dogged defensive battlers, few have been as memorable as Warren Sapp, whose us-against-the-world attitude transformed the Tampa Bay Yucks (as they were lampooned), into Super Bowl champions in 2002.

Drafted by the Buccaneers in 1995 out of the University of Miami, Sapp arrived in Tampa like a marching band. He was so loud he irritated many of his teammates, but his bravado on the field was a welcome addition for a team that was the equivalent of a 98-pound weakling.

Two years after drafting Sapp, the Bucs checked into the playoffs and although they lost to the eventual NFC champion Green Bay Packers, Sapp had a monumental game, making seven tackles,

three sacks, forcing two fumbles and recovering one. Three years after that, in 2000, Sapp recorded 16.5 sacks, a remarkable feat, since being a defensive tackle meant he was usually double-teamed by opposing blockers. Two years later, he was jawing with Green Bay head coach Mike Sherman, who accused Sapp of deliberately trying to injure Packers' lineman Chad Clifton with a hit that broke Clifton's pelvis.

"I don't play that way," Sapp said. "I know what a clean shot is. Front is front, back is back. I hit [Clifton] right in the mouth."

A lot of NFL players have wanted to zap Sapp in the mouth. Twice, he skipped his way through the opposing team's pre-game warm-up and earned warnings (and a fine) from the NFL. After the second incident, he ran onto the field and bumped into an official. Sapp was slapped with a $50,000 fine by the league but even that proved to be small potatoes compared to a 2007 incident that saw him hit with three unsportsmanlike conduct penalties on one play before being ejected and fined again, this time for $75,000.

"It's a slave system," Sapp said after his first fine. "Slave master say you can't do it, don't do it. They'll make an example out of you."

Giants' defensive end Michael Strahan, another Hall of Fame contender, once got into a verbal spat with Sapp after setting the league's single-season sack record with 22.5. Sapp was irked by the fact Strahan got the record when Green Bay quarterback Brett Favre appeared to simply fall down and allow Strahan to touch him for the record breaker. Sapp thought that was cheap and let Strahan know it.

"They won't give me one guy that will go one-on-one with me for four quarters twice a year so I can whoop the hell outta him for eight sacks," said Sapp. Strahan's response was: "When it comes to getting to the quarterback, I'm good. I'm sorry. I can't help it."

At his best, Sapp helped lead a ferocious Bucs defensive charge against Oakland in Super Bowl XXXVII. On that afternoon, the Raiders threw five interceptions and Oakland's quarterback Rich Gannon was sacked five times, and Warren Sapp couldn't stop smiling.

Strahan gets the defense pumped before defeating the Cowboys 21–17 on Jan. 13, 2008.

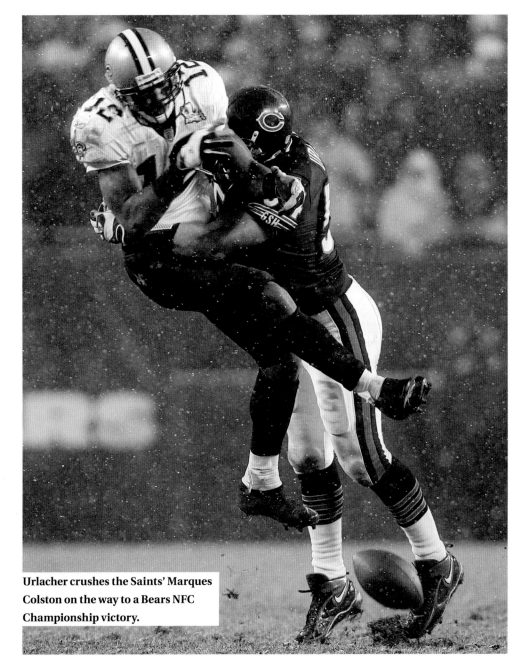

Urlacher crushes the Saints' Marques Colston on the way to a Bears NFC Championship victory.

Michael Strahan

Strahan is more than just a good quarterback hunter. In 2001, along with his record-setting sack count, he recorded 73 tackles and was named the league's Defensive Player of the Year. He was the leader among active players in 2007 with 141.5 sacks, which puts him in fifth place overall behind the next-to-unblockable Bruce Smith (who hit the 200 mark before retiring), Reggie White, Kevin Green and Chris Doleman.

Strahan came out of Texas Southern, an NCAA Division 1-AA school, where he tackled everything that moved. His first season in the NFL, in 1993, was hampered by a foot injury; his next three seasons saw him switch from right defensive end to left.

Finally, in 1997, Strahan recorded 14 sacks and established himself as a Pro Bowl player.

Ironically, after 14 seasons in the NFL, Strahan almost missed out on what he dearly wanted — a Super Bowl win. He was ready to retire in the summer of 2007 but changed his mind and reported late to training camp. In the end, he capped a stellar season with two tackles and a sack in the Giants' 17–14 triumph in Super Bowl XLII over the previously unbeaten New England Patriots.

"I waited 15 years," Strahan told New York fans, "and I never thought this would happen. And when it did, I never thought it would be of this magnitude."

Brian Urlacher

You couldn't go wrong with Brian Urlacher as your middle linebacker. In the grand tradition of the Bears' defense — think Bill George, Dick Butkus, Mike Singletary — Urlacher is the spark that lights the dynamite. With his strength, he can fill the gap and tackle ball carriers. With his speed, he can drop into pass coverage and make key interceptions. With his ferocity, he can blitz the quarterback and make him hurry his throw.

In 2006, with Chicago trailing Arizona by 20 points, Urlacher took charge by doing all three of those things to the utmost of his ability. He initiated his team's turnaround by stripping the ball from Edgerrin James, allowing Chicago to recover and score a key touchdown. After Chicago's stirring 24–23 win, Urlacher was credited with 18 tackles. The Bears went on to finish 13–3 that season and win the NFC championship game. They lost 29–17 to the Indianapolis Colts in Super Bowl XLI.

"Brian was born with certain physical tools, which you certainly can't teach," said Dick Jauron, his former head coach in Chicago. "But his attitude is really what makes him special."

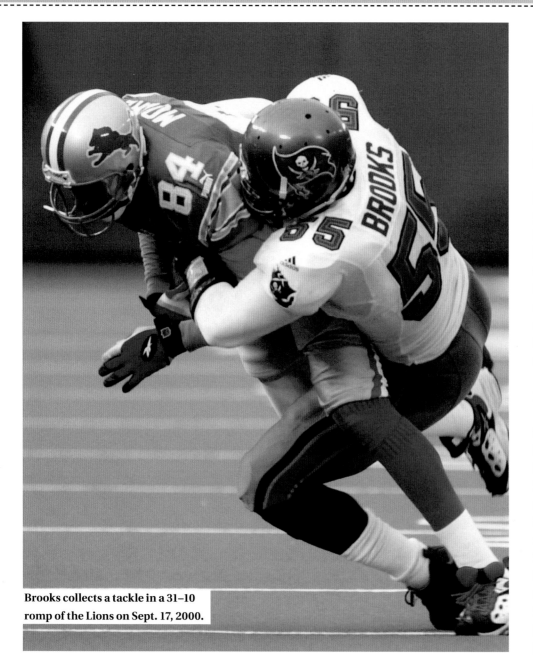

Brooks collects a tackle in a 31–10 romp of the Lions on Sept. 17, 2000.

Derrick Brooks

Derrick Brooks has to be a special player, otherwise he wouldn't have been asked to give one of his helmets to Peyton Manning, the Colts stud quarterback. Manning has a personal trophy case at home that now boasts Brooks' Tampa Bay Bucs helmet. In return, Brooks has one of Manning's helmets on display at his home.

"But I see his helmet doesn't have as many marks as mine," Brooks observed.

Thirteen years of banging heads with offensive linemen, receivers and running backs have left their mark on Brooks, who in return has done a far better job leaving his on the game. He has made more than 1,600 tackles for the Bucs. He is the prototype for the weakside linebacker who has to chase ball carriers and follow the play and, for his efforts, Brooks has been named to the Pro Bowl 10 times. Six other linebackers have gone to the Pro Bowl nine or more times, four are in the Hall of Fame — Mike Singletary, Jack Lambert, Lawrence Taylor and Henry Carson. The remaining two linebackers are Junior Seau and Derrick Thomas: Seau is still playing, and Thomas was tragically killed in a car crash in 2000.

Brooks' game is based on basic principles: "I never get satisfied. I stay humble. I stay hungry … trying to set the standard at this position every single year. There's always something I can do better."

He was close to perfection in 2002 when he was named the league's top defensive player. He returned four interceptions for touchdowns that season, a record for NFL linebackers, and added a touchdown on a fumble return. In Super Bowl XXXVII in 2003, he picked off an Oakland pass and ran it back 44 yards for the touchdown that sealed the deal. Just as amazing is the fact Brooks has never missed a game in his NFL career.

Rodney Harrison

Harrison has everything it takes to make the grade in Canton, but he may not get there. At strong safety Harrison is a two-time NFL record-setter. In 1997, he became the first player to return an interception, a fumble and a kickoff for a touchdown. For his career, he is the only player to have recorded 30 sacks and 30 interceptions. His postseason performances have also included four interceptions in four consecutive games, and there isn't a defensive back who hits harder than Harrison, which brings us to why he might not get enough Hall of Fame votes.

Twice (2004, 2006), *Sports Illustrated* polled NFL players and named Harrison as the league's dirtiest player. He has been fined more than $200,000 in his career and suspended for a helmet-to-helmet on legendary pass catcher Jerry Rice. Harrison drew a four-game suspension in 2007 for admitting he used a banned substance. He denied it was steroids but admitted it was a banned substance to "accelerate the healing process" from his knee and shoulder injuries of the previous two seasons.

How the voters view Harrison — great player or dirty player — will determine his post-football fate.

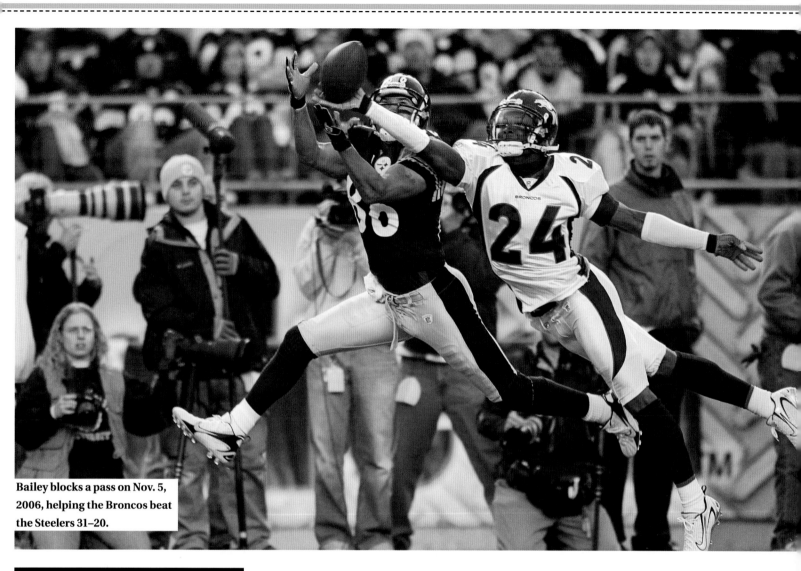

Bailey blocks a pass on Nov. 5, 2006, helping the Broncos beat the Steelers 31–20.

OTHER NOTABLE DEFENSIVE CANDIDATES

- **Dwight Freeney** defensive end, Indianapolis Colts
- **Ray Lewis** middle linebacker, Baltimore Ravens
- **John Lynch** safety, Denver Broncos
- **Julius Peppers** defensive end, Carolina Panthers
- **Junior Seau** linebacker, New England Patriots
- **Richard Seymour** defensive end, New England Patriots

Champ Bailey

Our last defensive candidate is a man whose first name takes a little living-up-to. Champ Bailey does just that. He's an eight-time Pro Bowler for the Denver Broncos at cornerback, where, if you make even the tiniest mistake, somebody scores and it's like getting your pants pulled down in front of 70,000 people.

Bailey was drafted by the Washington Redskins and learned his position from two of the masters, Deion Sanders and Darrell Green. The Broncos wanted to shore up their defense so badly they traded away running back Clinton Portis, who had amassed 7,715 yard rushing in just six seasons and who might be a Hall of Famer himself if he stays healthy.

In 2006, Bailey had the distinction of playing an entire season without being beaten for a touchdown. He picked off 10 passes and was a rock-steady tackler against the run. And with a name like Champ, you know he's got to be good.

Of course, Bailey and his NFL contemporaries are too busy worrying about winning a Super Bowl to think much about the Hall of Fame. But rest assured, when they leave the game they love, they'll want to be remembered as someone who made a difference, someone special.

For all players, the public realization of that moment is something to relish forever, and if, like Art Monk, they have to wait — they'll feel every bit as amazed as he did when Canton finally calls. ▮

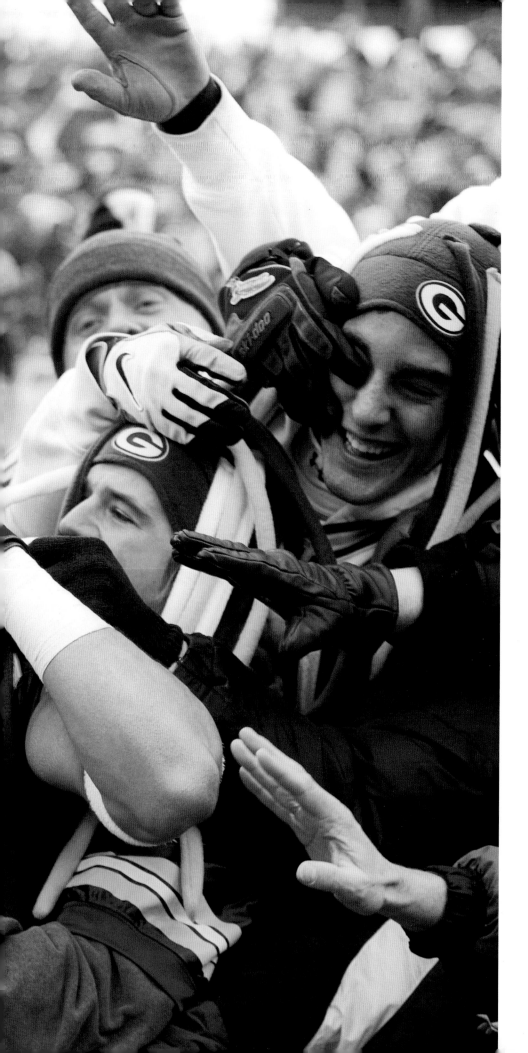

THE FRANCHISES

AFC EAST
Buffalo Bills
Miami Dolphins
New England Patriots
New York Jets

AFC NORTH
Baltimore Ravens
Cincinnati Bengals
Cleveland Browns
Pittsburgh Steelers

AFC SOUTH
Houston Texans
Indianapolis Colts
Jacksonville Jaguars
Tennessee Titans

AFC WEST
Denver Broncos
Kansas City Chiefs
Oakland Raiders
San Diego Chargers

NFC EAST
Dallas Cowboys
New York Giants
Philadelphia Eagles
Washington Redskins

NFC NORTH
Chicago Bears
Detroit Lions
Green Bay Packers
Minnesota Vikings

NFC SOUTH
Atlanta Falcons
Carolina Panthers
New Orleans Saints
Tampa Bay Buccaneers

NFC WEST
Arizona Cardinals
San Francisco 49ers
Seattle Seahawks
St. Louis Rams

BUFFALO
BILLS

Bruce Smith

TEAM ORIGINS: The origin of professional football in the city of Buffalo, New York, starts in the All American Football Conference (AAFC) in the 1940s. The Buffalo organization was known as the Buffalo Bisons. However, in 1947, there was a contest to rename the team. The winning name was "the Bills" in honor of western frontiersman, Buffalo Bill Cody. When the Bills joined the AFL in 1960, the same name was adopted and continues to this day. On Sept. 11, 1960, led by coach Buster Ramsey, the Buffalo Bills played their first game against the New York Titans, and lost 27–3. The first win in modern Buffalo Bills' history came against the Boston Patriots on Sept. 23, 1960, winning 13–0.

THE GLORY YEARS: The Buffalo Bills found success in the AFL in the mid 1960s. In 1964, under the guidance of coach Lou Saban and led by quarterback Jack Kemp, the Buffalo Bills won their first AFL Championship, defeating the San Diego Chargers 20–7 in front of a sold-out crowd at War Memorial Stadium in Buffalo. The next year, they repeated their success by defeating the San Diego Chargers 23–0, again in the AFL Championship game. The next year Lou Saban would leave the Bills to take a job at the University of Maryland.

Led by Hall of Fame coach Marv Levy and quarterback Jim Kelly, the Bills would find success and bring glory back to the Buffalo football scene in the early 1990s. Using the no-huddle offense, and led by power back Thurman Thomas, the Buffalo Bills would win the AFC championship four times in the 1990s (1990–1993). However, their success will always be tainted by their four consecutive Super Bowl losses, the only team in NFL history to do so.

CURRENT STATE OF THE FRANCHISE: The Buffalo Bills have been marred by inconsistency and disappointment. They have not made the playoffs since 1999 and have been through a carousel of coaches and general managers. The current quarterback situation is up in the air, with rookie Trent Edwards and former first-round pick J.P. Losman battling for the job throughout the 2007 season. The Bills did strike it rich in the 2007 draft by selecting Marshawn Lynch as the 12th overall pick. In his rookie season, he rushed for 1,115 yards and 7 touchdowns, second-most for all rookies in 2007. There is no doubt that he will become the face of the Bills' franchise for years to come.

DRAFT IMPACT
Jim Kelly (quarterback)
- drafted 14th overall from the University of Miami in 1983
- owns every major Buffalo Bills' passing record
- elected into the Pro Football Hall of Fame in 2002

Bruce Smith (defensive end)
- drafted first overall from Virginia Tech University in 1985
- current holder of the NFL career sack record
- defensive MVP in 1990

DRAFT FALLOUT
Ronnie Harmon (running back)
- drafted 16th overall from the University of Iowa in 1986
- career rushing high of 485 yards in 1987
- accused of "throwing" the Rose Bowl after he fumbled on the goal line

Tom Cousineau (linebacker)
- drafted first overall from Ohio State in 1979
- never played a game for the Bills; instead played for the Montreal Alouettes of the CFL for double the money the Bills had offered him

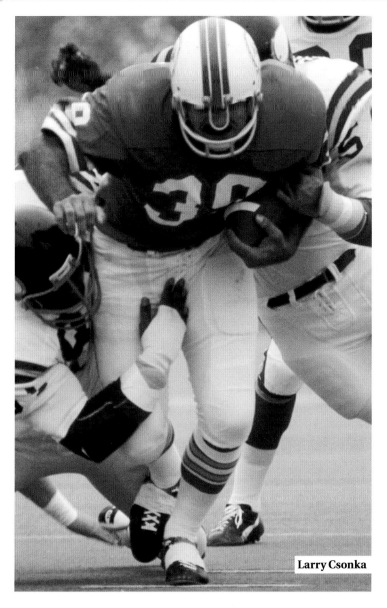

Larry Csonka

MIAMI DOLPIIINS

TEAM ORIGINS: In August of 1965, the AFL awarded its first expansion franchise to lawyer Joseph Robbie and actor Danny Thomas for 7.5 million dollars. The nickname "Dolphins" was chosen by a local media screening committee.

The Dolphins began their first season in the AFL under head coach George Wilson, who had coached the Detroit Lions to an AFL Championship in 1957. On Sept. 2, 1966, the Miami Dolphins played their first game in the Orange Bowl where they hosted the Oakland Raiders. Although the Dolphins got off to a quick start by returning a touchdown 95 yards on the opening kickoff, they eventually lost the game 23–14. The Dolphins finished the season 3–13, their first of four consecutive losing seasons. After the 1969 season Don Shula replaced Wilson as coach.

THE GLORY YEARS: Don Shula's hiring as head coach and vice president of football operations paid immediate dividends for the team. In his first year at the helm, the Dolphins recorded their first winning season, going 10–4 and making the playoffs for the first time. Although they would lose their first playoff game (21–14) against the Oakland Raiders, the success of the 1970 season helped build the momentum for a successful franchise through the 1970s and 1980s.

In 1972, that momentum peaked when the Miami Dolphins were undefeated through the regular season and went on to win the Super Bowl. They are the only team in NFL history to post a perfect season and win the Super Bowl. The next year, under the leadership of Bob Griese and the rugged play of running back Larry Csonka, the team won Super Bowl VIII 24–7 over the Minnesota Vikings. Csonka was named the Super Bowl MVP, rushing for 145 yards and two touchdowns.

In 1984, Dan Marino led the Dolphins back to the Super Bowl, but lost to the San Francisco 49ers. Marino was the face of the franchise through the 1980s and 1990s and led the Dolphins to multiple playoff appearances, shattering NFL records along the way.

CURRENT STATE OF THE FRANCHISE: In 2007, the Miami Dolphins had one of their worst seasons in franchise history, finishing 1–15. However, they have a plethora of young talent in the mix, including last year's first-round pick, explosive wide receiver Ted Ginn Jr. As well, they have the productive power back Ronnie Brown, who was limited in 2007 with an injury. The Dolphins now need to finally find a replacement for Dan Marino.

DRAFT IMPACT

Bob Griese (quarterback)
- drafted fourth overall from Purdue in 1967
- named to eight Pro Bowls
- named All-Pro five times throughout his career

Larry Csonka (running back)
- drafted with the 8th overall pick from Syracuse University in 1968
- Super Bowl MVP and Hall of Famer
- helped lead the Dolphins to their perfect season in 1972

DRAFT FALLOUT

David Overstreet (running back)
- drafted 11th overall from the University of Oklahoma in 1981
- signed with the Montreal Alouettes of the CFL after a contract dispute
- died in an automobile accident in 1984

Yatil Green (wide receiver)
- drafted 15th overall from the University of Miami in 1997
- tore his ACL in '97 and '98, both times before the regular season began
- collected 18 catches, for 234 yards and no touchdowns with Miami

NEW ENGLAND PATRIOTS

TEAM ORIGINS: The New England Patriots were established in 1960, when public relations executive William "Billy" Sullivan Jr. was awarded the eighth and final franchise in the inaugural season of the American Football League. Lou Saban was hired as the Boston Patriots first head coach and on Sept. 9, 1960, coach Saban led his team against the Denver Broncos in their first regular home game, where they were defeated 13–10. After playing at four different sites during the 1960s, the Patriots decided to settle in Foxborough, Massachusetts, in 1970. In 1971, the team was renamed the New England Patriots to honor all of the New England states.

THE GLORY YEARS: In 1996, the New England Patriots made their second Super Bowl appearance, led by former number one overall pick Drew Bledsoe. They would go on to lose to Brett Favre and the Green Bay Packers 35–21.

In 2001, an improbable run by then back-up quarterback Tom Brady propelled the New England Patriots into the Super Bowl again, where this time they upset the heavily favored St. Louis Rams, 20–17 on a last second, 48-yard field goal by Adam Vinatieri. This was the first of three Super Bowl victories in the next four years for the New England Patriots. In Super Bowl XXXVIII they defeated the Carolina Panthers 32–29, and followed that victory up the next year by defeating the Philadelphia Eagles 24–21 in Super Bowl XXXIX. Along the way, Tom Brady collected two Super Bowl MVP awards (Super Bowl XXXVIII and Super Bowl XXXVI).

CURRENT STATE OF THE FRANCHISE: The New England Patriots have continued their run of success. After ending the 2006 season with a loss to the Indianapolis Colts in the AFC Championship game, the Patriots reloaded in the offseason, adding Pro Bowl wide receiver Randy Moss, Pro Bowl linebacker Adelius Thomas and standout slot receiver Wes Welker. Loaded with talent, the New England Patriots went undefeated in the 2007 regular season, becoming only the second team in NFL history to do so (the 1972 Miami Dolphins being the first).

Although the season was magical, it was also a disappointment, as the Patriots were upset in Super Bowl XLII by the New York Giants 17–14. As well, questionable strategic practices (video taping opposing team's signals), have hurt the Patriots image and, more precisely, the image of their head coach, Bill Belichick. As penalty, the Patriots forfeited their first pick in the 2008 draft.

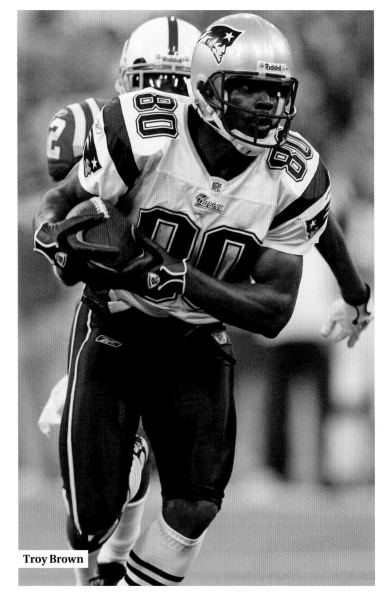

Troy Brown

DRAFT IMPACT

Troy Brown (wide receiver)
• drafted 198th overall from Marshall University in 1993
• Named to the Pro Bowl in 2001
• holds the Patriots' record for receptions

Willie McGinest (outside linebacker)
• drafted 4th overall from USC in 1994
• anchored the defense for three Super Bowl wins
• currently third on the New England sack list

DRAFT FALLOUT

Robert Edwards (running back)
• drafted 18th overall from the University of Georgia in 1998
• ran for 1,105 yards and 9 touchdowns in his rookie season
• career ended abruptly in 1999 after a flag football injury

Hart Lee Dykes (wide receiver)
• drafted 16th overall from Oklahoma State in 1989
• in 26 games he collected 83 receptions for 1344 yards
• fractured his eye in a bar fight ending his career

NEW YORK
JETS

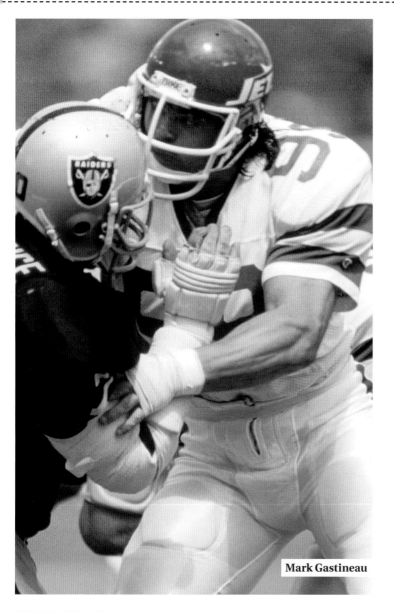

Mark Gastineau

TEAM ORIGINS: In 1959, Lamar Hunt established the American Football League (AFL) to rival the NFL. The New York Titans were one of the eight charter franchises. In 1963, after several years of financial turmoil, five New York businessmen bought the New York Titans for one million dollars and renamed the team the New York Jets.

THE GLORY YEARS: The early sixties were a mediocre decade for the Jets, but in 1966 the team drafted the most recognizable face the franchise has ever seen: Joe Namath. He was drafted in the first round, first overall, out of the University of Alabama. "Broadway Joe" was known for his charisma and playboy personality. The next year, in 1967, the Jets had a solid winning season, going 8–5–1, with Namath becoming the only player in NFL history to throw for over 4,000 yards in a season. In 1968, the Jets' success continued, finishing with an 11–3 record in the regular season and beating their AFL rivals the Oakland Raiders 27–23 in the AFL Championship game.

The Jets' victory over the Oakland Raiders in the AFL Championship game set up a matchup for the newly named "Super Bowl" — the final game of the year between the AFL champion and the NFL champion. Although the Jets were heavy underdogs going into the game, Joe Namath had guaranteed a victory over the Baltimore Colts. True to his word, Namath delivered a win for the Jets and was also named Super Bowl MVP. It was one of the greatest upsets in professional football history.

The New York Jets had some success in the late 1990s under the guidance of head coach Bill Parcells. Parcells, along with veteran quarterback Vinny Testaverde and All-Pro wide receiver Keyshawn Johnson, led the Jets to the 1999 AFC Championship game, but lost to eventual Super Bowl champs, John Elway and the Denver Broncos.

CURRENT STATE OF THE FRANCHISE: The New York Jets followed up a successful 2006 with a dismal 2007 season, going 4–12. Quarterback Chad Pennington seems to have thrown his last passes as a Jet, thus leaving the quarterback position void of a true starter, although second-year Kellen Clemens shows some signs of promise. If the Jets lack anything, it is the presence of a true star or a franchise player, something they have always had. In the late 1990s and early 2000s, it was Curtis Martin and Keyshawn Johnson. The defense is still solid, led by veteran Sean Ellis and last year's first round pick, cornerback Derrelle Revis.

DRAFT IMPACT

Joe Namath (quarterback)
- drafted first overall from the University of Alabama in 1966
- led the Jets to a win in Super Bowl III
- elected to the Pro Football Hall of Fame in 1985

Mark Gastineau (defensive end)
- drafted 41st overall from Arizona State in 1979
- held the single season sack record with 22 sacks until 2005
- five-time Pro Bowler and five-time All-Pro

DRAFT FALLOUT

John Wesley "Lam" Jones (wide receiver)
- drafted second overall from the University of Texas in 1980
- won a gold medal in track and field at the 1976 Olympics
- never caught more than 734 yards in a season

Blair Thomas (running back)
- drafted second overall from Penn State in 1990
- highest season total was only 728 yards rushing
- first in a long line of Penn State backs who never cut it in the NFL

BALTIMORE
RAVENS

TEAM ORIGINS: The Baltimore Colts left for Indianapolis in 1984. In 1996 Art Modell moved the Cleveland Browns to Baltimore. It was one of the most controversial moves in the history of professional sport, which still leaves a bitter taste in the mouths of Cleveland's sports fans.

The team was named in honour of Baltimore native Edgar Allen Poe's poem "The Raven." On Feb. 15, 1996, former Baltimore Colts head coach Ted Marchibroda was hired to coach the Ravens. His signing was 20 years and 1 day removed from when he was originally first named a head coach in Baltimore. The Baltimore Ravens took the field for the first time in front of 64,124 fans on Sept. 1, 1996, and defeated the Oakland Raiders 19–14.

THE GLORY YEARS: Although the history of the Baltimore Ravens has been brief, they have had success in the NFL since their inception in 1996. The Ravens were mediocre until 2000, when their dominating defense, led by future Hall of Famer Ray Lewis, exploded onto the scene. In 2000, they made an improbable run to the playoffs.

The simple formula of solid defense and a powerful running game proved to be successful for the Ravens as their playoff run turned into a shot at the Vince Lombardi trophy. In Super Bowl XXXV, the Ravens stuck to their formula, holding the New York Giants to seven points while Jamal Lewis ran for 102 yards and one touchdown; the Ravens won the game 34–7. Ray Lewis, the heart of the defense and the team's spiritual leader, was named the Super Bowl MVP. The Ravens' Super Bowl victory was followed with two division championships and four playoff appearances in the early 2000s.

CURRENT STATE OF THE FRANCHISE: After winning their division in 2006, but losing in the first round of the playoffs, the Baltimore Ravens took a turn south in the standings in 2007, going 5–11, last in NFC North. Injuries and age looked to be the catalyst for the drop in form; however, the disappointing season also cost head coach Brian Billick his job. Ray Lewis and Chris McAllister, the cornerstones of the Ravens' defense in the earlier part of the decade, have lost a step, and as the team continues to shift its image, younger players such as running back Willis McGhahee and defensive tackle Haloti Ngata are taking charge. These young, budding stars are the foundation for the Raven's future.

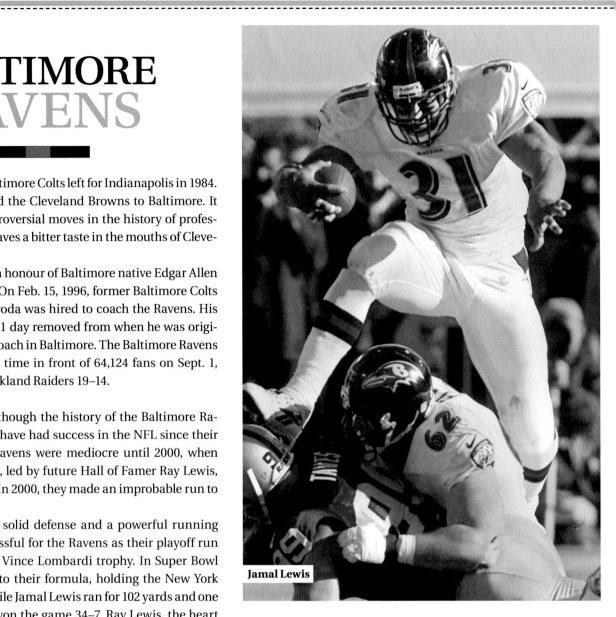

Jamal Lewis

DRAFT IMPACT

Jonathan Ogden (offensive tackle)
- drafted fourth overall from UCLA in 1996
- known for plowing the way for numerous 1,000-yard rushers
- an 11-time Pro Bowl selection
- a nine-time All-Pro selection

Jamal Lewis (running back)
- drafted fifth overall from the University of Tennessee in 2000
- helped pave the way to a Super Bowl championship in 2000
- third player in NFL history to rush for over 2,000 yards in a season
- is sixth in among active running backs in career yards with 9,105

DRAFT FALLOUT

Kyle Boller (quarterback)
- drafted 19th overall from the University of California in 2003
- has played only one entire 16-game season: 2004
- has only started 42 games in 5 seasons
- career marred by injuries and inconsistency

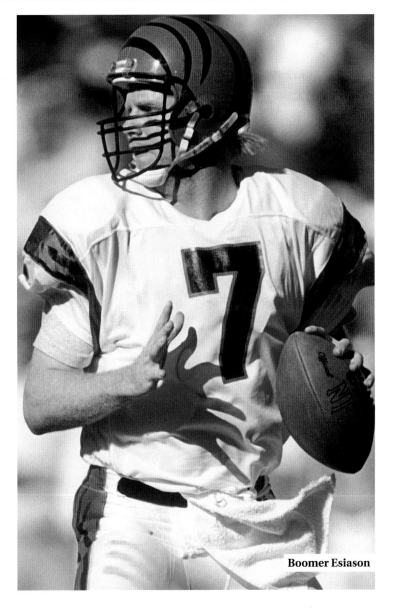

Boomer Esiason

DRAFT IMPACT

Ken Anderson (quarterback)
- drafted 67th overall from the University Augustana (Illinois) in 1971
- won the NFL MVP in 1981
- led the team to its first Super Bowl appearance in team history in 1982

Boomer Esiason (quarterback)
- drafted 38th overall from the University of Maryland in 1984
- led the Bengals to their second Super Bowl appearance in the 1980s
- 1988 NFL MVP

DRAFT FALLOUT

Ki-Jana Carter (running back)
- drafted first overall from Penn State in 1995
- touted to bring the team back to respectability
- tore his knee in his first preseason game and never fully recovered

Akili Smith (quarterback)
- drafted third overall from the University of Oregon in 1999
- lack of experience led to no more than three touchdowns in a season
- cut from the team after the 2002 season

CINCINNATI BENGALS

TEAM ORIGINS: Legendary coach Paul Brown, who led the Cleveland Browns to seven conference championships and three NFL championships, decided that in 1962, it was time to move on. Fresh from a five-year hiatus, the coach, in partnership with a group of investors, was awarded an expansion team for the city of Cincinnati in 1967. Brown decided to name his new team the "Bengals" in honor of Cincinnati's old professional AFL team in the late 1930s, and on Sept. 15, 1968, Brown led his Bengals onto the field where they beat the Denver Broncos 24–10, in front of 25,000 fans. The next week, they followed up that win with another, this time over the Buffalo Bills. But after winning their first two regular season games, a rare feat for an expansion team, they won only one more game in 1968, finishing the season 3–11.

THE GLORY YEARS: The Cincinnati Bengals won two division championships in the 1970s, but didn't reach the pinnacle of professional football, the Super Bowl, until 1982, where they were defeated by the San Francisco 49ers, 26–21. Seven years later, the Bengals would chart an almost identical path to Super Bowl XXIII, defeating the Buffalo Bills in the AFC Championship (as they did in '82), only to again be defeated, this time in heart-breaking fashion, by the 49ers. The Bengals, who were leading Super Bowl XXIII with 3:20 left in the game, were left to watch as Niners' quarterback Joe Montana marched his team 92-yards down the field and capped off an 11-play drive with a touchdown pass to John Taylor. It is one of two plays in NFL lore known simply as "The Drive."

CURRENT STATE OF THE FRANCHISE: After winning their division in 2005 under the leadership of Carson Palmer, the Bengals have since had struggles on and off the field. On the field they have underperformed, especially on defense, finishing near the bottom of the AFC in nearly every defensive category. Off the field, the Bengals have run into problems, specifically with talented wide receiver Chris Henry, who was arrested four times over a 14-month span. Henry was suspended for the first eight games of the 2007 season. Unfortunately, these struggles have blinded most from the talented group of individuals on the offensive side of the ball. It starts with the Bengals' quarterback Carson Palmer who, after recovering from knee surgery in 2005, is starting to look like the Pro Bowler they envisioned when they drafted him first overall. Complementing him is the talented and always entertaining wide receiver Chad Johnson and workhorse running back Rudi Johnson.

CLEVELAND
BROWNS

TEAM ORIGINS: In 1946, a rival football league known as the All America Football Conference (AAFC) was formed. The Cleveland Browns was one of seven teams to compete in the AAFC. After the league folded in 1950, the Browns joined the NFL. Under the guidance of head coach Paul Brown, they made their NFL debut on Sept. 16, 1950, with a dominant 35–10 victory over the Philadelphia Eagles. To everyone's surprise, the Browns ended up finishing their first season in the league by winning the NFL championship, defeating the Los Angeles Rams 30–28 on Christmas Eve, 1950.

THE GLORY YEARS: The Cleveland Browns won a total of four NFL championships between the years 1950 and 1964, and in the mid fifties, the Browns won back-to-back titles. In 1954, they lost two of their first three games, but rallied to win eight straight, finishing the season with a 9–3 record. On Dec. 26, 1954, the Browns routed the Detroit Lions 56–10 to win their second championship of the decade. In 1955, Paul Brown led his team to a 9–2–1 regular season record, and quarterback Otto Graham had one of his best statistical years, throwing for 15 touchdowns and only 8 interceptions. The Browns dominated the St. Louis Rams in the '55 Championship, winning 38–14. It would also be Otto Graham's last game as a professional. In 1964, running back Jim Brown had one of his best seasons ever, rushing for over 1,400 yards and leading the Browns to a 10–3–1 record. On December 27, 1965, Jim Brown led the Browns to their fourth championship, by shutting out the Baltimore Colts 27–0.

CURRENT STATE OF THE FRANCHISE: After going 4–12 in the 2006 season, the Browns bounced back in 2007, finishing just outside the playoffs with a much-improved 10–6 record. After years of not being able to find a quarterback, the Browns found themselves in 2007 with two potential All-Pros in Derek Anderson and their first-round pick, Brady Quinn. Anderson emerged as a bonified number-one pivot by throwing for 3,787 yards and 29 touchdowns. Most of his passes went to his two Pro Bowl receivers, wide receiver Braylon Edwards and tight end Kellen Winslow Jr., who each caught for over 1,000 yards. Jamal Lewis resurrected his career by rushing for 1,304 yards and nine touchdowns. With a young nucleus on offense and a solid defense-minded coach in Romeo Crennel, the Browns seem to have all the makings of a contender.

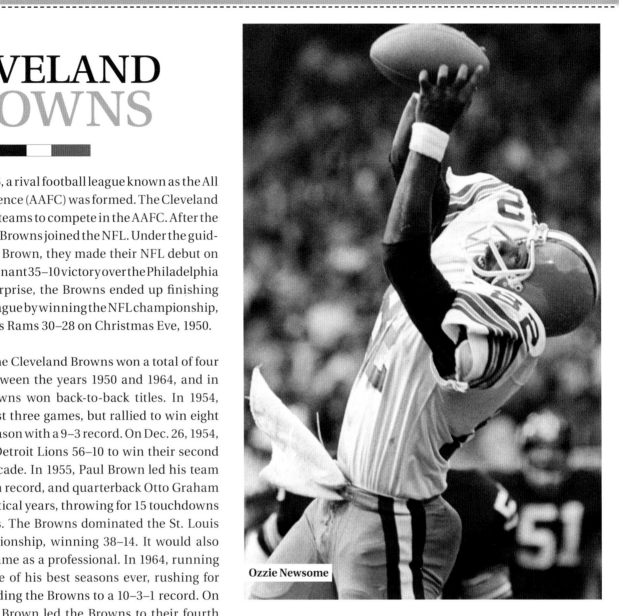

Ozzie Newsome

DRAFT IMPACT

Ozzie Newsome (tight end)
- drafted 23rd overall from the University of Alabama in 1978
- played 13 seasons with the Browns
- named a three-time Pro Bowler and seven-time All-Pro

Doug Atkins (defensive end)
- drafted 11th overall from the University of Tennessee in 1953
- named an eight-time Pro Bowler and 10-time All-Pro
- inducted into the Hall of Fame in 1982

DRAFT FALLOUT

"Touchdown" Tommy Vardell (fullback)
- drafted ninth overall from Stanford University in 1992
- amassed five touchdowns over four years with the Browns
- scored the only touchdown in the Detroit Lions' 1998 wild-card loss

Steve Holden (wide receiver)
- drafted 16th overall from Arizona State in 1973
- did not start a single game over 54 appearances with the Browns
- cut in the 1976 season

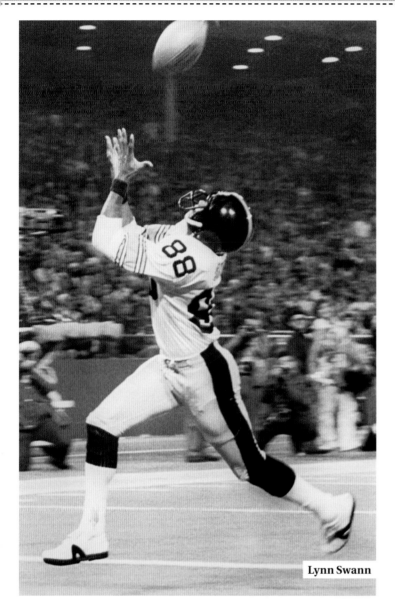

Lynn Swann

PITTSBURGH STEELERS

TEAM ORIGINS: The NFL's fifth oldest franchise was founded on July 8, 1933, by Arthur Joseph Rooney, and originally called the Pirates. In 1940, after seven years of struggling, Rooney decided to rename the team. Hoping a new blue-collar identity would change his team's fortunes, he decided on the "Steelers" in honor of the city's steel industry.

THE GLORY YEARS: It took the team a very long time to become successful, but when success came, it would continue for the next ten years. The NFL's first modern dynasty was born.

Under the leadership of head coach Chuck Noll and quarterback Terry Bradshaw, the Pittsburgh Steelers went on to dominate the NFL in the 1970s and win four Super Bowls. The first Super Bowl victory came in 1975, after going 10–3–1 in the regular season. Franco Harris rumbled for 153 yards and one touchdown, defeating the Minnesota Vikings 16–6. Harris took home the Super Bowl MVP. This would be the first of two Steelers' back-to-back championships. The following year they defeated the Dallas Cowboys in Super Bowl X, 21–17, with Lynn Swann capturing the Super Bowl MVP.

The Steelers were competitive for the duration of the 1970s, but did not make their next Super Bowl appearance until the latter part of the decade when they met rival Dallas in Super Bowl XIII in 1979. Terry Bradshaw put on a legendary performance, throwing for 318 yards and four touchdowns, en route to a 35–31 victory over the Cowboys. The next season, Bradshaw's encore was equally impressive, passing for over 300 yards and two touchdowns in a 31–19 romp over the St. Louis Rams. Bradshaw was named Super Bowl MVP for both games.

CURRENT STATE OF THE FRANCHISE: In 2006, the Pittsburgh Steelers recaptured some of their former glory by winning Super Bowl XL, 21–10 over the Seattle Seahawks. With the exception of head coach Bill Cowher, the foundation from that Super Bowl team is still intact today. Quarterback Ben Roethlisberger and running back Willie Parker are the foundation of the offense. Speed burner Santonio Holmes is the team's deep threat and the consistent and productive Heath Miller rounds out the exciting Pittsburgh offense. The defense is led by Pro-Bowl safety Troy Polamula. He is accompanied by veterans Casey Hampton, at defensive tackle, and James Farrior, at linebacker. After being eliminated in the first round of the playoffs in the 2007 season, look for the Steeler veterans to lead the resurgence.

DRAFT IMPACT

Franco Harris (running back)
- drafted 13th overall from Penn State in 1972
- a Super Bowl MVP and eight-time Pro-Bowl selection
- elected to the Hall of Fame in 1990

Lynn Swann (wide receiver)
- drafted 21st overall from USC in 1974
- played in three Pro Bowls and was named MVP in Super Bowl X
- elected to the Hall of Fame in 2001

DRAFT FALLOUT

Tim Worley (running back)
- drafted seventh overall from the University of Georgia in 1989
- posted a career best 770 yards and five touchdowns in his rookie year
- played four seasons for the Steelers; traded to the Bears in 1993

Troy Edwards (wide receiver)
- drafted 13th overall from Louisiana Tech in 1999
- caught a career best 714 yards with five touchdowns as a rookie
- played arena football in 2007 with the Grand Rapids Rampage

HOUSTON
TEXANS

TEAM ORIGINS: After the Houston Oilers left for Tennessee in 1997, the city of Houston was craving a team to fill their professional football needs. On Oct. 6, 1999, the NFL owners unanimously approved Bob McNair's application for an expansion franchise in Houston. The team began play in 2002.

On Jan. 21, 2001, Dom Capers was hired as the first head coach of the Houston Texans. That February, the expansion draft took place and Capers began to build a franchise. Some notable names that were taken in the expansion draft: former first-round pick, offensive tackle Tony Boselli; Super Bowl champion linebacker Jamie Sharper; and former Heisman Trophy winning quarterback Danny Wuerffel.

Houston had the first overall pick in the 2002 entry draft and took quarterback David Carr from Fresno State University. On Sept. 8, 2002, the Texans were ready to take the field and start their journey to NFL greatness against their state rivals, the Dallas Cowboys. In front of 69,604 fans, the Texans defeated the Cowboys 19–10. David Carr led the attack, throwing for two touchdowns, one to tight end Billy Miller for the first touchdown in the Texans' history.

THE GLORY YEARS: The Texans have yet to make the playoffs in their five-year existence in the NFL, but they have made steady progress. In 2007 they had one of their more successful seasons, going 8–8; most of that without star wide receiver Andre Johnson. Had he been healthy, it's a very good possibility that they would have made the playoffs for the first time.

CURRENT STATE OF THE FRANCHISE: The Texans in 2007 were a team that was riddled by injuries to key players. The worst of these injuries was a sprained knee to All-Pro wide receiver Andre Johnson. After going down in week two, the receiver did not return until week 11, but still collected 847 yards receiving and eight touchdowns. Johnson and quarterback Matt Schaub are the foundation of the Texans' offense. Provided Johnson can stay healthy, the two will be a deadly combination for years to come. The Houston defense is finally starting to take shape after years of mediocrity. Led by the 2006 Defensive Rookie of the Year, DeMeco Ryans, and the number-one pick in the 2006 draft, defensive end Mario Williams, the defense is becoming a dominant force in the AFC. The future looks bright for the Texans.

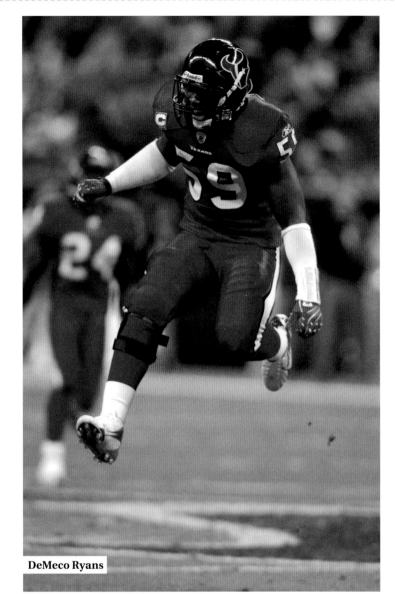

DeMeco Ryans

DRAFT IMPACT
Andre Johnson (wide receiver)
- drafted third overall from the University of Miami in 2003
- nominated to his second Pro Bowl and named All-Pro in 2006
- caught career highs in receptions (103) and yards (1,147) in 2006

DeMeco Ryans (linebacker)
- drafted in the second round from the University of Alabama in 2006
- named Defensive Rookie of the Year in 2006
- named to the Pro Bowl in only his second season

DRAFT FALLOUT
Tony Boselli (offensive tackle)
- first player taken in the expansion draft in 2002
- chosen to protect most-sacked-in-one-season quarterback David Carr
- never played a game with the team due to lingering injuries

David Carr (quarterback)
- drafted first overall from Fresno State University in 2002
- sacked an NFL record 76 times in a single season (2002)
- cut from the team in 2007, replaced by quarterback Matt Schaub

Marvin Harrison

INDIANAPOLIS COLTS

TEAM ORIGINS: After playing in Baltimore for almost 40 years, the Colts moved to Indianapolis in 1984. Although the fans in Baltimore were outraged, the Indianapolis fans welcomed the Colts with open arms.

THE GLORY YEARS: After drafting Peyton Manning first overall, out of the University of Tennessee in 1998, the Colts built a solid franchise around their new quarterback. Under Manning, they have won six division championships and have been to the playoffs eight times. In 2003, after finishing the season 12–4, the Colts blew out the Denver Broncos in their wild-card match-up, 41–10. Manning, the 2003 NFL MVP, threw for five touchdowns. Carrying the momentum from their first-ever home playoff win in Indianapolis, the Colts took to the road to face the Kansas City Chiefs. Manning was cool under pressure throwing for over 300 yards and three touchdowns as the Colts defeated the Chiefs 38–31. The following week, in the AFC Championship game, they faced their playoff nemesis, the New England Patriots, and were defeated 24–14.

In 2006, the Colts claimed their ninth regular-season division title, going 12–4. After steamrolling through the early rounds of the playoffs, the Colts once again met the New England Patriots in the AFC Championship game. Trailing 34–31 late in the fourth quarter, Manning hooked up with Reggie Wayne for two big plays to get into Patriots' territory. Running back Joseph Addai rushed up the middle for the score, sealing the 38–34 victory and sent the Indianapolis Colts to their first Super Bowl.

In Super Bowl XLI, Manning led the Colts to a 29–17 victory over the Chicago Bears and was named the game's MVP.

CURRENT STATE OF THE FRANCHISE: The Colts had a successful regular season in 2007 by all standards, finishing first in their division with a 13–3 record and capturing their tenth division crown. Despite this achievement, Indianapolis made an early exit in the divisional playoffs courtesy of the San Diego Chargers. Many around the Colts' camp felt the season was a disappointment, but the core group is still together and performing at a high level. All-Pro wide receivers Reggie Wayne and Marvin Harrison complement Manning, as well as emerging star running back Joseph Addai. The defense, led by 2007 NFL Defensive Player of the Year, safety Bob Sanders, is a solid group that will keep the Colts in games for years to come. Look for the Colts to reload and make another run to the Super Bowl.

DRAFT IMPACT

Peyton Manning (quarterback)
- drafted over Ryan Leaf with the first overall pick in 1998
- named to eight Pro Bowls and named All-Pro six times
- two-time NFL MVP (2003, 2004); 2007 Super Bowl MVP

Marvin Harrison (wide receiver)
- drafted 19th from the University of Syracuse in 1996
- broke the NFL's record for most receptions in a season (144) in 2002
- eight-time Pro Bowler and All-Pro

DRAFT FALLOUT

Steve Emtman (defensive lineman)
- drafted first overall from the University of Washington in 1992
- career year: three sacks, one interception and one touchdown
- played only three seasons with the Colts; is currently out of football

Quentin Coryatt (linebacker)
- drafted second overall from Texas A&M in 1992
- a solid yet undistinguished contributor; retired after only six years
- recorded a career-high 153 tackles and one sack in 1993

JACKSONVILLE
JAGUARS

TEAM ORIGINS: With already two professional football franchises in the state of Florida, Jacksonville was a long shot to get a franchise when it applied for a team in 1991. The NFL defied the critics as it awarded Jacksonville a franchise on Nov. 30, 1993. Tom Coughlin, who was the head coach at Boston College, was hired as the team's first coach. On Sept. 3, 1995, the Jaguars played their first regular season game against the Houston Oilers and were defeated 10–3 in front of 72,623 fans at Jacksonville Municipal Stadium. The Jaguars would finish that first season 4–12, but had the building blocks for a strong future.

THE GLORY YEARS: The Jaguars' rise to success was a quick one. In 1996, in only their second year of existence, they made the playoffs, going 9–7 in the regular season. Quarterback Mark Brunell was starting to develop into a solid NFL pivot and complementing him was wide receiver Keenan McCardell. The 1996 season had helped to propel the Jaguars to the next level, and after two more playoff appearances (1997 and 1998), they had the best year in their short existence. In 1999, going 14–2 in the regular season, it looked like this was going to be the season Brunell and company would not be denied.

The Jaguars were heavy favorites to represent the AFC in the Super Bowl going into the playoffs with a first-round bye. Sure enough, Jacksonville massacred the Miami Dolphins, their state rivals, 62–7 in the divisional round of the playoffs to advance to the AFC Championship. Coming off the big win, the Jaguars seemed primed to beat the Tennessee Titans and move on to the Super Bowl. Although Jacksonville led 14–10 at halftime, the Titans came out in the second half and shut down the Jaguars offense, and captured the AFC Championship with a 33–14 victory.

CURRENT STATE OF THE FRANCHISE: After winning the starting quarterback job in the 2007 training camp, David Garrard embraced the position and led his team to the playoffs for the first time since 2005. Complemented by veteran running back Fred Taylor and explosive back Maurice Jones-Drew, the Jaguars won their wild-card playoff game against the Pittsburgh Steelers, but were defeated by the New England Patriots the following week. With Garrard at the helm and Jones-Drew in the backfield, the Jaguars are a team with a lot of speed on offense. Look for them to continue the momentum, like they did in the mid 1990s, and contend for a Super Bowl in the very near future.

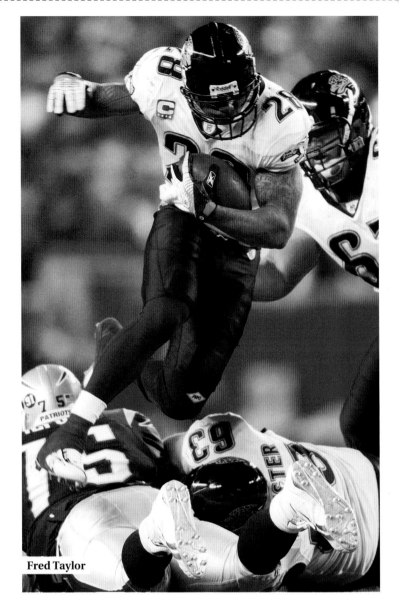

Fred Taylor

DRAFT IMPACT

Fred Taylor (running back)
- drafted ninth overall from the University of Florida in 1998
- one-time Pro Bowler and All-Pro
- rushed for over 1,000 yards seven times in his career with the Jaguars

Tony Boselli (offensive tackle)
- drafted second overall from USC in 1995
- five-time Pro Bowler and four-time All-Pro
- retired after the 2002 season due to injury

DRAFT FALLOUT

R. Jay Soward (receiver)
- drafted 29th overall from USC in 2000
- problems with substance abuse plagued his year-long NFL career
- played three seasons with the Toronto Argonauts of the CFL

Byron Leftwich (quarterback)
- drafted seventh overall from Marshall University in 2003
- released by the Jaguars in 2007; now a backup with the Atlanta Falcons
- never threw more than 15 touchdown passes in a season

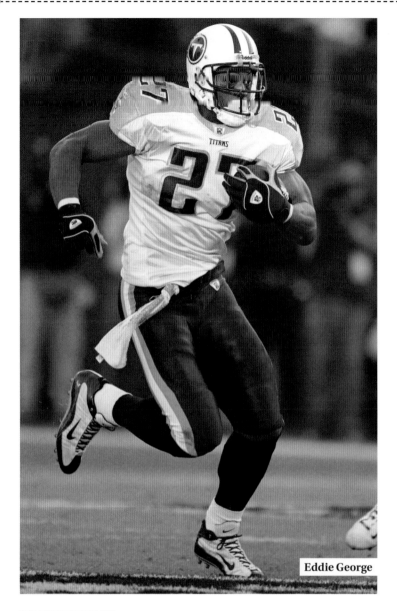

Eddie George

TENNESSEE TITANS

TEAM ORIGINS: After decades in Houston, the Oilers to moved to Tennessee in 1997. The team was to be located in Nashville, but the new stadium would not be ready until 1999. The Tennessee Oilers made their debut on Aug. 31, 1997, at the Liberty Bowl Stadium in Memphis.

Running back Eddie George ran for 216 yards on 35 carries and Al Del Greco kicked a winning field goal in overtime to defeat the Oakland Raiders 24–21. The move to a brand-new stadium in Nashville came with a brand-new name, too. The Oilers' moniker was shed in favor of a name that would allow Nashvillians to lay claim to their team, and so it would be that the team to represent Nashville, "The Athens of the South," would be the Titans.

THE GLORY YEARS: In 1999 the Titans won all of their home games, finishing the regular season 13-3. Eddie George rushed for 1,304 yards and was named to the Pro Bowl and "the Freak," Jevon Kearse, won the NFL's Defensive Rookie of the Year.

In their first playoff game at home in Tennessee, the Titans shocked the Buffalo Bills with a 22–16 last-second victory. Down by one point with 16 seconds left to play, and set to receive the ball from the kick-off, the Titans executed a special-team lateral play that saw Kevin Dyson race down the sidelines for the game winning touchdown. The play, which was surrounded by controversy (Buffalo insisted that the lateral was a forward pass), came to be coined "The Music City Miracle." The next week in the divisional playoff, the Titans upset the Indianapolis Colts, 19–16. In the AFC Championship game, trailing 14–10 at half time, the Titans came back and scored 23 second-half points en route to a 33–14 win.

In Super Bowl XXXIV, the Titans faced the high-powered offense of the St. Louis Rams. Despite a two-touchdown performance by Eddie George, the Titans came up short, literally. In one of the most exciting plays in Super Bowl history, Tennessee quarterback Steve McNair dumped a pass off to Kevin Dyson who was stopped one yard shy of the goal line as time expired.

CURRENT STATE OF THE FRANCHISE: If there is one thing head coach Jeff Fisher knows, it is how to develop a quarterback and build a championship team around him. In 2006, after drafting Vince Young with the third overall pick, Fisher did just that. Vince Young was named NFL Offensive Rookie of the Year in 2006, and the Titans posted a respectable 8–8 record. Fisher and Tennessee have since been rewarded with a return to the playoffs in 2007.

DRAFT IMPACT

Eddie George (running back)
- drafted 14th overall from Ohio State University in 1996
- winner of the Heisman Trophy
- four-time Pro Bowler and three-time All-Pro

Jevon "The Freak" Kearse (defensive end)
- drafted 16th overall from the University of Florida in 1999
- first player to be drafted, developed and star in a Tennessee uniform
- three-time Pro Bowler and one-time All-Pro

DRAFT FALLOUT

Adam "Pacman" Jones (defensive back)
- drafted sixth overall from the University of West Virginia in 2005
- suspended for the entire 2007 season for "off the field conduct"
- named All-Pro in 2006

Andre Woolfolk (defensive back)
- drafted 28th overall from the University of Oklahoma in 2003
- has never had more than one interception in a season
- only played 39 games in four seasons with the Titans

DENVER
BROCOS

TEAM ORIGINS: The Denver Broncos, founded by Earl Howsam and his two sons Lee and Bob, were one of the eight original American Football League (AFL) teams. The Broncos began their inaugural season by winning four of their first six games, but then took a slide, as they went on an eight-game winless streak, finishing their first season 4–9–1; last place in the AFL West.

THE GLORY YEARS: In 1987, the Broncos met the New York Giants in Super Bowl XXI and were soundly defeated 39–20. However, this proved to be a turning point for the franchise, as they were now looked upon as serious contenders in the NFL. The Broncos reached two more Super Bowls in the 1980s: Super Bowl XXII in 1988, where they were demolished 44–10 by the Washington Redskins; and Super Bowl XXIV in 1989 where they were hammered by the San Francisco 49ers, 55–10.

Denver quarterback John Elway was starting to get the reputation of never being able to win the big game. Nine long years later he would answer his critics. After defeating their AFC rivals, the Pittsburgh Steelers 24–21 in the 1998 AFC Championship, Elway would again be on his way to the Super Bowl, this time against defending champs Brett Favre and the Green Bay Packers. John Elway and power back Terrell Davis plowed their way through the Green Bay defense, scoring four rushing touchdowns on their way to a 31–24 win. Terrell Davis scored three of the four touchdowns and was named Super Bowl MVP.

The next year, the Broncos repeated as Super Bowl champions, defeating the Atlanta Falcons 34–19. Elway threw for over 300 yards and a touchdown, and ran for a score as well. Elway was named Super Bowl MVP. It would be his last game.

CURRENT STATE OF THE FRANCHISE: After Elway's retirement, the Broncos have been looking for a quarterback to continue the legacy of success that Elway installed during his 15-year career. The Broncos think they have found that with their 2006 first-round pick Jay Cutler, who has demonstrated his talents with leadership ability and a strong arm. Cutler has a new favorite target he will be passing to for years to come: blooming star receiver Brandon Marshall, who caught 102 receptions and 1,325 yards in 2007. On the defensive side of the ball, All-Pro Champ Bailey leads a young but eager defense. When the younger talent begins to jell, look for an updated version of the "Orange Crush" defense.

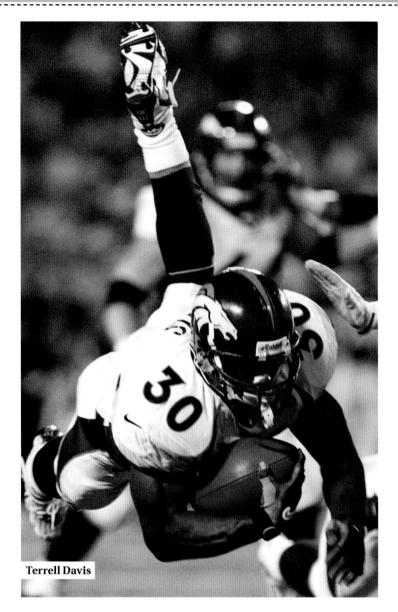

Terrell Davis

DRAFT IMPACT

Terrell Davis (running back)
- drafted 196th overall from the University of Georgia in 1995
- one of only five players to run for over 2,000 yards in a season (1998)
- named the 1998 NFL MVP

Tom Jackson (linebacker)
- drafted 88th overall from Louisville University in 1973
- a key player on the "Orange Crush" defense
- three-time Pro Bowler and four-time All-Pro

DRAFT FALLOUT

Marcus Nash (wide receiver)
- drafted 30th overall from the University of Tennessee in 1998
- played one season for the Broncos and recorded only four catches
- retired from professional football by 2000

Tommy Maddox (quarterback)
- drafted 25th overall from UCLA in 1992
- played only two seasons with the Broncos
- passed for five touchdown and nine interceptions in 1992

KANSAS CITY
CHIEFS

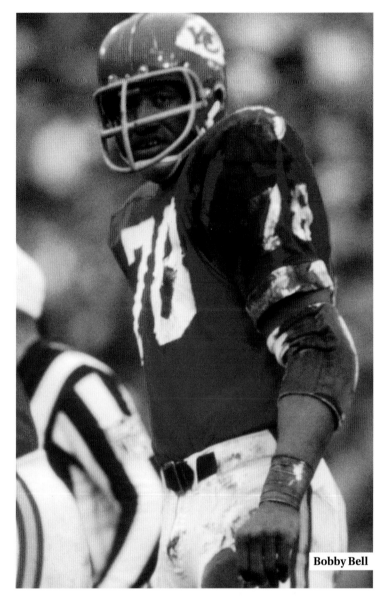

Bobby Bell

TEAM ORIGINS: After three seasons as the Dallas Texans, owner Lamar Hunt (the man who started the AFL) moved his team to Kansas City in 1963. Under the leadership of Hank Stram, the Kansas City Chiefs won their first game over the Denver Broncos, dominating the contest 59–7. However, the Chiefs struggled during the remainder of the season, finishing 5–7–2. As well, the team had to deal with the tragic death of running back Stone Johnson, who fractured his vertebra in a preseason game against the Oakland Raiders, and died ten days later. The Chiefs retired his No. 33 in his honor.

THE GLORY YEARS: Success came early for the Kansas City Chiefs. After only three years in Kansas City, the Chiefs were the first team to ever play in the newly formed game between the NFL champion and the AFL champion — the game that would go on to be called the "Super Bowl." In 1966, Hall of Fame quarterback Len Dawson led the team to an 11–2–1 record. In the first-ever Super Bowl, Dawson threw for 211 yards and one touchdown, but it was not enough. The Green Bay Packers defeated the Chiefs 35–10.

In 1969, after going 11–3 in the regular season and defeating their arch rivals, the Oakland Raiders, in the AFL Championship game, the Kansas City Chiefs got another shot at Super Bowl glory when they faced the Minnesota Vikings in Super Bowl IV. The second time around, Len Dawson would not be denied. Despite being underdogs against the Minnesota defense, the Chiefs scored 16 points in the first half and never looked back, defeating the Vikings 23–7. Dawson completed 17 of 22 passes for 142 yards and one touchdown on his way to Super Bowl MVP honors.

CURRENT STATE OF THE FRANCHISE: After making the playoffs in 2006, the Chiefs hit a snag in 2007, finishing the season 4–12, last place in the AFC West. The Chiefs have some of the major puzzle pieces in place: an All-Pro running back in Larry Johnson; a budding star at wide receiver in last year's first round pick Dwayne Bowe; and a future Hall of Famer in tight end Tony Gonzalez. The Chiefs' main issue is the lack of a bona fide number-one quarterback. Look for them to fill this need through the draft. On the defensive side of the ball, head coach Herm Edwards has a young foundation of players, such as linebacker Derrick Edwards and defensive end Tamba Hali, which could become some of the NFL's finest.

DRAFT IMPACT

Bobby Bell (linebacker/defensive end)
- drafted 56th overall (AFL) from the University of Minnesota in 1963
- drafted 16th overall (NFL) by the Minnesota Vikings in 1963
- inducted into the Hall of Fame in 1983

Derrick Thomas (linebacker)
- drafted fourth overall from the University of Alabama in 1989
- a nine-time Pro Bowler and eight-time All-Pro
- died on Feb. 8, 2000, as a result of injuries from a car accident

DRAFT FALLOUT

Harvey Williams (running back)
- drafted 21st overall out of Louisiana State in 1991
- never started a game and never gained more than 447 yards rushing
- released by the Chiefs in 1994

Todd Blackledge (quarterback)
- drafted seventh overall from Penn State in 1983
- posted 29 touchdowns and 38 interceptions over a seven-year career
- never played a full season in the NFL due to injuries

OAKLAND RAIDERS

TEAM ORIGINS: The Raiders, who were originally supposed to be located in Minnesota, were the AFL's eighth franchise. On Sept. 11, 1960, the Raiders played their first game, losing to the Houston Oilers 37–22 at Kesar Field in San Francisco (Raider home games would be held in San Francisco until 1962). Head coach Eddie Erdelatz led the Raiders to a modest 6–8 record that year, and was fired two games into the next season. The Raiders would not have a winning season until 1963 when Al Davis arrived from San Diego to take over both GM and head coaching duties.

THE GLORY YEARS: Under head coach John Madden, the 1976 Raiders posted a 13–1 regular season record. Oakland faced the New England Patriots in the divisional playoffs and fell behind early. Entering the fourth quarter down 21–10, the Raiders rallied to within four points, and were the beneficiaries of a controversial pass interference call that set up the game winning touchdown. The momentum from that 24–21 win carried through to the AFC Championship game where the Raiders easily defeated the Pittsburgh Steelers 24–7. In Super Bowl XI, the Raiders would play a talented Minnesota team who had visited the Super Bowl three times in the previous seven years. The Raiders would hand the Vikings another Super Bowl loss with a dominating 32–14 victory.

The Raiders returned to the big show in 1981. After upsetting the San Diego Chargers in the AFC Championship game, 34–27, the Raiders rode into Super Bowl XV against the Philadelphia Eagles on the arm of quarterback Jim Plunkett. Plunkett threw for 261 yards and three touchdowns, and was named the Super Bowl MVP. The Raiders went on to beat the Eagles, 27–10.

After the team relocated to Los Angeles, the Raiders made another Super Bowl appearance, this time facing the Washington Redskins in Super Bowl XVIII. In arguably the best performance of his life, Hall of Fame running back Marcus Allen racked up 191 yards on the ground and two touchdowns. Allen was named the Super Bowl MVP, and the Raiders crushed the Redskins, 38–9.

CURRENT STATE OF THE FRANCHISE: After going to the Super Bowl in 2002, there has been a steady decline in the Bay Area. Oakland was awarded the first pick in the 2007 draft, selecting quarterback JaMarcus Russell out of Louisiana State. After a lengthy holdout, Russell did little to improve the Raiders' record as they finished 2007 at 4–12. The Raiders will need to continue adding young talent and building around JaMarcus Russell in order to again contend.

Marcus Allen

DRAFT IMPACT

Marcus Allen (running back)
- drafted 12th overall from USC in 1982
- winner of the Heisman Trophy in 1981
- named Super Bowl MVP in 1984 and NFL MVP in 1985

Fred Biletnikoff (wide receiver)
- drafted 11th overall from Florida State in 1965
- named Super Bowl MVP in 1977
- six-time Pro Bowler and six-time All-Pro

DRAFT FALLOUT

Todd Marinovich (quarterback)
- drafted 27th overall from USC in 1991
- Threw 8 touchdowns and 9 interceptions in two years with Oakland
- arrested for drug possession and sexual assault

Rickey Dudley (tight end)
- drafted ninth overall from Ohio State in 1996
- never caught more then 787 yards in a season
- released by the Raiders at the end of the 2000 season

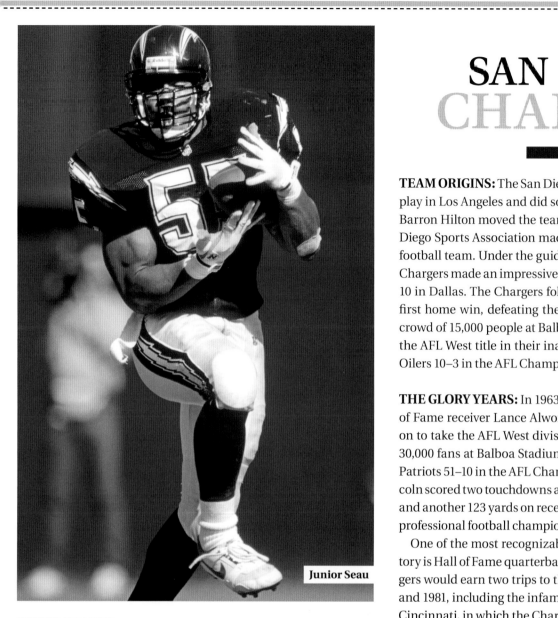

Junior Seau

SAN DIEGO CHARGERS

TEAM ORIGINS: The San Diego Chargers were originally slated to play in Los Angeles and did so for one year in 1960. In 1961, owner Barron Hilton moved the team to San Diego after the Greater San Diego Sports Association made a strong pitch for the professional football team. Under the guidance of head coach Sid Gillman, the Chargers made an impressive debut, beating the Dallas Texans 26–10 in Dallas. The Chargers followed up their debut win with their first home win, defeating the Oakland Raiders 44–0 in front of a crowd of 15,000 people at Balboa Stadium. The Chargers captured the AFL West title in their inaugural year, but lost to the Houston Oilers 10–3 in the AFL Championship game on Dec. 24, 1961.

THE GLORY YEARS: In 1963, the San Diego Chargers, led by Hall of Fame receiver Lance Alworth, posted an 11–3 record and went on to take the AFL West division title. On Jan. 24, 1964, in front of 30,000 fans at Balboa Stadium, the Chargers trounced the Boston Patriots 51–10 in the AFL Championship game. Fullback Keith Lincoln scored two touchdowns and collected 206 yards on the ground and another 123 yards on receptions. To date it is the Chargers only professional football championship.

One of the most recognizable faces in San Diego Chargers' history is Hall of Fame quarterback Dan Fouts. Under Fouts, the Chargers would earn two trips to the AFC Championship game in 1980 and 1981, including the infamous –59 degrees Fahrenheit game in Cincinnati, in which the Chargers lost 27–7.

The Chargers would win the AFC Championship once, in 1994, when they defeated the heavily favored Pittsburgh Steelers 17–13 to advance to Super Bowl XXIX. They then lost to the San Francisco 49ers, 49–26.

CURRENT STATE OF THE FRANCHISE: The road to glory may not be far away for the Chargers. After making the playoffs in 2006 with the best record in the NFL (14–2), the Chargers were eliminated in the second round. In 2007, they advanced to the AFC Championship, this time losing to the New England Patriots.

Charger fans, though, have plenty to look forward to in 2008. Led by arguably the best player in the NFL, running back LaDainian Tomlinson, the Chargers are poised to make another deep run in the playoffs. Their defense is led by All-Pro linebacker Shawne Merriman and emerging star cornerback, Antonio Cromartie. This current crop of San Diego Chargers may turn out to be the powerhouse of the NFL.

DRAFT IMPACT

LaDainian Tomlinson (running back)
- drafted fifth overall from Texas Christian University in 2001
- currently ranks third on the all-time rushing touchdown list
- five-time Pro Bowl selection and five-time All-Pro

Junior Seau (linebacker)
- drafted fifth overall from Southern California University in 1990
- considered the face of the franchise in the 1990s and early 2000s
- helped lead the team to its only Super Bowl appearance in 1994

DRAFT FALLOUT

Ryan Leaf (quarterback)
- drafted second overall from Washington State University in 1998
- career QB rating of 50.0, with 36 interceptions and 14 touchdowns
- was a member of four teams in a career that spanned five years

Mossy Cade (defensive back)
- drafted sixth overall from the University of Texas in 1984
- was traded to Green Bay for a 1986 first-round pick; never played a down for the Chargers

DALLAS
COWBOYS

TEAM ORIGINS: At the 1960 annual NFL meetings, Clint Murchison Jr. and Bedford Wynne were awarded an expansion franchise for the Dallas area. Originally named the "Steers," the franchise changed its name to the "Rangers" in honor of the local baseball team that was going to cease operations in 1960. However, the baseball Rangers decided to play the 1960 season, so Murchison and Wynne, in order to avoid any confusion, chose the name "Cowboys." On Sept. 24, 1960, the Cowboys opened to the Pittsburgh Steelers and were defeated 35–28.

THE GLORY YEARS: Under legendary head coach Tom Landry, the Cowboys would arrive at the dance five times between 1971 and 1979, and first taste Super Bowl success in 1972. The Cowboy defense, which held San Francisco to three points in the NFC Championship game, would again stymie its opponent as Dallas defeated Miami 24–3 in Super Bowl VI. Quarterback Roger Staubach passed for two touchdowns and was named MVP.

The 1977 Cowboys dominated the regular season with a 12–2 record, and rolled into Super Bowl XII the clear favorite over an inexperienced Denver Bronco squad. The Cowboys would win 27–10.

There was a long draught of football success in the Lone Star State for the next 14 years, but fortunes began to change when Dallas drafted quarterback Troy Aikman in 1989 and running back Emmitt Smith in 1990. The 1992 season saw the youthful Cowboys, now under head coach Jimmy Johnson, return to the Super Bowl. Led by Troy Aikman's MVP performance — an aerial attack of 273 yards and four touchdowns — the Cowboys defeated the Buffalo Bills in Super Bowl XXVII, 52–17. They would go on to do the same the next year, defeating Buffalo 30–13 at Super Bowl XXVIII, with MVP Emmitt Smith rushing for 132 yards and two touchdowns.

Dallas added one more Vince Lombardi Trophy to the mantle in 1996, defeating the Pittsburgh Steelers 27–17 in Super Bowl XXX. That victory tied the Cowboys with the 49ers as the only two five-time Super Bowls champs.

CURRENT STATE OF THE FRANCHISE: The Dallas Cowboys hope to reclaim the success they had in the 1990s with quarterback Tony Romo, who has emerged as one of the NFL's best. With All-Pro Terrell Owens as his top receiving threat, Marion Barber in the backfield and pass rusher Demarcus Ware harassing NFL quarterbacks, Romo and the Cowboys have all the tools to bring a Super Bowl back to the Lone Star State.

David LaFleur

DRAFT IMPACT
Troy Aikman (quarterback)
• drafted first overall from UCLA in 1989
• led the Cowboys to three Super Bowl titles in the 1990s
• inducted into the Hall of Fame in 2006

Emmitt Smith (running back)
• drafted 17th overall from the University of Florida in 1990
• Named 1993 NFL MVP and the 1994 Super Bowl MVP
• Set the all-time rushing record with 18,355 yards over his career

DRAFT FALLOUT
David LaFleur (tight end)
• drafted 22nd overall from Louisiana State in 1997
• caught a career-high seven touchdowns and 322 yards in 1999
• only amassed 12 touchdowns between 1997 and 2000

Mike Sherrard (wide receiver)
• drafted 18th overall from UCLA in 1986
• collected five touchdowns in 16 games with Dallas
• attempted a comeback in 1989 after a broken leg in 1987

Frank Gifford

DRAFT IMPACT

Phil Simms (quarterback)
- drafted seventh overall from Morehead State in 1979
- leader on two Super Bowl teams
- named MVP in Super Bowl XXI

Frank Gifford (wide receiver)
- drafted first overall from the USC in 1952
- named the NFL MVP in 1956
- inducted into the Hall of Fame in 1977

DRAFT FALLOUT

Tyrone Wheatley (running back)
- drafted 17th overall from the University of Michigan in 1995
- never collected more than 583 yards in a season with the Giants
- missed 17 days of training camp before ending a contract hold-out

Derek Brown (tight end)
- drafted 14th overall from Notre Dame in 1992
- only played four seasons with the Giants
- never amassed more than 56 yards in a season

NEW YORK
GIANTS

TEAM ORIGINS: New York businessman Tim Mara purchased the New York Football Giants for 500 dollars in 1925, and the team made its debut with head coach Bob Folwell in October of the same year. Although they lost the contest 14–0 to the Frankford Yellow Jackets, it was a great day for New York football fans, as it was the first professional football game in New York's history — a tradition that has lasted for more than 80 years.

THE GLORY YEARS: The Giants won four NFL championships before the NFL–AFL merger in 1966. Since then, the Giants have been Super Bowl champions three times.

In 1986, under legendary coach Bill Parcells, the Giants finished the regular season 14–2. In the divisional playoff, New York demolished the San Francisco 49ers to move on to the NFC Championship, where they faced the Washington Redskins. The Giants' defense carried the team, shutting out the Redskins 17–0. In Super Bowl XXI, quarterback Phil Simms threw for 268 yards and three touchdowns to lead the Giants past the Denver Broncos, 39–20.

The Giants were not absent from the big game for long, returning to football's grandest stage in 1991. This time their opponent would be the heavily favored Buffalo Bills. Ottis Anderson rushed for 102 yards and one touchdown, but it was a missed field goal in the dying seconds by Buffalo kicker Scott Norwood that sealed the deal for the Giants' second Super Bowl, as they hung on to win by one point, 20–19.

In 2007 at Super Bowl XLII, the Giants, led by Eli Manning, pulled off one of the most electrifying upsets in modern sports' history as they toppled the New England Patriots who were projected as two-touchdown favorites. Manning's MVP performance included 255 yards through the air and two touchdown passes, while the Giants' defense allowed only 14 points and sacked Patriot quarterback Tom Brady five times. The Giants won 17–14 on a touchdown pass from Manning to Plaxico Burress with only 38 seconds left on the clock.

CURRENT STATE OF THE FRANCHISE: Coming off one of the biggest wins in franchise history, the New York Giants are on cloud nine. On offense, Eli Manning is developing into one of the NFL's elite quarterbacks, while running back Brandon Jacobs is proving to be a bruiser. The defense is led by aging, but effective defensive end Micheal Strahan. Surrounding him on defense is a group of young players including defensive end Justin Tuck, who collected two sacks and a forced fumble in Super Bowl XLII.

PHILADELPHIA EAGLES

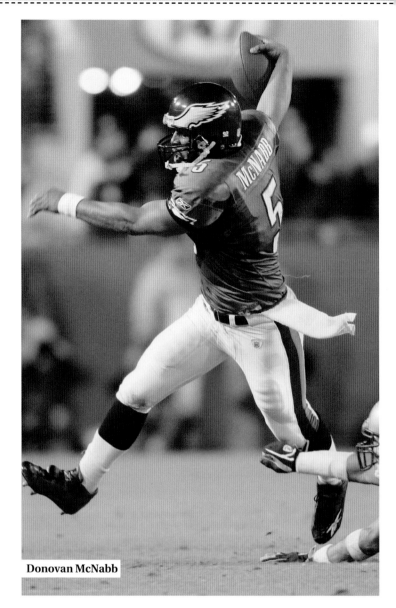

Donovan McNabb

TEAM ORIGINS: After moving the team from Frankford, Pennsylvania, in 1933 to the City of Brotherly Love, owners Bert Bell and Lud Wray decided to change the name from the Yellow Jackets to the Eagles, in honor of the symbol of the National Recovery Administration. On Oct. 15, 1933, the Eagles made a less-than-stellar debut, being blown out 56–0 by the New York Giants. The Eagles' first win came on Nov. 5, 1933, when they defeated the Cincinnati Reds 6–0. They finished the season 3–5–1.

THE GLORY YEARS: Before the NFL–AFL merger in 1966, the Philadelphia Eagles won three NFL championships (1948, 1949, 1960). Since then, the Eagles have been to two Super Bowls and to five NFC Championship games. In 1980, under the guidance of head coach Dick Vermeil and their strong-armed quarterback Ron "Jaws" Jaworski, the Eagles finished 12–4, top of their division.

Jaworski had a career year in 1980, passing for 3,529 yards and 27 touchdowns and being named to his first and only Pro Bowl. The Eagles would roll through the playoffs, beating the Minnesota Vikings 31–16, and then defeating the Dallas Cowboys in the NFC Championship game 20–7. In Super Bowl XV, the Eagles were grounded as the Oakland defense dismantled Jaworski and the Eagles offense, intercepting the quarterback three times. The Eagles were never a threat in the game, and lost 27–10.

In 2005, the Eagles made their Super Bowl return after falling one game shy of the Super Bowl for three consecutive years, from 2002–2004. Quarterback Donovan McNabb led the Eagles (without their star receiver Terrell Owens) to the promised land over the Atlanta Falcons, 27–10.

In Super Bowl XXXIX, wide receiver Terrell Owens made his return from a horrific ankle injury that had sidelined him for the latter part of the regular season and the playoffs. Although Owens caught a game-high 122 yards, and despite the Eagles having 357 total passing yards and three touchdowns, New England defeated Philadelphia 24–21.

CURRENT STATE OF THE FRANCHISE: The Eagles are a team in limbo, teetering on whether to rebuild or to reload and make another run for the playoffs. The one thing the Eagles are missing is a bona fide star, the likes of Terrell Owens. After an unimpressive 2007 campaign, Donovan McNabb needs to recapture his playoff form. If that can happen, look for the Eagles to give it another shot before going into the rebuilding stage.

DRAFT IMPACT

Donovan McNabb (quarterback)
- drafted second overall from Syracuse University in 1999
- appeared in four NFC Championship games and one Super Bowl
- named to five Pro Bowls

Reggie White (defensive end)
- drafted fourth overall from the University of Tennessee in 1984
- nicknamed "The Minister of Defense"
- led the league in sacks twice and made the Pro Bowl seven times

DRAFT FALLOUT

Jon Harris (defensive end)
- drafted 25th overall from the University of Virginia in 1997
- only played two seasons with the Eagles
- collected only two sacks in his professional career

Kenny Jackson (wide receiver)
- drafted fourth overall from Penn State in 1984
- most successful season in 1985; caught 692 yards and one touchdown
- caught five passes in his 1990–1991 comeback with the Eagles

Sammy Baugh

WASHINGTON
REDSKINS

TEAM ORIGINS: On Feb. 13, 1937, team owner George Preston Marshall got approval from the NFL to move his team to Washington from the Boston area. On Sept. 16, 1937, the Washington Redskins played their first game and also recorded their first victory, defeating the New York Giants 13–3. That first season in Washington proved to be one of the most successful for an inaugural team as Hall of Fame quarterback Sammy Baugh led the Redskins past the Chicago Bears 28–21 for the 1937 NFL Championship.

THE GLORY YEARS: The Washington Redskins' most successful seasons (three Super Bowl wins in four appearances) came under the guidance of Hall of Fame coach Joe Gibbs.

The first Super Bowl win occurred in 1983. After a 7–1 regular season (shortened due to strike), the Redskins blew through their longtime rivals, the Dallas Cowboys, 31–17 in the NFC Championship game. In Super Bowl XVII against the Miami Dolphins (the Redskins first since 1973, also against the Dolphins) running back John Riggins dominated, rushing for 166 yards and one touchdown. The Redskins won 27–17 and Riggins was named Super Bowl MVP.

The Redskins returned to Super Bowl glory a few years later in 1988. In the NFC Championship game against the Minnesota Vikings, Redskin quarterback Doug Williams broke a 10–10 deadlock in the fourth quarter with a seven-yard touchdown pass to Gary Clark. The Vikings made a final push for victory, but were thwarted at the goal line with a blocked pass by speedy defensive back Darrell Green. In Super Bowl XXII, Doug Williams passed for 340 yards and four touchdowns as the Redskins pounded the Denver Broncos 42–10. Williams' performance earned him the Super Bowl MVP.

Super Bowl XXVI in 1992 marks the last time the Redskins have won the Vince Lombardi Trophy. Quarterback Mark Rypien led the Redskins to victory over the Buffalo Bills, 37–24. Rypien was named Super Bowl MVP. This victory marked the end of the Joe Gibbs era, as he left football to pursue his passion for NASCAR.

CURRENT STATE OF THE FRANCHISE: The 2007 season weighed heavily on the Redskins as safety Sean Taylor was murdered in his Miami home on November 27th. Playing with heavy hearts, the Redskins rallied for their former teammate and made the playoffs. The Redskins lost more than a player in Taylor, but a team leader. Washington is hoping that rookie LaRon Landry can help fill that role, along with running back Clinton Portis and quarterback Jason Campbell.

DRAFT IMPACT

Sammy Baugh (quarterback/running back)
- drafted sixth overall from Texas Christian University in 1937
- helped the Redskins win two NFL championships
- inducted into the Hall of Fame in 1963

Ark Monk (wide receiver)
- drafted 18th overall from Syracuse University in 1980
- named to three Pro Bowls
- elected to the Hall of Fame in 2008

DRAFT FALLOUT

Heath Shuler (quarterback)
- drafted third overall from the University of Tennessee in 1994
- in three seasons with the Redskins, only passed for 2,403 yards, 13 touchdowns and 19 interceptions.

Michael Westbrook (wide receiver)
- drafted fourth overall from the University of Colorado in 1995
- punched out running back Stephen Davis at training camp in 1997
- fights Mixed Martial Arts; first win over former NFL Pro Jarrod Bunch

CHICAGO
BEARS

TEAM ORIGINS: The NFL's second oldest franchise was born as the Decatur Staley Football Club from Decatur, Illinois, in 1920, the same year the American Professional Football Association was formed. Led by George Halas, the team moved to Chicago in 1921, and by 1922, the same year the APFA changed its name to the National Football League, the team was named the Chicago Bears — partly in homage to the Chicago Cubs, who would share Cubs Park (Wrigley Field) with the Bears.

THE GLORY YEARS: Between 1920 and 1966, George Halas led his team to eight NFL Championships, either as a player or as a head coach, or both.

It would not be until the 1980s that the Bears were again Champions. In 1984, two significant moments shaped the Bears. First, on October 7, Walter Payton became the NFL's all-time leading rusher, accomplishing the milestone in a win over the New Orleans Saints; second, on December 30, the Chicago Bears advanced, for the first time in franchise history, to the NFC Championship game with a 23–19 victory over the Washington Redskins. The Bears lost the game, but it would set the stage for huge success.

In 1985, defensive coordinator Buddy Ryan and head coach Mike Ditka formed "The Monsters of Midway." Led by Hall of Fame middle linebacker Mike Singletary, the Monsters led the league in every major defensive category. Chicago finished the regular season 15–1. After shutting out the Los Angeles Rams in the NFC Championship game, 24–0, the Bears were on their way to Super Bowl XX.

A dominating defense and strong leadership on offense by Walter Payton and quarterback Jim McMahon led the Bears to a 46–10 rout of the New England Patriots, which even saw rookie defensive tackle William "The Fridge" Perry, rush for a one-yard touchdown. (Since then only Super Bowl XXIV has had a larger point differential).

CURRENT STATE OF THE FRANCHISE: After returning to the Super Bowl in 2006, Chicago missed the playoffs in 2007. The team's strength is on defense, led by middle linebacker Brian Urlacher; free safety Mike Brown patrols the secondary and defensive tackle Tommy Harris stuffs the middle of the defensive line. The Bears have yet to find a consistent quarterback. 2003 first-rounder Rex Grossman is failing to live up to expectations. As well, Cedric Benson continues to disappoint after being made the go-to running back in 2007.

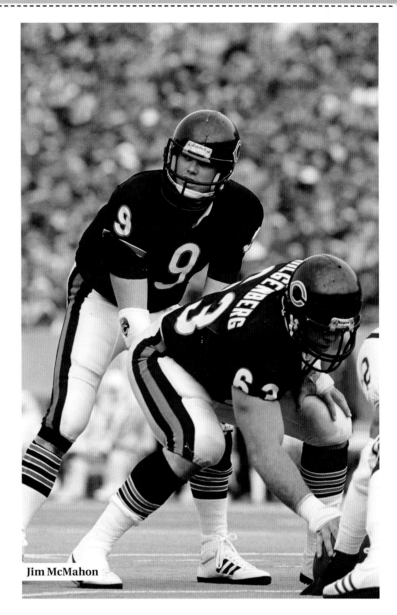

Jim McMahon

DRAFT IMPACT

Walter "Sweetness" Payton (running back)
- drafted fourth overall from Jackson State in 1975
- named to nine Pro Bowls
- broke the all-time rushing record in 1984

Jim McMahon (quarterback)
- drafted fifth overall from Brigham Young University in 1982
- the first recipient of the Davey O'Brien National Quarterback Award
- named All-Pro and nominated to the Pro Bowl in 1985

DRAFT FALLOUT

Curtis Enis (running back)
- drafted fifth overall from Penn State in 1998
- posted a career-high 916 yards in his second season
- only played three seasons in the NFL, collecting 1,497 yards

Cade McNown (quarterback)
- drafted 12th overall from UCLA in 1999
- tossed 16 touchdowns and 19 interceptions in 25 NFL games
- relegated to a fourth-string quarterback after the 2000 season

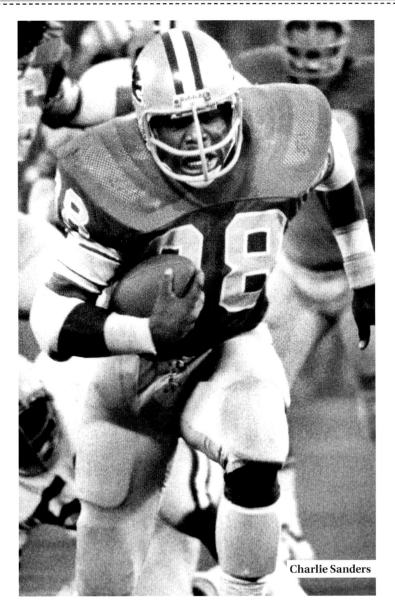

Charlie Sanders

DRAFT IMPACT

Barry Sanders (running back)
• drafted third overall from Oklahoma State in 1989
• 10-time Pro Bowler and 10-time All-Pro
• Rookie of the Year in 1989; NFL MVP in 1991 and 1997

Charlie Sanders (tight-end)
• drafted 74th overall from the University of Minnesota in 1968
• seven-time Pro Bowler and six-time All-Pro
• Lions' leader or co-leader for most receptions in six of his ten seasons

DRAFT FALLOUT

Andre Ware (quarterback)
• drafted seventh overall from the University of Houston in 1990
• Heisman Trophy winner
• scored five touchdowns over four seasons (14 games) in Detroit

Charles Rogers (receiver)
• drafted second overall from Michigan State in 2003
• Heisman Trophy winner
• only played 15 games with the Lions over three seasons

DETROIT
LIONS

TEAM ORIGINS: Detroit radio executive George A. Richards purchased the Portsmouth Spartans for $7,952.08 in 1934 and moved them to Detroit. The Detroit Lions won their inaugural game over the New York Giants 9–0 on Sept. 23, 1934. In the same year, one of the NFL's oldest traditions was established as the Lions hosted the Chicago Bears on Thanksgiving Day — it was the first in a long tradition of Lions' Thanksgiving football games. Detroit finished the season with a 10–3 record.

THE GLORY YEARS: Detroit was an NFL powerhouse in the 1950s. Under head coach Buddy Parker, Detroit won back-to-back titles in 1952 and 1953, and would add another in 1957, the season Parker resigned. The 1950s also saw the emergence of a great rivalry as the Lions and the Cleveland Browns would face-off four times for the NFL Championship, with the Browns only win coming in 1954.

The Lions' first championship win against the Browns took place in Cleveland on Dec. 28, 1952. After a successful 9–3 campaign, the Lions were tied with the Los Angeles Rams for the NFC title. The Lions defeated the Rams easily in the Conference Championship game, 31–21, earning themselves a trip the NFL Championship. Although the Lions had the better record, the Browns were the more experienced team. Detroit, however, surprised Cleveland, 17–7, to claim their second NFL Championship (the first since 1935).

Hall of Fame quarterback Bobby Layne guided the Lions to a 10–2 regular season in 1953. The Lions met the Browns again in the championship game, and narrowly escaped defeat with a 17–16 victory. Detroit's third and final championship of the 1950s — a 59–14 shellacking of the Browns — came under head coach George Wilson, who took the reins upon Parker's departure. The Motor City has not had a professional football championship since.

CURRENT STATE OF THE FRANCHISE: After starting 6–2 in 2007, the Lions looked like they were going to make their first playoff appearance in nine years. However, the Lions lost seven of their last eight games, finished out of the hunt with a 7–9 record.

Disappointing is an understatement when describing the Lions in recent years. Despite having a defensive-minded coach in Rod Marinelli, the Lions ranked dead last in total defense in 2007. Their poor offensive production is also surprising considering the talent they have on the field. Led by veteran quarterback Jon Kitna, and young and talented wide receivers Roy Williams and Calvin Johnson, the Lions have the makings of a devastating threesome.

GREEN BAY
PACKERS

TEAM ORIGINS: As far as legendary goes, the Green Bay Packers share company with sporting's elite: the New York Yankees, the Montreal Canadiens and the Boston Celtics. The Packers were founded in 1919 in a dingy editorial room at the *Green Bay Press-Gazette*. In 1921, they joined the NFL and finished their first season under head coach and owner, Curly Lambeau, 3–2–1.

THE GLORY YEARS: The Packers' long and storied history includes nine NFL championships and 19 division titles. Since the NFL–AFL merger, they have won three Super Bowls. Most notable are the victories in Super Bowls I and II, which have served to forever cement the legacy of the green and gold.

In 1966, Green Bay posted a 12–2 regular-season record, and quarterback Bart Starr was named the NFL MVP. The Packers then defeated the Dallas Cowboys in the NFL Championship game, 34–27, for the right to face the AFL Champion Kansas City Chiefs in Super Bowl I. The Packers dominated, cruising to a 35–10 victory. Starr would be named Super Bowl MVP.

In 1967, Green Bay again faced Dallas for the NFC title. On New Year's Eve in Green Bay, with temperatures dropping to –13 Fahrenheit and a wind chill of –43, the Cowboys and Packers played in what is now known as the "Ice Bowl." Bart Starr's last-minute quarterback sneak gave the Packers their second consecutive Super Bowl appearance, inching out the Cowboys 21–17.

In Super Bowl II, the Packers faced the Oakland Raiders. Starr passed for over 200 yards and one touchdown to lead the Packers to victory. Starr was once again named the MVP.

There was a long draught of championships for Green Bay, until a kid out of Southern Mississippi University brought the team back to glory. Brett Favre collected three NFL MVPs, seven All-Pro nods and nine Pro Bowl nominations in his career with the Packers. In 1997, he led the Pack back to the big game, defeating the New England Patriots 35–21 in Super Bowl XXXI.

CURRENT STATE OF THE FRANCHISE: On Mar. 4, 2008, Green Bay reached the end of an era as Brett Favre retired. The hole at quarterback will be filled by 2005 first-round pick Aaron Rodgers. The young pivot will be supported by other youngsters such as wide receiver Greg Jennings and running back Ryan Grant. Veteran wide receiver Donald Driver is now in position to become Green Bay's leader. On defense, linebacker A.J. Hawk and sack-machine Aaron Kampman will continue terrorizing opposing offenses.

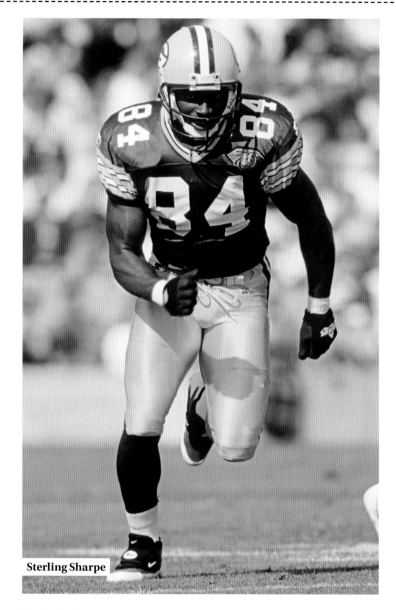

Sterling Sharpe

DRAFT IMPACT

Bart Starr (quarterback)
- drafted 200th overall from the University of Alabama in 1956
- led Green Bay to six division titles, five NFL titles and two Super Bowls
- inducted into the Hall of Fame in 1977

Sterling Sharpe (wide receiver)
- drafted seventh overall from the University of South Carolina in 1988
- five time Pro Bowler and five-time All-Pro
- ended career after 1994 when he suffered a devastating neck injury

DRAFT FALLOUT

Tony Mandarich (offensive lineman)
- drafted second overall from Michigan State in 1989
- collected one fumble recovery in 45 games with Green Bay
- attempted a brief comeback with the Indianapolis Colts in 1996

Jamal Reynolds (defensive end)
- drafted 10th overall from Florida State in 2001
- played three seasons with the Packers before being released in 2003
- collected three sacks and two fumble recoveries in 18 games

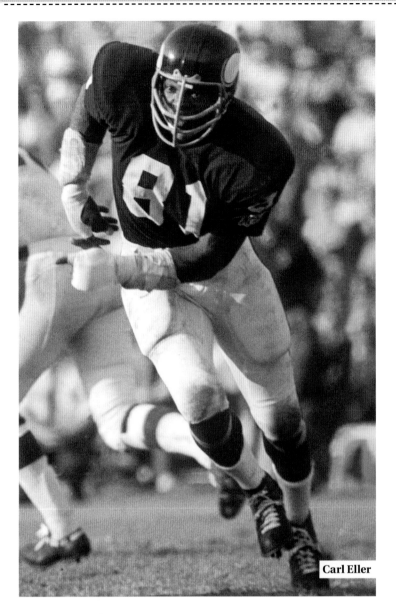

Carl Eller

MINNESOTA VIKINGS

TEAM ORIGINS: In January 1960, the NFL awarded Minnesota and five local businessmen its 14th franchise. The group of men had previously arranged for the team to play in the AFL, but withdrew to be part of NFL's expansion instead. On Sept. 17, 1961, the Vikings made one of the most impressive debuts in NFL history. Rookie quarterback Fran Tarkenton passed for 250 yards and four touchdowns and ran for a score as the Vikings upset the Chicago Bears 37–13. Unfortunately, they lost their next seven games, and finished the season 3–11.

THE GLORY YEARS: Minnesota has been successful throughout their history with 16 division championships and four Super Bowl appearances, yet the Vikings have yet to claim the top prize. Their first big success came in 1969, when the Vikings won their second straight division title, finishing with a 12–2 record. The Vikings' defense, "the Purple People Eaters," held all opponents to just 133 points. Minnesota defeated the Cleveland Browns 27–7 in the NFL Championship game to enter their first Super Bowl against the Kansas City Chiefs. Minnesota would prove to be no match for the Chiefs as Kansas dismantled the People Eaters to the tune of 23–7.

Fran Tarkenton and Minnesota parted ways in 1967 when he was traded to the New York Giants. The Vikings, however, needed help at quarterback and decided to trade back for the future Hall of Famer in 1972. Tarkenton led the Vikings to six division championships and three Super Bowl appearances in his second tour with Minnesota, yet, even the great Tarkenton would not be able to get the Vikings over the Super Bowl hump.

CURRENT STATE OF THE FRANCHISE: The Vikings have not made the playoffs since 2004. The team was competitive throughout the 2007 season and made strides to becoming a championship team again. It started with drafting the 2007 Offensive Rookie of the Year, Adrian Peterson, out of the University of Oklahoma. Peterson ran for 1,341 yards and 12 touchdowns, despite missing two games due to injury. His greatest accomplishment of the year came on Nov. 4, when he broke Jamal Lewis's single game rushing record by racking up 296 yards and three touchdowns.

Complementing Peterson is quarterback Tavaris Jackson, the second-year pro out of Alabama State. Jackson showed the flashes of brilliance and frustration that come with being a young quarterback. However, the Vikings may have eased the pressure on him by signing free agent wide receiver Bernard Berrian in the offseason.

DRAFT IMPACT

Fran Tarkenton (quarterback)
- drafted 29th overall from the University of Georgia in 1961
- at retirement he owned every significant passing record including passing yards, passing touchdowns and pass completions

Carl Eller (defensive end)
- drafted sixth overall from the University of Minnesota in 1964
- foundation of the "Purple People Eaters" defense in the 1970s
- named to six Pro Bowls

DRAFT FALLOUT

D.J. Dozier (running back)
- drafted 14th overall from Penn State in 1987
- never amassed over 257 rushing yards in a season
- scored seven touchdowns in five career NFL seasons

Troy Williamson (wide receiver)
- drafted seventh overall from the University of South Carolina in 2005
- collected 79 receptions in 39 games with Minnesota
- only three touchdowns with the Vikings before they traded him in 2008

ATLANTA FALCONS

TEAM ORIGINS: Rankin M. Smith, a successful insurance executive, was awarded the NFL's 15th franchise on Jun. 30, 1965. By Christmas Eve, 1965, the Falcons had already broken a franchise record by selling nearly 45,000 season tickets. On Sept. 11, 1966, the Falcons took to the field against the Los Angeles Rams. Although the Falcons kept the game close, the Rams prevailed, edging out the Falcons 19–14.

THE GLORY YEARS: The Falcons have been to the playoffs eight times and won their division three times. Their best year occurred in 1998, when they went 14–2 in the regular season, won their division and advanced well into the playoffs. The Falcons were led by running back Jamal Anderson as he rushed for 1,846 yards and scored 16 touchdowns.

In their divisional playoff showdown against the San Francisco 49ers, the Falcons jumped ahead to a 14–0 lead. Although the 49ers fought back, the Atlanta defense prevailed and they won the contest 20–18. The next week, in the NFC Championship game. The Falcons were heavy underdogs in the matchup, and the Vikings took a 20–7 lead late in the second quarter.

However, a late score in the second quarter cut the lead to 20–14. The game ended in a tie. In overtime, veteran kicker Morten Anderson answered the prayers of the Atlanta faithful and kicked a 39-yard field goal to send the team to Super Bowl XXXIII.

In Super Bowl XXXIII, the Falcons had to face Denver Broncos' John Elway, Terrell Davis and company for football's ultimate prize. Hall of Fame quarterback Elway proved too much for the Falcons, as he guided Denver to a 33–19 win. Still, the 1998 season was deemed a major success for the franchise and helped the team take that next step in development.

CURRENT STATE OF THE FRANCHISE: After pleading guilty to dog fighting charges on Aug. 24, 2007, quarterback Michael Vick, the cornerstone of the franchise, missed the entire season. Vick is currently serving a 23-month jail sentence. Wide receiver Roddy White is now the main offensive threat, after collecting 1,202 yards and six touchdowns in 2007.

On defense, first-round pick defensive end Jamaal Anderson looks to make a big splash in his second year as a pro (perhaps living up to his name in Atlanta). Supporting him will be cornerback DeAngelo Hall, a two-time Pro Bowler who is the jewel on the defense and who looks to lead the Falcons back to championship glory.

Keith Brooking

DRAFT IMPACT

Keith Brooking (linebacker)
- drafted 12th overall from Georgia Tech in 1998
- served as the foundation of the Atlanta defense for the last 10 years
- five-time Pro Bowler and two-time All-Pro

Bob Whitfield (offensive tackle)
- drafted eighth overall from Stanford University in 1992
- anchored the line and opened holes for running back Jamal Anderson, who led the Falcons to a NFC Championship in 1998

DRAFT FALLOUT

Michael Booker (cornerback)
- drafted 11th overall from the University of Nebraska in 1997
- collected six interceptions in three seasons with the Falcons

Bruce Pickens (cornerback)
- drafted third overall from the University of Nebraska in 1991
- plagued with injuries for most of his career
- collected two interceptions and one sack in 1992, his healthy season
- played for three teams in 1993, being shipped to his fourth in 1995

CAROLINA PANTHERS

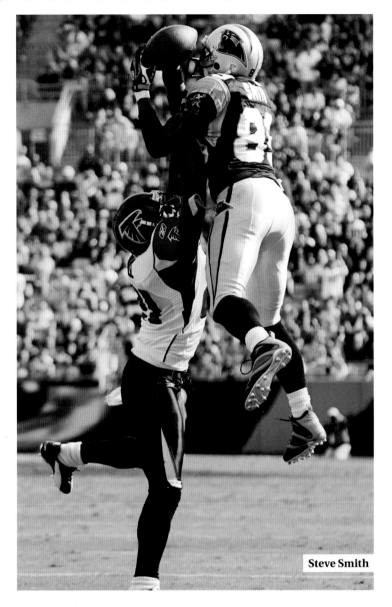

Steve Smith

DRAFT IMPACT

Steve Smith (wide receiver)
• drafted 74th overall from the University of Utah in 2001
• three-time Pro Bowler and two-time All-Pro
• is currently the face of the Panthers' franchise

Julius Peppers (defensive end)
• drafted second overall from the University of North Carolina in 2002
• cornerstone of the defense; made two playoff trips in the last five years
• named three-time Pro Bowler and two-time All-Pro

DRAFT FALLOUT

Rae Carruth (wide receiver)
• drafted 27th overall from the University of Colorado in 1997
• was convicted of a conspiracy to murder his girlfriend in 1999
• currently serving a 18–24 year prison sentence

Tim Biakabutuka (running back)
• drafted eighth overall from the University of Michigan in 1996
• retired from football after six injury-plagued seasons
• career high–718 yards and six touchdowns in 1999

TEAM ORIGINS: On Oct. 26, 1993, a meeting of NFL owners unanimously selected the Carolina Panthers as the 29th team in the NFL, and the first expansion team since 1976. Carolina named former Pittsburgh Steelers' defensive coordinator Dom Capers as the team's first head coach. After drafting quarterback Kerry Collins with the fifth overall pick in 1995, the Panthers took to the field against the Atlanta Falcons on Sept. 3, 1995. In their first game, the Panthers took the favored Falcons into overtime. However, they came up short and lost their debut 23–20.

THE GLORY YEARS: In only their second year of existence, the Panthers defied the odds and went 12–4 in the 1996 regular season and captured their first West Division title. In their first playoff game in team history, the Panthers defeated the Dallas Cowboys (the defending Super Bowl Champions) 26–17. However, the magical season ended the next week in the NFC Championship, when the Panthers lost to the Green Bay Packers 30–13.

In 2003, quarterback Jake Delhomme came off the bench to lead the Panthers to an 11–5 regular-season record and an NFC South Division Championship. In the divisional playoff game against the St. Louis Rams, wide receiver Steve Smith sent his team to its second NFC Championship game by catching a 69-yard touchdown pass in the second overtime. This catch gave the Panthers the momentum they needed to advance to their first Super Bowl

In Super Bowl XXXVIII, the Carolina Panthers were up against the biggest challenge of their short existence: The New England Patriots, whose dynasty was in full swing. The teams fought like two heavyweight champions, punch for punch, throughout the whole game. Quarterback Jake Delhomme passed for 323 yards and three touchdowns, but in the end the Patriots got the final punch in. With four seconds left, Adam Vinatieri kicked the game-winning field goal, giving the Patriots a 32–29 victory and ending the magical run of the 2003 Panthers.

CURRENT STATE OF THE FRANCHISE: The 2007 season was a disappointing one for Carolina, who finished 7–9, missing the playoffs for the second straight year. Quarterback Delhomme, who was limited by injuries in 2007, looks to regain the chemistry with his star wide receiver Steve Smith, who had another 1,000 yard season. Complementing the aerial attack is the emergence of 2006 first-round pick, running back DeAngelo Williams, who is poised to have a breakout season.

NEW ORLEANS
SAINTS

TEAM ORIGINS: On Nov. 1, 1966, the NFL awarded its 16th franchise to the city of New Orleans. The announcement was made on All Saints' Day, so the owners thought it was appropriate to name the team after the day on which it was born. On Dec. 27, 1966, Tom Fears was named the team's first head coach. Finally, after almost a year of preparation, the New Orleans Saints took to the field on Sept. 17, 1967, in front of 80,879 fans at Tulane Stadium. Despite a 94-yard kickoff return for a touchdown by rookie running back John Gilliam, the Saints were defeated 27–13 by the Los Angeles Rams.

THE GLORY YEARS: It wasn't until 1987 that the Saints finally made the playoffs, and they have only made it five times since. In 2000, head coach Jim Haslett led the Saints to a 10–6 record and their second division title. On Dec. 30, 2000, they hosted the St. Louis Rams on wild-card weekend. Quarterback Aaron Brooks led the Saints to their first-ever playoff victory as he passed for four touchdowns, three to wide receiver Willie Jackson.

In 2006, one year after the devastating effects of Hurricane Katrina, the Saints returned home to New Orleans. It was one of the most inspiring seasons in the NFL's history. Playing in their first game at home, a *Monday Night Football* national television broadcast, the Saints held Michael Vick and the Falcons to only three points, as they stormed to victory 23–3. The season was also a great success: the Saints finished with a 10–6 record, and their third division title.

In the NFC divisional playoff game, running back Deuce McAllister rushed for 143 yards and a touchdown, on the team's way to a 27–24 victory over the Philadelphia Eagles, advancing the Saints to their first NFC Championship game in team history. However, the magic ran out. Despite the Saints trailing by only two points at halftime, the Chicago Bears ended the Saints' season, defeating them 39–14.

CURRENT STATE OF THE FRANCHISE: In 2007, the Saints stumbled their way to a disappointing 7–9 record. Quarterback Drew Brees still leads the team on offense, and with Reggie Bush in the backfield, there is always a chance he will break away and run for a score. Marques Colston, a seventh-round pick in 2006, continued to spite draft observers, catching 1,206 yards, and 11 touchdowns in his second year as a pro. If Brees and Colston can continue this chemistry, more success is just beyond the horizon in the Saints' future.

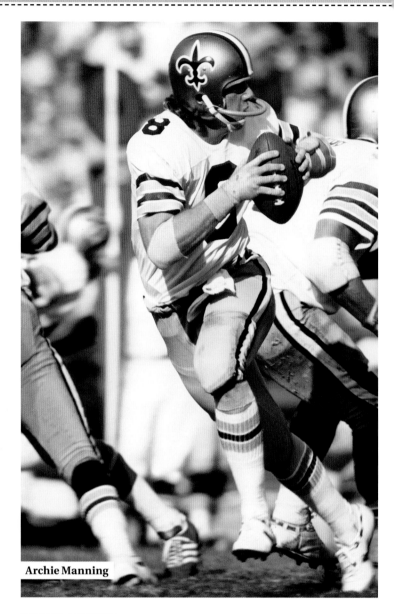

Archie Manning

DRAFT IMPACT

Archie Manning (quarterback)
- drafted second overall from the University of Mississippi in 1971
- two-time Pro Bowler and one-time All-Pro
- finished his career with 23,911 yards, 125 touchdowns, 55.2 QB rating
- father of Super Bowl MVP quarterbacks Peyton and Eli Manning

Willie Roaf (offensive tackle)
- drafted eighth overall from Louisiana Tech in 1993
- anchored the line for nine years; helped lead the Saints to the 2000 playoffs
- 11-time Pro Bowler and 10-time All-Pro

DRAFT FALLOUT

Ricky Williams (running back)
- drafted fifth overall from the University of Texas in 1999
- collected 1,000 rushing yards in 2000 and 1,245 in 2001
- left for the Miami Dolphins in 2002
- suspended by the league four times for substance abuse violations
- played with the Toronto Argonauts of the CFL in 2006

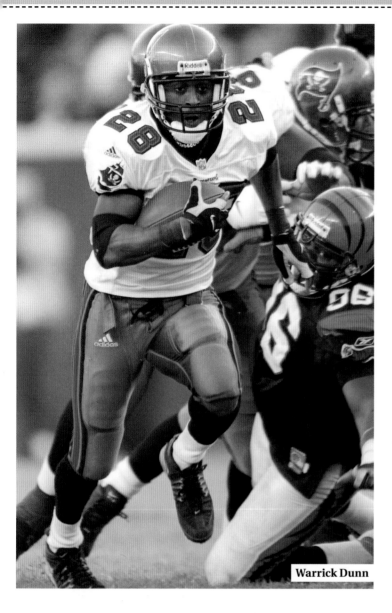

Warrick Dunn

TAMPA BAY
BUCCANEERS

TEAM ORIGINS: Tampa Bay was awarded the NFL's 27th franchise back in 1976. A group of trustees awarded the name "Buccaneers" to the team after a local pirate legend. John McKay was named the Buccaneers' first head coach. The 1976 season would go down in infamy as one of the worst seasons in professional sports, as the Buccaneers went winless for the season, finishing with a 0–14 record.

THE GLORY YEARS: The Bucs were the laughingstock of the NFL for pretty much their first 20 years of existence in the league. In 1996, Tony Dungy made an immediate impact by building one of the best defenses in the league. In 1997, in only Dungy's second year, the Buccaneers made the playoffs for the first time since 1982. That season proved to be the start of a great Buccaneers' run, which lasted for the next ten years, with two NFC Championship appearances and one Super Bowl title.

In 2002, under the leadership of head coach Jon Gruden, the Buccaneers had one of their most successful regular seasons ever. The team finished 12–4 and after rolling over the San Francisco 49ers in the divisional playoffs, 31–6, the Bucs were ready to face their biggest challenge of the season — the Philadelphia Eagles. The Bucs defense was dominant on that day, allowing only ten points to be scored, winning the NFC Championship 27–10.

Coach Jon Gruden now faced his old team, the Oakland Raiders, on professional football's grandest stage in Super Bowl XXXVII. The Bucs defense was well prepared and it showed on the field. Raider's quarterback Rich Gannon threw five interceptions, two of those to safety Dexter Jackson, the game's MVP. Brad Johnson passed for two touchdowns and 215 yards to help the cause. In the end, it was never close, as the Bucs toppled the Raiders 48–21 to claim their first-ever Super Bowl.

CURRENT STATE OF THE FRANCHISE: In 2007, Jon Gruden and veteran quarterback Jeff Garcia led the Buccaneers to their sixth division title. Although the regular season was successful, their early exit in the playoffs was a disappointment. The offense is still led by Jeff Garcia, and his favorite target is Joey Galloway who, at the age of 36, had another 1,000-yard receiving season. The defense is led by veteran Ronde Barber, but look for fourth overall pick, defensive end Gaines Adams, to take more of a leadership role in the years to come. The foundation of this team is still a powerful defense.

DRAFT IMPACT

Warren Sapp (defensive tackle)
- drafted 12th overall from the University of Miami in 1995
- anchored a defense that would take the team to the playoffs five times
- seven-time Pro Bowler and six-time All-Pro

Warrick Dunn (running back)
- drafted 11th overall from Florida State University in 1997
- named Walter Payton Man of the Year in 2004 for his charity work
- three-time Pro Bowler

DRAFT FALLOUT

Bo Jackson (running back)
- drafted first overall from the University of Auburn in 1986
- Jackson instead decided to play baseball for the Kansas City Royals
- returned to play football with the Raiders in 1987

Ricky Bell (running back)
- drafted first overall from the USC in 1977
- rushed for 1,263 yards and seven touchdowns in 1979
- sadly, died of heart disease in 1984 at the age of 29

203

ARIZONA CARDINALS

TEAM ORIGINS: After 28 years as the St. Louis Cardinals, owner Bill Bidwell moved the team out to the desert in 1988. On *Monday Night Football*, the Cardinals made their Arizona debut in front of 67,139 fans against their NFC East divisional rivals, the Dallas Cowboys, losing 17–14. The new Arizona Cardinals were competitive, and looked good starting the season 7–4, but as was too often the case with the Cardinals, the team suffered a collapse to finish the season 7–9.

THE GLORY YEARS: The Arizona Cardinals have been haunted by mediocrity, failure and flat out embarrassment as a franchise. From poor free-agent signings to draft busts and general mismanagement, the Cards have never been a true contender in the southwest.

In 1998, there was a gleam of light at the end of the tunnel. Quarterback Jake Plummer, who was already a southwest household name because of his excellent college career at Arizona State, led the Cardinals to their most successful season in the desert, going 9–7. On Dec. 27, the Cardinals hosted the San Diego Chargers. In the dying seconds of a 13–13 tie, kicker Chris Jacke nailed a 52-yard field goal to lift Arizona to its first playoff berth. Although the Cardinals were double-digit underdogs against the Cowboys in the ensuing wild-card game, they came out as though they belonged in the playoffs. Plummer threw for two touchdowns, as the Cards won 20–7. The win broke the longest postseason winless draught in professional sports, as the franchise had not won a playoff game since the 1947 NFL Championship. The next week, the magic ran out when the Minnesota Vikings ended the dream by beating the Cards 41–21 in the divisional playoff.

CURRENT STATE OF THE FRANCHISE: The year 2008 will mark the tenth anniversary of the Cardinals' playoff run. Every year, it seems, optimists predict that the franchise will break out of its slump and return to the playoffs. They are loaded with tons of young talent, such as Heisman Trophy quarterback Matt Leinhart, and Pro Bowl wide receivers Larry Fitzgerald and Anquan Boldin. Veteran running back Edgerrin James has the experience to lead the Cardinals to playoff greatness like he did with Peyton Manning and the Indianapolis Colts. Each year, however, due either to injury, or just underperformance, the Cardinals seem to go on one of their infamous losing skids and miss the playoffs. Maybe the tenth anniversary of their playoff run will inspire this current group of Cardinals to return to the playoffs, and perhaps their first taste of true NFL glory.

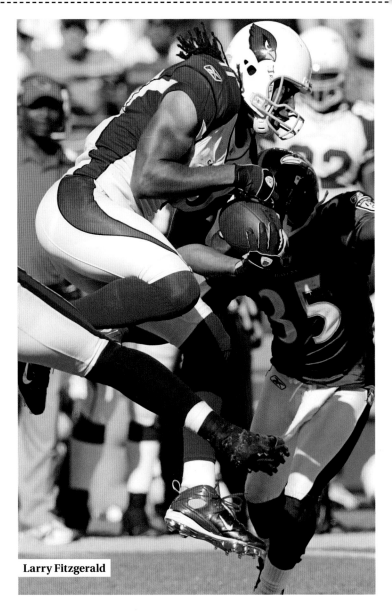

Larry Fitzgerald

DRAFT IMPACT

Larry Fitzgerald (wide receiver)
• drafted third overall from the University of Pittsburgh in 2004
• posted a career-high 103 receptions in 2005
• two-time Pro Bowler and one-time All-Pro

Anquan Boldin (wide receiver)
• drafted 54th overall from Florida State in 2003
• named Offensive Rookie of the Year in 2003
• two-time Pro Bowler

DRAFT FALLOUT

Andre Wadsworth (defensive end)
• drafted third overall from Florida State in 1998
• plagued by various injuries and a lengthy initial contract hold out
• collected eight sacks in three seasons with the Cardinals

Wendell Bryant (defensive tackle)
• drafted 12th overall from the University of Wisconsin in 2002
• collected 1.5 sacks in 29 games with the Cardinals
• suspended in 2004 for violation of the substance abuse policy

SAN FRANCISCO
49ERS

ORIGINS: The San Francisco 49ers were established in 1946 after the city petitioned for five years to bring professional football to San Francisco. Its original owner was trucking executive Tony Morabito, who spent $25,000 to get charter into the All America Football Conference (AAFC). The first game took place against the New York Yankees at Kezar Stadium, in which the 49ers lost 21–7. However, the 49ers ended on a good note, going 9–5 in their first season of the AAFC. When the AAFC ceased operations in 1949, the 49ers joined the NFL the following year. Their first season in the NFL was tough under coach Lawrence T. Shaw, as the 49ers finished with a dismal 3–9 record.

THE GLORY YEARS: The San Francisco 49ers ended the 1970s by drafting two key players, one who would serve as the foundation of the team, and the other who would help establish the dynasty San Francisco enjoyed in the 1980s. Joe Montana, a third-round steal, and Dwight Clark and 10th-round pick, became the duo famous for the play simply known as "The Catch," which propelled the 49ers into their first Super Bowl appearance and victory in 1982.

That Super Bowl XVI victory was the first of four championship seasons in the 1980s for the 49ers, including Super Bowl wins in 1985, 1989 and 1990. For the 49ers, the 1980s were great draft years as well, as the club selected two Hall of Famers: Ronnie Lott (first round, 1981), and arguably the greatest player ever, Jerry Rice (first round, 1985). The combination of solid drafting and signing of key free agents, along with acquiring Steve Young in a trade with the Tampa Bay Buccaneers in 1987, helped the 49ers carry their success into the early and mid-1990s. This run was highlighted by a then-record fifth Super Bowl win in 1995.

CURRENT STATE OF THE FRANCHISE: The 49ers have only made two playoff appearances in the 2000s (2001 and 2002), only making it out of the wild-card round once in 2002. In the last five seasons, the 49ers have had losing records and have focused on rebuilding their once glorious franchise through the draft. In 2005, with the first-overall pick, they drafted Alex Smith out of the University of Utah, and with their third-round pick they drafted Frank Gore out of the University of Miami. The franchise also boasts blue-chip tight end prospect Vernon Davis and the 2007 Defensive Rookie of the Year, Patrick Willis, at middle linebacker. The 49ers are establishing the foundation for success in the years to come.

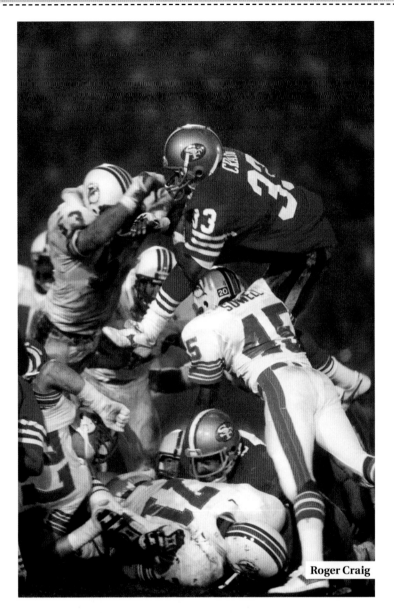

Roger Craig

DRAFT IMPACT

Joe Montana (quarterback)
- drafted 82nd overall from the University of Notre Dame in 1979
- led the 49ers to three Super Bowl championships
- two-time MVP (1989, 1990)

Roger Craig (running back)
- drafted 49th overall from the University of Nebraska in 1983
- four-time Pro Bowler and four-time All-Pro
- collected a career-high 1,502 yards in 1988

DRAFT FALLOUT

Jim Druckenmiller (quarterback)
- drafted 27th overall from Virginia Tech in 1997
- played two years for the 49ers, throwing one touchdown
- retired in 2002 after stints in the Arena Football League and the XFL

Reggie McGrew (defensive end)
- drafted 24th overall from the University of Florida in 1999
- played only 10 games in his first season due to injuries
- collected one sack in 22 games with the 49ers

SEATTLE
SEAHAWKS

TEAM ORIGINS: On Jun. 4, 1974, the NFL announced that Seattle would have a professional football team by 1976. In 1975, a year before the Seahawks would play their first game, 59,000 season ticket applications were received. Finally, after two years of waiting, the Seattle Seahawks stepped onto the field, led by head coach Jack Patera, to play the St. Louis Cardinals. The Seahawks were competitive, but their last-second Hail Mary was intercepted, and they lost 30–24.

THE GLORY YEARS: Seattle's first taste of success came in 1983 when the franchise squeaked into the playoffs with a 9–7 record. After two successful playoff victories, one over the Denver Broncos in the wild-card weekend and the next weekend over the Miami Dolphins, the Seahawks went to their first Conference Championship game. The magic ran out, though, as the Los Angeles Raiders rolled over the Seahawks 30–14. Seattle would go on to make 10 playoff appearances in 25 years.

In 2005, the Seahawks dominated the NFC, winning the NFC West Division title with a 13–3 record. Running back Shaun Alexander led the offense, rushing for 1,880 yards and 27 touchdowns, on his way to being named the NFL MVP. Quarterback Matt Hasselbeck developed into a quality starter and made the Pro Bowl, hooking up with his favorite receiver Darrell Jackson.

The Seahawks hosted the Washington Redskins in the divisional playoff, where Hasselbeck rallied the troops after losing Shaun Alexander to a concussion. Seattle won 20–10, ending their 21-year playoff winless streak. The next week, in the NFC Championship game, the Seahawks hosted the Carolina Panthers with Alexander back in the lineup. Hasselbeck passed for 219 yards and two touchdowns while Alexander rushed for two more, as the Seahawks thrashed the Panthers 34–14 and advanced to their first Super Bowl in franchise history. Despite losing in Super Bowl XL to the Pittsburgh Steelers, the season was a success story for the Seahawks.

CURRENT STATE OF THE FRANCHISE: The Seahawks are still Super Bowl contenders. After winning their fourth consecutive NFC West Division title in 2007, the Seahawks stumbled in the divisional playoffs, falling 42–20 to the Green Bay Packers. Former MVP Shaun Alexander, who hadn't broke the 1,000-yard mark since 2005, was released by the Seahawks on Apr. 22, 2008, after the team signed free-agent running backs Julius Jones and T.J. Duckett, in an attempt to revitalize the running game.

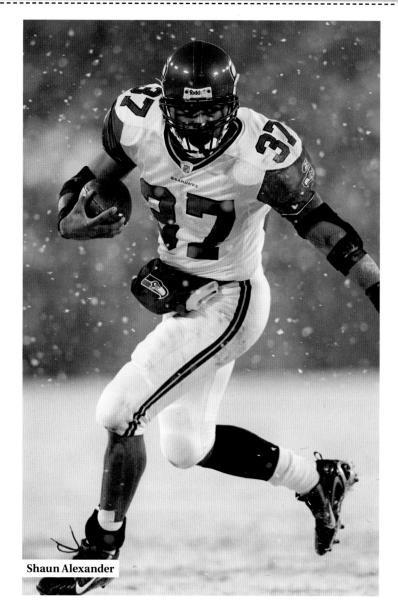

Shaun Alexander

DRAFT IMPACT

Steve Largent (wide receiver)
- traded to Seattle from the Houston Oilers in his first NFL season
- broke every major receiving record including most receptions, most receiving yards and most receiving touchdowns at his retirement

Shaun Alexander (running back)
- drafted 19th overall from the University of Alabama in 2000
- currently the only Seahawk to be named NFL MVP (2005)
- ran a career-high 1,880 yards in 2005

DRAFT FALLOUT

Brian Bosworth (linebacker)
- drafted first overall (supplemental draft) from Oklahoma in 1987
- collected four sacks in 24 games with Seattle
- retired due to injuries after only three seasons with the Seahawks

Rick Mirer (quarterback)
- drafted second overall from the University of Notre Dame in 1993
- has played for five teams in eight seasons
- in 80 career games has thrown 50 touchdowns and 76 interceptions

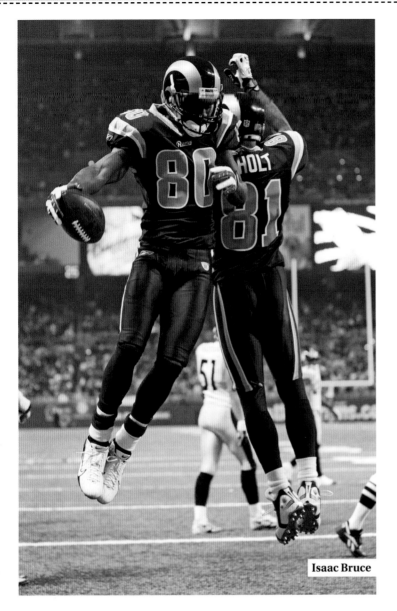

Isaac Bruce

ST. LOUIS
RAMS

TEAM ORIGINS: The Rams have called Cleveland, Los Angeles and St. Louis home over their 71-year history. In 1988, the St. Louis football faithful were trying to get another team to the Midwest in the wake of the Cardinals departure. In 1995, they got their wish as the Los Angeles Rams relocated after being unable to get funding for a new stadium. In their first season in St. Louis, under head coach Rich Brooks, the Rams finished a sub-par 7–9.

THE GLORY YEARS: In 1999, after signing quarterback Trent Green, the Rams were set to make their first playoff push in St. Louis. Green tore his ACL in preseason action and was out for the year. In a classic case of "blessing in disguise," Green's injury opened the door for an undrafted free-agent quarterback named Kurt Warner. Kurt Warner shocked the NFL. The former quarterback from the Arena Football League passed for 4,353 yards and 41 touchdowns on his way to an MVP award. Warner and company: veteran receiver Isaac Bruce, explosive rookie receiver Torry Holt and running back Marshall Faulk, finished the regular season 13–3, booking their first playoff appearance in 10 years.

In the divisional playoff, the Rams showed no signs of playoff rust and steamrolled over the Minnesota Vikings 49–37. In the NFC Championship, the Tampa Bay Buccaneers defense would hold the Rams to only 11 points. Instead of the Rams offense winning the game, the defense held the Bucs to a minuscule six points, sending the Rams to Super Bowl XXXIV.

In one of the most memorable Super Bowls in the modern era, Kurt Warner would pass for 467 yards, and two touchdowns against the Tennessee Titans. But it was the defense that would again shine for the Rams, as linebacker Mike Jones stopped Tennessee star receiver Kevin Dyson at the one-yard line as time expired to give the Rams their first Super Bowl victory. Warner was named the game's MVP, capping off one of the most remarkable individual seasons in NFL history.

CURRENT STATE OF THE FRANCHISE: After signing a huge multi-year extension in 2007, quarterback Marc Bulger had one of the most disappointing seasons of his career, missing four games due to injury and leading the Rams to the second-worst record in the NFL (3–13). The Rams' engine on offense, running back Steven Jackson, was slowed by injuries in 2007, although he still carried for over 1,000 yards. Veteran wide receiver Isaac Bruce left the team in 2008, leaving Torry Holt as the main passing threat.

DRAFT IMPACT

Orlando Pace (offensive tackle)
- drafted first overall from Ohio State in 1997
- helped lead the team to two Super Bowls
- six-time All-Pro and seven-time Pro Bowler

Isaac Bruce (wide receiver)
- drafted 33rd overall from the University of Memphis in 1994
- four-time Pro Bowler and three-time All-Pro
- left the Rams in 2008 for the division rival San Francisco 49ers

DRAFT FALLOUT

Lawrence Phillips (running back)
- drafted sixth overall from the University of Nebraska in 1996
- traded to the Dolphins in 1998 in the middle of his second season
- arrested for assault with a deadly weapon

Trung Canidate (running back)
- drafted 31st overall from the University of Arizona in 2000
- career-high 441 yards and 5 touchdowns in 2001
- retired in 2004 after being released by the Washington Redskins

SUPER BOWL HISTORY

Super Bowl I – Jan. 15, 1967
Memorial Coliseum, Los Angeles, California
Green Bay Packers   35
Kansas City Chiefs   10
MVP: Bart Starr, QB, Green Bay

Super Bowl II – Jan. 14, 1968
Orange Bowl, Miami, Florida
Green Bay Packers   33
Oakland Raiders   14
MVP: Bart Starr, QB, Green Bay

Super Bowl III – Jan. 12, 1969
Orange Bowl, Miami, Florida
New York Jets   16
Baltimore Colts   7
MVP: Joe Namath, QB, New York

Super Bowl IV – Jan. 11, 1970
Tulane Stadium, New Orleans, Louisiana
Kansas City Chiefs   23
Minnesota Vikings   7
MVP: Len Dawson, QB, Kansas City

Super Bowl V – Jan. 17, 1971
Orange Bowl, Miami, Florida
Baltimore Colts   16
Dallas Cowboys   13
MVP: Chuck Howley, LB, Dallas

Super Bowl VI – Jan. 16, 1972
Tulane Stadium, New Orleans, Louisiana
Dallas Cowboys   24
Miami Dolphins   3
MVP: Roger Staubach, QB, Dallas

Super Bowl VII – Jan. 14, 1973
Memorial Coliseum, Los Angeles, California
Miami Dolphins   14
Washington Redskins   7
MVP: Jake Scott, S, Miami

Super Bowl VIII – Jan. 13, 1974
Rice Stadium, Houston, Texas
Miami Dolphins   24
Minnesota Vikings   7
MVP: Larry Csonka, RB, Miami

Super Bowl IX – Jan. 12, 1975
Tulane Stadium, New Orleans, Louisiana
Pittsburgh Steelers   16
Minnesota Vikings   6
MVP: Franco Harris, RB, Pittsburgh

Super Bowl X – Jan. 18, 1976
Orange Bowl, Miami, Florida
Pittsburgh Steelers   21
Dallas Cowboys   17
MVP: Lynn Swann, WR, Pittsburgh

Super Bowl XI – Jan. 9, 1977
Rose Bowl, Pasadena, California
Oakland Raiders   32
Minnesota Vikings   14
MVP: Fred Biletnikoff, WR, Oakland

Super Bowl XII – Jan. 15, 1978
Superdome, New Orleans, Louisiana
Dallas Cowboys   27
Denver Broncos   10
co-MVP:Randy White, DT, Dallas
Harvey Martin, DE, Dallas

Super Bowl XIII – Jan. 21, 1979
Orange Bowl, Miami, Florida
Pittsburgh Steelers   35
Dallas Cowboys   31
MVP: Terry Bradshaw, QB, Pittsburgh

Super Bowl XIV – Jan. 20, 1980
Rose Bowl, Pasadena, California
Pittsburgh Steelers   31
Los Angeles Rams   19
MVP: Terry Bradshaw, QB, Pittsburgh

Super Bowl XV – Jan. 25, 1981
Louisiana Superdome, New Orleans, Louisiana
Oakland Raiders   27
Philadelphia Eagles   10
MVP: Jim Plunkett, QB, Oakland

Super Bowl XVI – Jan. 24, 1982
Pontiac Silverdome, Pontiac, Michigan
San Francisco 49ers   26
Cincinnati Bengals   21
MVP: Joe Montana, QB, San Francisco

Super Bowl XVII – Jan. 30, 1983
Rose Bowl, Pasadena, California
Washington Redskins   27
Miami Dolphins   17
MVP: John Riggins, RB, Washington

Super Bowl XVIII – Jan. 22, 1984
Tampa Stadium, Tampa, Florida
Los Angeles Raiders   38
Washington Redskins   9
MVP: Marcus Allen, RB, Los Angeles

Super Bowl XIX – Jan. 20, 1985
Stanford Stadium, Palo Alto, California
San Francisco 49ers   38
Miami Dolphins   16
MVP: Joe Montana, QB, San Francisco

Super Bowl XX – Jan. 26, 1986
Louisiana Superdome, New Orleans, Louisiana
Chicago Bears   46
New England Patriots   10
MVP: Richard Dent, DE, Chicago

Super Bowl XXI – Jan. 25, 1987
Rose Bowl, Pasadena, California
New York Giants   39
Denver Broncos   20
MVP: Phil Simms, QB, New York

Super Bowl XXII – Jan. 31, 1988
Jack Murphy Stadium, San Diego, California
Washington Redskins   42
Denver Broncos   10
MVP: Doug Williams, QB, Washington

Super Bowl XXIII – Jan. 22, 1989
Joe Robbie Stadium, Miami, Florida
San Francisco 49ers   20
Cincinnati Bengals   16
MVP: Jerry Rice, WR, San Francisco

Super Bowl XXIV – Jan. 28, 1990
Louisiana Superdome, New Orleans, Louisiana
San Francisco 49ers   55
Denver Broncos   10
MVP: Joe Montana, QB, San Francisco

Super Bowl XXV – Jan. 27, 1991
Tampa Stadium, Tampa, Florida
New York Giants   20
Buffalo Bills   19
MVP: Ottis Anderson, RB, New York

Super Bowl XXVI – Jan. 26, 1992
Metrodome, Minneapolis, Minnesota
Washington Redskins   37
Buffalo Bills   24
MVP: Mark Rypien, QB, Washington

Super Bowl XXVII – Jan. 31, 1993
Rose Bowl, Pasadena, California
Dallas Cowboys   52
Buffalo Bills   17
MVP: Troy Aikman, QB, Dallas

Super Bowl XXVIII – Jan. 30, 1994
Georgia Dome, Atlanta, Georgia
Dallas Cowboys   30
Buffalo Bills   13
MVP: Emmitt Smith, RB, Dallas

Super Bowl XXIX – Jan. 29, 1995
Joe Robbie Stadium, Miami, Florida
San Francisco 49ers   49
San Diego Chargers   26
MVP: Steve Young, QB, San Francisco

Super Bowl XXX – Jan. 28, 1996
Sun Devil Stadium, Tempe, Arizona
Dallas Cowboys   27
Pittsburgh Steelers   17
MVP: Larry Brown, CB, Dallas

Super Bowl XXXI — Jan. 26, 1997
Louisiana Superdome, New Orleans, Louisiana
Green Bay Packers   35
New England Patriots   21
MVP: Desmond Howard, KR-PR, Green Bay

Super Bowl XXXII — Jan. 25, 1998
Qualcomm Stadium, San Diego, California
Denver Broncos   31
Green Bay Packers   24
MVP: Terrell Davis, RB, Denver

Super Bowl XXXIII — Jan. 31, 1999
Pro Player Stadium, Miami, Florida
Denver Broncos   34
Atlanta Falcons   19
MVP: John Elway, QB, Denver

Super Bowl XXXIV — Jan. 30, 2000
Georgia Dome, Atlanta, Georgia
St. Louis Rams   23
Tennessee Titans   16
MVP: Kurt Warner, QB, St. Louis

Super Bowl XXXV — Jan. 28, 2001
Raymond James Stadium, Tampa, Florida
Baltimore Ravens   34
New York Giants   7
MVP: Ray Lewis, LB, Baltimore

Super Bowl XXXVI — Feb 3, 2002
Louisiana Superdome, New Orleans, Louisiana
New England Patriots   20
St. Louis Rams   17
MVP: Tom Brady, QB, New England

Super Bowl XXXVII — Jan. 26, 2003
Qualcomm Stadium, San Diego, California
Tampa Bay Buccaneers   48
Oakland Raiders   21
MVP: Dexter Jackson, FS, Tampa Bay

Super Bowl XXXVIII — Feb 1, 2004
Reliant Stadium, Houston, Texas
New England Patriots   32
Carolina Panthers   29
MVP: Tom Brady, QB, New England

Super Bowl XXXIX — Feb 6, 2005
Alltel Stadium, Jacksonville, Florida
New England Patriots   24
Philadelphia Eagles   21
MVP: Deion Branch, WR, New England

Super Bowl XL — Feb 5, 2006
Ford Field, Detroit, Michigan
Pittsburgh Steelers   21
Seattle Seahawks   10
MVP: Hines Ward, WR, Pittsburgh

Super Bowl XLI — Feb 4, 2007
Dolphin Stadium, Miami, Florida
Indianapolis Colts   29
Chicago Bears   17
MVP: Peyton Manning, QB, Indianapolis

Super Bowl XLII — Feb 3, 2008
University of Phoenix Stadium, Glendale, Arizona
New York Giants   17
New England Patriots   14
MVP: Eli Manning, QB, New York

ADDITIONAL CAPTIONS

Pg 9: Bart Starr lines up to take the snap in the 1966 NFL Championship game against the Cleveland Browns. Green Bay won the game 23–12.

Pg 11: O.J. Simpson sidesteps a New York Jets defender at Shea Stadium in 1973.

Pg 13: Thurman Thomas takes a break between downs in 1997, during a 22–13 victory over the Detroit Lions.

Pg 15: The New York Giants celebrate winning Super Bowl XLII, a 17–14 upset of the New England Patriots.

Pg 26: Sweetness runs the ball against the Oakland Raiders in 1977 preseason action. Payton would lead the league in regular-season rushing yards with 1,852.

Pg 29: Terry Bradshaw watches the defense work in a 24–13 victory over the Oakland Raiders in the 1974 AFC Championship game. The Steelers went on to win their first Super Bowl.

Pg 32: Jim Brown powers through a pile of Giants in his 1963 MVP season.

Pg 35: Dick Butkus flies through the air to make a crushing stop on the Los Angeles Rams on Dec. 8, 1968. The Bears won the game 17–16.

Pg 38: John Elway looks to pass in a 21–20 loss to the Los Angeles Raiders on Dec. 4, 1988. Elway tossed two touchdowns, three interceptions and was sacked three times in the game.

Pg 41: Brett Favre drops back to pass in a 31–17 win over the Carolina Panthers on Nov. 18, 2007. The Packers would post a 13–3 record in 2007 and return to the playoffs for the first time since their wild-card loss in 2004.

Pg 44: Forrest Gregg yells from the sidelines during a 13–0 victory over the San Francisco 49ers on Dec. 10, 1960.

Pg 47: Deacon Jones on the sidelines in 1970, one of his eight Pro Bowl seasons.

Pg 50: Dan Marino drops back to pass on Dec. 5, 1999. Despite a three-touchdown performance from Marino, the Dolphins lost 37–34 to the Indianapolis Colts. It was Marino's last season.

Pg 53: Joe Montana warms up for a game against the Los Angeles Raiders on Sept. 12, 1982. The 49ers lost 23–17 on the way to a 3–6 record in the nine game strike-shortened 1982 season.

Pg 56: Walter Payton rushes against Los Angeles Rams defensive back LeRoy Irvin during the 1985 NFC Championship game on Jan. 12, 1986. The Bears won 24–0 on their way to crushing the New England Patriots 46–10 for their first Super Bowl.

Pg 59: Jerry Rice runs with the ball in a 16–6 victory over the Atlanta Falcons on Nov. 19, 2000, his last season with the 49ers.

Pg 62: Barry Sanders rushes for a total of 75 yards on the day in a 26–17 loss to the Green Bay Packers on Nov. 21, 1993. Despite only playing in 13 games in 1993, Sanders still rushed for over 1,100 yards.

Pg 65: Deion Sanders runs with the ball in a 20–17 win over the San Francisco 49ers on Nov. 10, 1996.

Pg 68: Gale Sayers carries the ball in 1967 at Wrigley Field. He appeared in 13 of 14 games that season.

Pg 71: Emmitt Smith breaks a tackle against the Oakland Raiders in his career year, 1995. Emmitt posted at least one touchdown in 15 of 16 games that season on his way to a total of 25.

Pg 74: Roger Staubach looks to pass in a loss to the Atlanta Falcons on Nov. 21, 1976. It was one of only three regular-season losses for the Cowboys.

Pg 77: Fran Tarkenton, looking down field for the pass, scrambles out of the pocket to collect a few of his 3,674 career-rushing yards.

Pg 80: Lawrence Taylor on the rush against the Washington Redskins in the first game of the 1988 season. L.T. collected two sacks on the day and 15.5 on the season.

Pg 83: Johnny Unitas poses for photographers at Colts training camp in the mid 1960s.

Pg 86: Reggie White reads the offense during a 27–17 victory over the San Francisco 49ers in the NFC divisional playoff on Jan. 6, 1996.

Pg 88: Max McGee catches one of two touchdowns in the Packers 35–10 rout of the Kansas City Chiefs in Super Bowl I.

Pg 100: Tom Brady passes the ball under pressure from Kamerion Wimbley of the Cleveland Browns on Oct. 7, 2007. Brady passed for 265 yards and three touchdowns as the Patriots crushed the Browns 34–17, on the way to a perfect season.

Pg 162: LaDainian Tomlinson leaps to score a one-yard touchdown against the Tennessee Titans to seal the Chargers 17–6 AFC wild-card victory on Jan. 6, 2008.

Pg 174: Green Bay wide receiver Ruvell Martin celebrates the Packers NFC North division title with fans after a 34–14 drubbing of the Detroit Lions in the last regular season game of the year. The Packers would advance to the NFC Championship game where they would lose to the eventual Super Bowl champion New York Giants.

ACKNOWLEDGMENTS

Steve Cameron of Firefly Books was the driving force behind this project. Not only was he a tactful editor but a beacon of encouragement, especially when he sent e-mails that read, "Good job. You only have 18 more biographies to go." Thanks, Steve. It's your turn to buy the next round of beers, though.

George Johnson and I have shared many laughs over the years covering sports. He is delightfully skeptical; a wickedly funny guy who can recite every Monty Python skit ever done. The *Calgary Herald* is lucky to have him as its main sports columnist, as was I to have him as a contributor on this book.

A special thanks goes to Derek Iwanuk for his Joe Montana like deftness when compiling both the statistical information and the franchise stories. As well, designer Jamie Hodgson deserves a special thanks for his ability to plow through revisions — much the way Reggie White plowed through offensive lines — and, of course, a great design.

I forced a lot of people to listen as I bounced names, storylines and ideas off of them, but David Naylor and Matthew Sekeres, my *Globe and Mail* colleagues, did more than their share when it mattered, and it was appreciated. A special thanks also goes to *Globe and Mail* sports editor Steve McAllister for allowing me to adjust my work schedule so I could spend time researching what receiving records Jerry Rice didn't hold.

Without those people, this book never would have happened.

PHOTO CREDITS

FURTHER READING

Bradshaw, Terry, and Colin P. Cohn. *No Easy Game.* Chicago: Fleming H. Revell Co., 1979.

Curran, Bob. *The $400,000 Quarterback or: The League That Came in From the Cold.* Toronto: Signet Books, 1969.

Fleder, Rob, editor. *The Football Book.* New York: Sports Illustrated Books, 2005.

Fitzgerald, Ed. *The Johnny Unitas Story.* New York: Tempo Books, 1968.

Grimley, Will, editor. *The Sports Immortals: 50 of Sports' All-Time Greatest as Selected by the Sports Staff of The Associated Press.* Eaglewood Cliffs, New Jersey: Stratford Books, 1972.

Kramer, Jerry, and Dick Schaap. *Distant Replay.* New York: G. P. Putnam's Sons, 1985.

Kramer, Jerry. *Instant Replay.* Edited by Dick Schaap. Toronto: The New American Library of Canada Ltd., 1968.

Taylor, Lawrence, and David Falkner. *LT: Living on the Edge.* New York: Random House, 1987.

MacCambridge, Michael. *America's Game: The Epic Story of How Pro Football Captured a Nation.* New York: Random House, 2004.

Maramiss, David. *When Pride Still Mattered.* New York: Touchstone Books, 2000.

Montana, Joe, and Dick Schaap. *Montana.* Nashville: Turner Publishing, 1995.

Nielsen, Nancy J. *Eric Dickerson.* Mankato, Minnesota: Crestwood House, 1988.

Paolantonio, Sal. *The Paolantonio Report: The Most Overrated and Underrated Players, Teams, Coaches & Moments in NFL History.* Chicago: Triumph Books, 2007.

Rand, Jonathan. *300 Pounds of Attitude: The Wildest Stories and Craziest Characters the NFL Has Ever Seen.* Connecticut: The Lyons Press, 2006.

Rice, Jerry, and Brian Curtis. *Go Long! My Journey Beyond the Game and the Fame.* New York: Ballantine Books, 2007

Rushin, Steve. *1954-1994: How We Got Here.* New York: Time Inc., 1994.

Sahadi, Lou. *The Long Pass.* New York: Bantam Book, 1969.

Sanders, Deion, and Jim Nelson Black. *Power, Money & Sex: How Success Almost Ruined My Life.* Nashville, Tennessee: Word Publishing, 1998.

Sayers, Gale, and Al Silverman. *I Am Third.* New York: Bantam Books, 1970.

Vancil, Mark, editor. *Marino: On the Record.* San Francisco: Collins Publishers, 1996.

Wiebusch, John, editor. *Lombardi.* Chicago: Follett Publishing Co. 1971.

Zimmerman, Paul. *A Thinking Man's Guide to Pro Football.* New York: Warner Paperback, 1972.

Additional resources include the network of NFL.com websites, *Sports Illustrated*/SI.com, *The Sporting News*/TSN.com, ESPN/ESPN.com, as well as pro-football-reference.com, sportsecyclopedia.com and drafthistory.com.

INDEX